MW00627594

THE FUT
EDUCATION RESEARCH AT IES
ADVANCING AN EQUITY-ORIENTED SCIENCE

Adam Gamoran and Kenne A. Dibner, *Editors*

Committee on the Future of Education Research at the Institute of
Education Sciences in the U.S. Department of Education

Board on Science Education

Division of Behavioral and Social Sciences and Education

A Consensus Study Report of

The National Academies of
SCIENCES · ENGINEERING · MEDICINE

THE NATIONAL ACADEMIES PRESS
Washington, DC
www.nap.edu

THE NATIONAL ACADEMIES PRESS   500 Fifth Street, NW   Washington, DC 20001

This activity was supported by a contract between the National Academy of Sciences and the U.S. Department of Education (Award No. 9199-00-21-C-0002). Any opinions, findings, conclusions, or recommendations expressed in this publication do not necessarily reflect the views of any organization or agency that provided support for the project.

International Standard Book Number-13: 978-0-309-27539-2
International Standard Book Number-10: 0-309-27539-3
Digital Object Identifier: https://doi.org/10.17226/26428

Additional copies of this publication are available from the National Academies Press, 500 Fifth Street, NW, Keck 360, Washington, DC 20001; (800) 624-6242 or (202) 334-3313; http://www.nap.edu.

Printed in the United States of America

Cover Credit: Elizabeth Hora

Suggested citation: National Academies of Sciences, Engineering, and Medicine. 2022. *The Future of Education Research at IES: Advancing an Equity-Oriented Science.* Washington, DC: The National Academies Press. https://doi.org/10.17226/26428.

The National Academies of
SCIENCES · ENGINEERING · MEDICINE

The **National Academy of Sciences** was established in 1863 by an Act of Congress, signed by President Lincoln, as a private, nongovernmental institution to advise the nation on issues related to science and technology. Members are elected by their peers for outstanding contributions to research. Dr. Marcia McNutt is president.

The **National Academy of Engineering** was established in 1964 under the charter of the National Academy of Sciences to bring the practices of engineering to advising the nation. Members are elected by their peers for extraordinary contributions to engineering. Dr. John L. Anderson is president.

The **National Academy of Medicine** (formerly the Institute of Medicine) was established in 1970 under the charter of the National Academy of Sciences to advise the nation on medical and health issues. Members are elected by their peers for distinguished contributions to medicine and health. Dr. Victor J. Dzau is president.

The three Academies work together as the **National Academies of Sciences, Engineering, and Medicine** to provide independent, objective analysis and advice to the nation and conduct other activities to solve complex problems and inform public policy decisions. The National Academies also encourage education and research, recognize outstanding contributions to knowledge, and increase public understanding in matters of science, engineering, and medicine.

Learn more about the National Academies of Sciences, Engineering, and Medicine at **www.nationalacademies.org**.

The National Academies of
SCIENCES · ENGINEERING · MEDICINE

Consensus Study Reports published by the National Academies of Sciences, Engineering, and Medicine document the evidence-based consensus on the study's statement of task by an authoring committee of experts. Reports typically include findings, conclusions, and recommendations based on information gathered by the committee and the committee's deliberations. Each report has been subjected to a rigorous and independent peer-review process and it represents the position of the National Academies on the statement of task.

Proceedings published by the National Academies of Sciences, Engineering, and Medicine chronicle the presentations and discussions at a workshop, symposium, or other event convened by the National Academies. The statements and opinions contained in proceedings are those of the participants and are not endorsed by other participants, the planning committee, or the National Academies.

For information about other products and activities of the National Academies, please visit www.nationalacademies.org/about/whatwedo.

About the Cover

"A Light to the Nation"

Image Created by Elizabeth Hora, Northwestern University

In keeping with the messages in this report, the image on the cover represents the tremendous opportunity and potential presented by the diversity of U.S. public school students. In a manner evocative of satellite images of the United States at night, this map depicts every public school district in the United States by district size and percentage of students of color. Just as this image glows, so too does the diversity of the U.S. population. Ultimately, U.S. students deserve an education research agenda as diverse and promising as the students themselves.

Preface

The Institute of Education Sciences (IES) in the U.S. Department of Education asked the National Academy of Sciences (NAS) to convene an expert panel to provide advice on the future of education research. I chaired the panel, and this volume is our response.

Serving on this panel was a serious task. I am proud of the diligence and responsiveness with which my colleagues and I undertook this responsibility, and I am grateful to have had the chance to work with such thoughtful, creative, and dedicated colleagues. Likewise I appreciate the expert guidance and hard work of several members of the NAS staff, particularly our study director, Kenne Dibner, and the director of the Board on Science Education, Heidi Schweingruber, without whom this work could not have been carried out.

The hallmark of an NAS report is its reliance on scientific evidence as the basis for its findings, conclusions, and recommendations. To meet this standard, the committee considered the existing research literature, examined data on IES funding patterns, sought data on grantees and reviewers, conferred with a broad range of relevant experts, and relied on members' own professional judgments to identify gaps and needs for the future of education research.

Our task was especially challenging because our charge focused on the future, whereas the evidence and judgments we considered reflected the past and present. Releasing this report in a still-ongoing global pandemic especially drove home the uncertainty of the future. Recent events have also spurred a racial reckoning that has brought renewed attention to structural inequalities in our society. In contemplating these issues, we considered changes over time in the progress of education research; in the practices of teaching, learning, and leadership at all levels of the education system; and in the social context of education. We then anticipated how those changes position us for a future that is different from the past and present and, consequently, what education research is needed to prepare us for that future.

Another distinctive challenge of our task is that education research is an intensely diverse field, encompassing different disciplines, areas of focus, methodological approaches, and epistemological assumptions, not to mention varied values and commitments on the part of researchers as well as those in practice and policy. Fortunately, our mandate was *not* to consider how to meet the needs of education research; instead, our charge was to consider what research and, correspondingly, research capacity is needed to meet the future educational needs of the nation, as laid out in IES's founding document, the Education Sciences Reform Act of 2002 (as amended in 2004). This necessarily means that the report cannot satisfy all constituencies of the field of education research. Instead, its contribution is to advise IES on what research must be prioritized and pursued, and what capacity must be built, to respond to the future education needs of the nation. If IES follows the committee's recommendations, we are confident that its leadership of the field over the next two decades will be as profoundly influential as it was during its first two decades.

IES is to be commended for its willingness to engage with its various constituencies, including researchers, parents, students, teachers, educational leaders and other practitioners, designers of education programs, and policy makers, through the vehicle of this committee's task. Few organizations willingly seek independent advice on how to carry out the core functions of their work. IES's leadership has taken a chance in seeking this advice because, as they may have anticipated, the report calls for fundamental changes in the structure of IES's research funding competition, and these changes will involve substantial work for IES staff. Some of the committee's recommendations can be implemented quickly and easily, but others will take hard intellectual and logistical effort. We recognize and appreciate the commitment to this work, which illustrates that IES staff are motivated by a desire to maximize the impact of their scarce resources and contribute optimally to the improvement of education.

It is not an exaggeration to assert that the fate of our nation rests on the success of our education system. More than any other institution, education is central both to our social cohesion and our economic productivity. The federal government is wise to invest not only in the education system itself, but also in research that can point the way toward addressing the serious challenges at hand. The Institute of Education Sciences must carry the torch that illuminates the way forward.

Adam Gamoran, *Chair*
Committee on the Future of Education Research
at the Institute of Education Sciences

Acknowledgments

The Committee on the Future of Education Research at the Institute of Education Sciences (IES) was charged with offering advice to IES that could be used to inform the 2023 grantmaking cycle. In order to achieve this task, the committee agreed to do the work of a full National Academies consensus study on a shortened timeline. A number of people devoted time and energy to supporting our work, and we owe a sincere debt of gratitude to all involved.

First, we wish to extend a thank you to IES staff and leadership for their willingness to engage in this project. Throughout this process, Mark Schneider, director of IES; Elizabeth Albro, commissioner of the National Center for Education Research; Joan McLaughlin, commissioner of the National Center for Special Education Research; and Anne Ricciuti, deputy director of the Office of Science at IES were on hand to provide resources, answer committee questions, and offer insight. We are profoundly grateful for their support.

We also wish to extend our thanks for the contributions of the many scholars who presented to the committee so that we might bring in outside expertise: your insights were invaluable, and each presentation informed our thinking in some way. Thank you also to Elizabeth Hora of Northwestern University for designing the image used on the cover of this report.

This Consensus Study Report was reviewed in draft form by individuals chosen for their diverse perspectives and technical expertise. The purpose of this independent review is to provide candid and critical comments that will assist the National Academies in making each published report as sound as possible and to ensure that it meets the institutional standards for quality, objectivity, evidence, and responsiveness to the study charge. The review comments and draft manuscript remain confidential to protect the integrity of the deliberative process.

We thank the following individuals for their review of this report: Prudence L. Carter, Department of Sociology, Brown University; David J. Francis, Department of Psychology, University of Houston; Lynn S. Fuchs, Department of Special Education, Vanderbilt University; Learning Supports, American Institutes for Research; Ray C. Hart, Office of the Executive Director, Council of the Great City Schools; Fiona Hollands, Department of Education Policy and Social Analysis, Teachers College, Columbia University; Venessa Keesler, AEM Corporation, Herndon, VA; Julie A. Marsh, Rossier School of Education and Sol Price School of Public Policy, University of Southern California; Roy D. Pea, David Jacks Professor of Education and Learning Sciences and H-STAR Institute, Stanford University; William R. Penuel, Institute of Cognitive Science and School of Education, University of Colorado Boulder; Beth D. Tuckwiller, Special Education and Disability Studies, The George Washington University; and George L. Wimberly, Professional Development and Diversity Officer, American Educational Research Association, Washington, DC.

Although the reviewers listed above provided many constructive comments and suggestions, they were not asked to endorse the conclusions or recommendations of this report nor did they see the final draft before its release. The review of this report was overseen by Michael J. Feuer, Dean and Professor, Graduate School of Education and Human Development, George Washington University, and James S. House, Angus Campbell Distinguished University Professor of Survey Research, Public Policy and Sociology, Institute for Social Research, University of Michigan. They were responsible for making certain that an independent examination of this report was carried out in accordance with the standards of the National Academies and that all review comments were carefully considered. Responsibility for the final content rests entirely with the authoring committee and the National Academies.

The committee wishes to extend its gratitude to the staff of the Division of Behavioral and Social Sciences and Education (DBASSE), in particular to Heidi Schweingruber, director of the Board on Science Education, whose strategic thinking and dedication helped ensure an incisive report, and to Leticia Garcilazo Green, who in her capacity as a research associate supported all elements of report production, from editing chapters to formatting report drafts. She has served as a full partner throughout the entirety of this process, and has made this work both enjoyable and efficient. Margaret Kelly's expert administrative leadership enabled smooth meetings and report production. Kirsten Sampson Snyder of the DBASSE staff deftly guided us through the National Academies review process, and Paula Whitacre provided invaluable editorial assistance.

Finally, the committee wishes to thank Adam Gamoran, study chair, for his seasoned leadership of a complex project. Adam's ability to listen to multiple perspectives and forge connections across ideas has enabled a forward-looking report that speaks to multiple audiences. His willingness to lead us toward robust consensus has infinitely strengthened this report, and the committee is deeply grateful for his wisdom.

Kenne A. Dibner, *Study Director*
Committee on the Future of Education
Research at the Institute of Education Sciences

Contents

xvii

Summary

In 2002, Congress passed the Education Sciences Reform Act of 2002 (ESRA), authorizing the creation of the Institute of Education Sciences (IES) as the research arm of the Department of Education, and crystallizing the federal government's commitment to providing "national leadership in expanding fundamental knowledge and understanding of education from early childhood through postsecondary study" (ESRA, 2002). In the 20 years since its founding, IES has had a field-defining impact on education research in the United States.

IES's activities are accomplished through four centers: the National Center for Education Research (NCER), the National Center for Education Statistics (NCES), the National Center for Education Evaluation and Regional Assistance, and the National Center for Special Education Research (NCSER).[1] This report focuses on NCER and NCSER. The two centers support a wide range of research activities with the broad goal of improving the quality of education in the United States. These research activities span from infancy through adulthood and across multiple education settings, depending on the center. NCER and NCSER also support the development of the next generation of education researchers through various training programs including predoctoral, postdoctoral, early career, and research methods training programs. The centers fund these activities through a

---

[1] In December 2004, Congress reauthorized the Individuals with Disabilities Education Act and, in doing so, authorized NCSER as part of IES. NCSER began operation on July 1, 2005.

competitive grant process, and the funding to support research programs is dependent on annual funding appropriated by Congress.

As the 20th anniversary of ESRA approaches, it is time to consider ways that IES can improve its current research activities and plan for future research and training in the education sciences. Such an examination can ensure that IES-funded research moves the field forward on issues that are of critical importance to education and special education policy and practice and that improve learner outcomes.

THE COMMITTEE'S CHARGE AND APPROACH

In response to a request from the Institute of Education Sciences, the National Academies of Sciences, Engineering, and Medicine through its Board on Science Education convened the Committee on the Future of Education Research at the Institute of Education Sciences to provide guidance on the future of education research at the National Center for Education Research and the National Center for Special Education Research. The committee was tasked with providing guidance on critical problems and issues where new research is needed, how to organize the request for applications, new methods and approaches, and new and different kinds of research training investments.

Research and training activities funded by the two centers have transformed education research and generated substantial insights for education policy and practice. However, the landscape of education and education research have changed substantially since the founding of IES due in large part to the portfolio of work funded by NCER and NCSER. These changes have consequences for how NCER and NCSER need to operate in order to effectively maintain their leadership role in education research.

The committee identified five themes that reflect both advances in education research since the founding of IES and major issues that education will face over the next decade: (1) equity in education, (2) technology in education, (3) use and usefulness of education research, (4) heterogeneity in education, and (5) implementation. These themes formed the lens through which the committee approached its task and developed guidance. The committee's recommendations are intended to help NCER and NCSER continue to produce transformative education research that will allow IES to maintain its status as the premier funder of education research.

KEY FINDINGS AND RECOMMENDATIONS

New Problems and Issues: Project Types and Topics

NCER and NCSER use both project types (Exploration, Development and Innovation, Initial Efficacy and Follow-up, Systematic Replication, and Measurement) and topics to organize grant competitions. Project types are important for NCER and NCSER's internal processes, as different types of projects result in different request for application (RFA) requirements and different budgets. These project types have also played a *normative* role in shaping education research, defining a process through which interventions *ought* to be developed and evaluated—moving from exploration to development to efficacy and finally to replication.

This structure was developed around the fundamental assumption that the challenges facing schools could be addressed by developing and testing interventions that could be packaged and that would increase student achievement across different school and community contexts. Twenty years into this science, however, it is now clear that this model does not account for the complexities of implementation, nor does it reflect what is now known about how evidence influences or drives changes in practice and policy.

Thus, the committee concluded that the current project type structure needs to be revised. The committee proposes an updated framework for the types of research one might undertake that would better reflect (a) the realities of the heterogeneous contexts in which research in education takes place, and (b) the actual ways in which research is used and engaged in education settings.

RECOMMENDATION 4.1:
IES should adopt new categories for types of research that will be more responsive to the needs, structures, resources, and constraints found in educational organizations. The revised types of research should include
- **Discovery and Needs Assessment**
- **Development and Adaptation**
- **Impact and Heterogeneity**
- **Knowledge Mobilization**
- **Measurement**

The committee also concluded that while the current set of topics does a good job of representing the field, the way that topics intersect with the present project types poses a challenge. Under the existing project type structure and given IES's emphasis on designs that allow for causal inferences, topic areas that can be more readily studied with causal designs (i.e., large samples, randomized interventions) are viewed as more competitive by reviewers. Further, NCER and NCSER's focus on student outcomes means that studies that would focus solely on other outcomes in the system are not eligible for funding. And, if investigators focused on outcomes other than those at the level of students are to make their proposal competitive, it means they likely have to change their research questions to focus on students and/or divert project resources to ensure they are meeting IES requirements. As a result, some of the most pressing topics given the current context of education have not received the attention warranted and need focused attention.

RECOMMENDATION 5.1:
Existing constraints or priorities in the RFA structure and review process have narrowed the kinds of studies within topics that are proposed and successfully funded. In order to expand the kinds of studies that are proposed and successfully funded in NCER and NCSER, IES should consider the following:

- Allowing use of outcomes beyond the student level (classroom, school, institution, district) as the primary outcome
- Expanding the choice of research designs for addressing research questions that focus on why, how, and for whom interventions work

In advance of these structural changes, however, the committee recognizes that the current moment of racial reckoning and responding to COVID-19 requires immediate scholarly attention. Given the issues in education that are emerging at breakneck pace and the subsequent demand for assistance from the field, the committee thinks that designating separate competitions for certain topics is warranted in order to signal their importance even though these topics might technically be "fundable" in existing competitions.

RECOMMENDATION 5.2:
Within each of its existing and future topic area competitions, IES should emphasize the need for research focused on equity.

RECOMMENDATION 5.3:
In order to encourage research in areas that are responsive to current needs and are relatively neglected in the current funding portfolio, NCER and NCSER should add the following topics:

- Civil rights policy and practice
- Teacher education and education workforce development
- Education technology and learning analytics

RECOMMENDATION 5.4:
IES should offer new research competitions under NCSER around these topics:
- Teaching practices associated with improved outcomes for students with disabilities
- Classroom and school contexts and structures that support access and inclusion to improved outcomes for students with disabilities
- Issues specific to low-incidence populations

The topics listed above represent priorities identified by the committee based on our understanding of the current state of education research. This list is not intended to be exhaustive or restrictive; rather, these topics are examples of the types of topics that emerge through consistent, focused engagement with the field. Indeed, the committee recognizes that education research is perennially evolving in response to both the production of knowledge as well as the circumstances in the world. For this reason, the committee advises that the list of topics funded by the centers should also evolve in order to remain responsive to the needs of the field. This responsiveness is a necessary component of fulfilling the obligations laid out in ESRA: in order to "sponsor sustained research that will lead to the accumulation of knowledge and understanding of education," it is important to fully understand not only what knowledge has accumulated, but also where the existing gaps are.

RECOMMENDATION 5.5:
IES should implement a systematic, periodic, and transparent process for analyzing the state of the field and adding or removing topics as appropriate. These procedures should incorporate:
- Mechanisms for engaging with a broad range of stakeholders to identify needs
- Systematic approaches to identifying areas where research is lacking by conducting syntheses of research, creating evidence gap maps, and obtaining input from both practitioners and researchers
- Public-facing and transparent communication about how priority topics are being identified

Methods and Approaches

IES will also need to re-orient its investment in methods and measures. In developing guidance on research to advance new methods and approaches the committee kept in mind that IES's charge requires that the Institute maintain a focus on "what works." Since causal questions are inherently comparative, descriptive work is also needed to conceptualize and describe current practices and the context of schools as a means for full understanding of the comparisons being made. Also, in order to fully understand why and how a particular intervention or program is working, the questions of what works and how it works need to be pursued in concert.

In reviewing the balance of funded work on methods and measures to date, the committee identified key gaps that need to be addressed moving forward. The committee recommends:

RECOMMENDATION 6.1:
IES should develop competitive priorities for research on methods and designs in the following areas:
- Small causal studies
- Understanding implementation and adaptation
- Understanding knowledge mobilization
- Predicting causal effects in local contexts
- Utilizing big data

RECOMMENDATION 6.2:
IES should convene a new competition and review panel for supporting qualitative and mixed-methods approaches to research design and methods.

To respond to the new study types and priority topics and to support the continued growth of methods, new measures and new approaches to measurement will be required. For this reason, we offer a recommendation for IES to consider related to measurement research that will support continued growth in other parts of NCER and NCSER's portfolio.

RECOMMENDATION 6.3:
IES should develop a competitive priority for the following areas of measurement research:
- Expanding the range of student outcome measures
- Developing and validating measures beyond the student level (e.g., structural and contextual factors that shape student outcomes; teacher outcomes; knowledge mobilization)
- Developing and validating measures related to educational equity
- Using technology to develop new approaches and tools for measurement

Training Programs

The training portfolio offered by NCER and NCSER is an important and vital function that has helped strengthen the education research field, and it is imperative that these programs continue to be offered to education research scientists. While IES continues these programs, there is also a need for more equitable opportunities and transparency in the offered trainings within both NCER and NCSER. Data that look at who is participating in the training programs are not readily available, and we do not know about the success of training as there are no obvious indicators of success created by IES. There is also a clear opportunity to build on current programs and expand trainings in methods to attend to the high demand among researchers. Finally, IES can implement a variety of strategies that can help broaden participation within its training programs and in turn, continue to strengthen a highly reputable portfolio. The committee recommends:

RECOMMENDATION 7.1:
IES should develop indicators of success for training, collect them from programs, and then make the information publicly available. IES should report the data it already collects on the success of programs and pathways of trainees post-training.

RECOMMENDATION 7.2:
IES should build on its current strengths in methods training and expand in the following areas:
- Methods to address questions of how and why policies and practices work
- Methods that use machine learning, predictive analytics, natural language processing, administrative data, and other like methods

To fully meet the needs of the field as outlined in ESRA, IES has a responsibility to ensure that its training programming is reaching populations of scholars and researchers who need it most. As the committee notes in this report, this is an important issue of equity in the education research community. In addition, there is tangible value in ensuring that the field of education research is diverse insofar as it improves the overall quality of eventual research, increases the likelihood that issues of equity will be taken up in research, and supports the ultimate identity-building of future researchers.

RECOMMENDATION 7.3:
IES should collect and publish information on the racial, ethnic, gender, disability status, disciplinary, and institutional backgrounds (types of institutions including Historically Black Colleges and Universities and Minority-Serving Institutions) of applicants and participants in training at both the individual and institutional levels.

RECOMMENDATION 7.4:

IES should implement a range of strategies to broaden participation in its training programs to achieve greater diversity in the racial, ethnic, and institutional backgrounds of participants. These strategies could include

- Implementing targeted outreach to underrepresented institution types
- Supporting early career mentoring
- Requiring that training program applications clearly articulate a plan for inclusive programming and equitable participation
- Offering supplements to existing research grants to support participation of individuals from underrepresented groups
- Funding short-term research opportunities for undergraduate and graduate students

RFA and Review

The committee concluded that the explicitness of the RFAs used by NCER and NCSER was one of the strengths of the IES grant review system, even as the detailed requirements result in lengthy proposals. Similarly, the committee viewed the review process of IES as a strength. Unlike other agencies (e.g., National Science Foundation), IES program officers have no role in the review process, other than to encourage applicants and provide guidance on the RFAs. Thus, the determination for funding arises only in relation to the final proposal score and the cut-score for that particular year.

Despite these strengths, the committee identified three central challenges that undermine the effectiveness: (1) IES does not publicly share information on its applicants, reviewers, and grantees, making it impossible to track whether the application and review process is resulting an equitable distribution of awards, and if not where in the process disparities are introduced; (2) the current procedures do not provide IES with sufficient information throughout the process to assess the potential impact of projects, including the significance of individual proposals, and the extent to which proposals collectively cohere as a program of research; and (3) the current procedures undermine IES's ability to be timely and responsive to the needs of the education research community. To address these challenges, the committee recommends:

RECOMMENDATION 8.1:

IES should regularly collect and publish information on the racial, ethnic, gender, disciplinary, and institutional backgrounds of applicants and funded principal investigators (PIs) and co-PIs, composition of review panels, and study samples.

RECOMMENDATION 8.2:
IES should review and fund grants more quickly and re-introduce two application cycles per year.

The committee thinks that attending to the larger structural issues facing NCER and NCSER (see Recommendations 4.1 and 5.1–5.5) will serve to help ensure that funded research is better positioned to be useful for practitioners and policy makers. However, the effects of implementing these recommendations may take several years to emerge, and the committee notes that the field needs useful research as soon as possible. For this reason, we offer two recommendations that may help ameliorate some of the challenges related to usefulness that the committee laid out. First, we suggest that the RFA adjust expectations around collaboration so that stakeholders in communities engaged in funded research are fully included in project planning.

RECOMMENDATION 8.3:
For proposals that include collaborating with LEAs and SEAs, the RFA should require that applicants explain the rationale and preliminary plan for the collaboration in lieu of the current requirement for a letter of support. Upon notification of a successful award, grantees must then provide a comprehensive partnership engagement plan and letter(s) of support in order to receive funding.

The committee also noted the current lack of a consistent plan for engaging practitioner and policy maker perspectives in the application and review process. There are multiple ways that IES might want to leverage these communities, ranging from consistent participation on panels to separate working groups, but the committee notes that practitioner and policy maker communities should be involved in determining the mechanism that works best for IES. The ultimate goal of this work is for IES to define a role for these communities that is both distinct and meaningful, such that these already burdened professionals can maximize their valuable time and effort.

RECOMMENDATION 8.4:
IES should engage a working group representing the practitioner and policy maker communities along with members of the research community to develop realistic mechanisms for incorporating practitioner and policy maker perspectives in the review process systematically across multiple panels.

Enabling Recommendations

Throughout this report, the committee returns to two major issues that constrain IES's ability to support research that attends to the needs of *all* students. The first issue is the lack of consistent reporting and analysis related to who applies and is funded in NCER and NCSER competitions, which limits the extent to which IES can ensure that funded research and researchers truly represent the needs of the communities they are intended to serve. Second, IES is afforded a relatively modest budget compared to other federal science agencies. The committee agreed that in order for IES to truly achieve the vision of these recommendations, it is critical to also address both of these issues. As such, the committee recommends:

RECOMMENDATION 9.1:
In addition to implementing the recommendations highlighted above, NCER and NCSER should conduct a comprehensive investigation of the funding processes to identify possible inequities. This analysis should attend to all aspects of the funding process, including application, reviewing, scoring, and monitoring progress. The resulting report should provide insight into barriers to funding across demographic groups and across research types and topics, as well as a plan for ameliorating these inequities.

RECOMMENDATION 9.2:
Congress should re-examine the IES budget, which does not appear to be on par with that of other scientific funding agencies, nor to have the resources to fully implement this suite of recommendations.

REFERENCE

Education Sciences Reform Act (ESRA). (2002). Title I of P.L. 107-279.

1

Introduction

A seismic shift in the landscape of public education in the United States occurred at the beginning of the 21st century. Building on decades of momentum, the years 2000–2004 saw federal and state governments passing a suite of policies that would affect virtually every stakeholder in the public education system, and usher in a new era in how the government interacts with schools. Ideas like "accountability" and "school choice," though not new to individuals already steeped in the work of education policy and teaching, became common parlance in public discourse around education. Education policy at all levels, most notably articulated in the federal No Child Left Behind Act of 2001, placed accountability for student achievement at the heart of the education enterprise and called upon stakeholders to employ evidence-based programming and practices in the service of that aim. Equally important was the new federal insistence on exposing disparities in achievement among students from a variety of demographic subgroups.

In support of those policy efforts, Congress passed the Education Sciences Reform Act of 2002 (ESRA), authorizing the creation of the Institute of Education Sciences (IES) as the research, evaluation, statistics, and assessment arm of the Department of Education, and crystallizing the federal government's commitment to providing "national leadership in expanding fundamental knowledge and understanding of education from early childhood through postsecondary study" (ESRA, 2002). The overarching goal of this legislation was to build and share reliable information on education with a broad base of constituents and intended audiences, including parents, educators, students, researchers, policy makers, and the general public. Specifically, ESRA mandates that IES share information on (a) the condition and progress of education in the United States, including early childhood education and special education; (b) educational practices that support learning and improve academic achievement and access to educational opportunities for all students; and (c) the effectiveness of federal and other education programs. With regard to research, the agency's charge is to build and disseminate a robust evidence of knowledge gained from "scientifically valid research activities" (ESRA, 2002). In the 20 years since its founding, IES has had a field-defining impact on education research in the United States.

Indeed, it is hard to overstate the role that IES has played in shaping the landscape of education research in the United States. In the intervening two decades since its founding, IES has provided funding for education research and statistics through contracts with both public and private research institutions, competitive awards to institutions around the country, and investments in research training programs, grants, and contracts. The work of IES is driven by an emphasis on using scientific research to guide education policy and practice. The agency's focus on rigor in its funded research has shaped the enterprise of education research, from who has access to research training, to what counts as high-quality research, to what questions researchers are encouraged to ask.

At the same time, the landscape of public education in the United States has changed since IES was founded in 2002, resulting in a different constellation of priorities and political realities than existed at the time IES was founded. As the 20th anniversary of ESRA approaches, it is time to consider ways that IES can improve its current research activities and plan for future research and training in the education sciences. Such an examination can ensure that IES-funded research moves the field forward on issues that are of critical importance to education and special education policy and practice and that improve learner outcomes.

STUDY SCOPE AND APPROACH

In response to a request from the Institute of Education Sciences, the National Academies of Sciences, Engineering, and Medicine through its Board on Science Education convened the Committee on the Future of Education Research at the Institute of Education Sciences to provide guidance on the future of education research at the National Center for Education Research (NCER) and the National Center for Special Education Research (NCSER).[1] IES directs two additional centers not included in this study: the

---

[1] Whereas NCER was created when IES was established by ESRA in 2002, NCSER came along 2 years later through a 2004 amendment to ESRA.

National Center for Education Statistics (NCES)[2] and the National Center for Education Evaluation and Regional Assistance (NCEE). In focusing on the future of educational research at NCER and NCSER, IES tasked the committee with identifying critical problems and issues, new methods and approaches, and new and different kinds of research training investments (see Box 1-1).

This statement of task is directly focused on helping NCER and NCSER strategically fund education research in the coming decade. Given this focus, a committee was assembled with expertise in the four primary elements of the charge. The committee members have a broad range of expertise including education policy, methods in education research, education leadership, education technology, cognition and student learning, training in education research, social-emotional learning, and early learning. In addition,

---

BOX 1-1
Statement of Task

The National Academies of Sciences, Engineering, and Medicine will convene an ad hoc committee to inform the Institute of Education Sciences (IES) National Center for Education Research and National Center for Special Education Research on

- Critical problems or issues on which new research is needed;
- How best to organize the request for applications issued by the research centers to reflect those problems/issues;
- New methods or approaches for conducting research that should be encouraged and why; and
- New and different types of research training investments that would benefit IES.

The committee will consider the policy and practice needs for education and special education research, as well as the balance across basic and applied research. The committee's work will be informed by documents that encompass the research mission and vision of IES, including the Education Sciences Reform Act (ESRA), Standards for Excellence in Education Research (SEER) principles, and detailed descriptions of the IES research and research training programs, as well input from IES staff, IES-funded researchers, and education leaders and practitioners.

---

[2] IES concurrently commissioned two other studies from the National Academies. One addresses key strategic issues related to the National Assessment of Educational Progress program, including opportunities to contain costs and increase the use of technology. The second study addresses NCE"s portfolio of activities and products, operations, staffing, and use of contractors, focusing on the center's statistical programs.

the committee was composed of scholars working in general education as well as in special education contexts, with several individuals who conduct research across settings. Several committee members are current or former practitioners and/or administrators in both K–12 and higher education settings. For more information on committee members, see Appendix F.

Interpreting the Statement of Task

One of the primary tasks facing a National Academies committee is to determine the bounds of its statement of task. Accordingly, the committee made judgments about the scope of its work. The statement of task clearly directs the committee to focus on NCER and NCSER and excludes other parts of IES such as NCEE and the Regional Education Laboratories within it. However, there were two issues the committee considered that are primarily in the purview of other units in IES, but that have implications for NCER and NCSER.

The first issue is "dissemination" of research and use of evidence generated by research conducted within NCER and NCSER. Based on materials provided to the committee by IES, the committee understood that IES categorizes dissemination of research findings as the purview of the What Works Clearinghouse (WWC) in NCEE. The theory of change, in this sense, is that research funded by NCER and NCSER that meets WWC standards can be included in the WWC repository, where it can be accessed by practitioners and policy makers in search of scientific evidence to support decision making. However, as the committee describes throughout this report, a contemporary understanding of how evidence is used by education stakeholders demands that knowledge mobilization become integrated into the work of researchers from the outset, and so these considerations are within the bounds of this committee's work.

The second issue is the review processes that govern who receives grants from NCER and NCSER. Reviews are managed by the Office of Science, which is outside of NCER and NCSER, but the committee's statement of task clearly asks the committee to address "how best to organize the request for applications issued by the research centers to reflect those problems/issues." So, while the organization of the Office of Science is out of scope, issues pertaining to how to organize reviews for NCER and NCSER are in scope, as confirmed by the IES deputy director for science in her testimony to the committee. Further, to the extent that WWC standards inform how researchers are designing and implementing their projects such that their research could be included in the repository (see more on the WWC in Chapters 2 and 4, and throughout this report), the committee considered

WWC standards as an implicit factor in the request for application (RFA) process, although stops short of commenting on the WWC itself.

Along those same lines, the committee interpreted the statement of task's four bullets as the primary tasks relevant to our work, and for this reason, focused on the research centers' activities that have direct bearing on future investments in critical problems or issues, new approaches or methods, training, and organization of RFAs. As described in Chapter 3, NCER and NCSER support research activities across multiple grant competitions, ranging from annual Education Research and Methods grant competitions to funding for Research and Development centers and Research Networks. One of the mechanisms is the Small Business Innovation Research (SBIR) competitions, which provide "seed funding to for-profit small businesses to develop and evaluate new education technology products to improve education and special education" (IES website, 2022).[3] Although the committee recognizes the value of this work, we note that the purpose of SBIR grants does not align with the specific tasks outlined in our scope, and therefore have not addressed this program.

The committee recognized that IES is both guided and constrained by the legislative language in ESRA. For this reason, the committee regularly returned to the legislative language included in ESRA to guide deliberations. As the committee made judgments about the future of NCER and NCSER, we continually reviewed ESRA text to ensure that our recommendations were within bounds.

Approach to Gathering and Assessing Evidence

The committee met five times over an 8-month period—four times completely virtually and once in a hybrid virtual/in-person setting. In addition, subgroups of the committee met throughout this period on an as-needed basis. After reviewing the expertise within the committee itself, the committee invited testimony from a number of outside experts in order to augment its expertise. The committee also considered documentation of organizational structure and programming as provided by IES staff, and invited commentary from the public via an open call for input. For details about who provided testimony to the committee and the topics covered, see Appendix A. For a description of public commentary, see Appendix B.

In addition to hearing from outside experts and soliciting public input, the committee sought additional input on scholarly areas in which we deemed further expertise was necessary. The committee commissioned five short papers to help synthesize existing evidence in the field and frame

---

[3] This sentence was modified after release of the report to IES to remove the suggestion that the use of SBIR competitions was a new mechanism for NCER. See https://ies.ed.gov/sbir/solicitations.asp.

our recommendations. These papers focused on (1) the scope of loss, both personal and educational, facing the nation in the wake of the COVID-19 pandemic; (2) the ways that scholarly understandings of learning have evolved and grown since the founding of IES in 2002; (3) what is known about how evidence is used in education policy and practice; (4) the impact of interventions aimed at supporting diversity, equity, and inclusion in academic peer-review processes; and (5) an analysis of what research topics have been funded through NCER and NCSER since their founding. These papers and their findings have all been considered as scholarly input into the committee's work. See Appendix C for a list of commissioned papers, and Appendix D for a full description of the methods used in the analysis of funding at NCER and NCSER.

Published, peer-reviewed literature remains the gold standard by which the committee made its judgments. Committee members relied on a combination of peer-reviewed published literature, the input of experts, and their own professional experience in reaching conclusions and developing recommendations. The committee's statement of task does not call for a synthesis of specific bodies of scholarship. Instead, we were asked to apply our professional judgment to a discrete set of recommendations about the future of IES, an assignment that requires deep expertise across education contexts and content areas, as well as a breadth of professional experience as IES grantees, reviewers, and research consumers. This particular statement of task demanded that the committee consider the prevailing evidence in their respective fields as the foundation for their expert judgment: that is, in the absence of a specific body of evaluative literature about IES, committee members were called upon to apply their own expertise in making recommendations. The committee was not asked to conduct original research or evaluations on how well IES is meeting its stated mandates: Indeed, the committee was directed to focus its energies on the future rather than perseverate over past events. When determining conclusions and formulating recommendations, the committee relied on our professional expertise to interpret multiple kinds of evidence: documents and information provided by IES staff, the five commissioned background papers, and oral testimony regarding the state of education research in the United States, as well as committee members' own experiences as producers and consumers of education research. Throughout our deliberations, committee members collaborated to ensure collective agreement on how the evidence was interpreted: that is, one individual's understanding of the literature in their field was not sufficient evidence to support a claim. The committee took particular care to not offer judgment in the absence of sufficient supporting evidence. In such cases, the committee attempted to elucidate ongoing issues or concerns for IES to consider as it moves forward. The conclusions and recommendations outlined in this report, and the process used to author it, reflect the full consensus judgment of the Committee on the Future of Education Research at the Institute of Education Sciences.

THE CURRENT CONTEXT OF EDUCATION AND CROSSCUTTING THEMES

As the committee began to address its charge, it became clear that to make recommendations about the future of education research at IES, it needed first to understand how the work of NCER and NCSER fits into the current landscape of education and education research in the United States. In doing so, the committee considered how that education landscape has changed since the founding of IES and whether these changes might have consequences for how NCER and NCSER should operate. The committee also considered how the advances in education research generated by IES's investments to date should inform a renewed set of priorities for the agency.

Current Context

The social and political context of education in the United States is quite different now than when IES was established. The past 20 years have seen major social and political shifts that both directly and indirectly impact education. Support for public education, politically and economically, has vacillated over this time, creating challenges for K–12 and higher education in providing high-quality learning experiences, retaining staff, and maintaining facilities. Political polarization and ideological differences have become heightened, embroiling educators and education decision makers in conflicts that often do not have much to do with student learning and student well-being. These kinds of tensions have become more visible during the COVID-19 pandemic, as exemplified by protests and often open conflict in school board meetings (Kamenetz, 2021).

The student population across preK–12 and higher education has also shifted over the past 20 years, with greater ethnic and racial diversity and growing numbers of students in K–12 who do not speak English as a first language (Irwin et al., 2021). Over this same period, income inequality in the United States has grown considerably, with consequences for the home and community contexts of students (Gamoran, 2015). PreK–12 schools have also become increasingly segregated by class and race (Reardon et al., 2021; Reardon & Owens, 2014; An & Gamoran, 2009). These trends pose increasing challenges for school systems that serve large numbers of students living in poverty, which all too often are the same school systems that have fewer economic resources in the first place.

There have also been rising concerns over the past two decades about the overall well-being of students—their mental health, their sense of belonging in school, and their social and emotional growth (National Academies of Sciences, Engineering, and Medicine, 2019a). While the alarm about students' overall well-being likely reflects issues in the broader society, schools are both called upon to support and nurture learners and themselves can be toxic and unsafe environments. The rise of school shootings, for example, and disciplinary practices that are differentially applied such that Black, Latinx, and Indigenous students and those with disabilities are more likely to suffer negative consequences are in-school phenomena that threaten learners' health and well-being (GAO, 2018; Gregory, Skiba, & Mediratta, 2017; Beland & Kim, 2016).

The COVID-19 pandemic, in concert with renewed public attention to issues of racial justice, has spotlighted the pernicious inequities that trouble the nation in a wide range of areas, including its education system (NASEM, 2021a). The impacts on schools and communities are innumerable: In addition to unprecedented disruption to schooling and staffing crises, the nation is dealing with profound personal and familial loss as the COVID-19 death toll continues to rise (NASEM, 2021b).

It is not yet possible to articulate a comprehensive analysis of the full scale of loss facing schools and communities, in part because the crisis is still ongoing. Though much media attention has been paid to the notion of "learning loss" as a result of interference with in-person schooling, the committee acknowledges a series of challenges in interpreting existing evidence around this concern. Beyond student achievement, however, there remains an abundance of open questions about how the pandemic will impact education going forward. Among them, what kind of support will communities need to be able to support student learning in the wake of the death of over 940,000 individuals in the United States? How will the nature of schooling change as a result of shifts made during the pandemic? What lessons can be learned from decisions to shift to remote schooling, and what role will technology play in schools going forward? What is the role of schools in attending to the social-emotional needs of students, families, and communities, and what is the role of families in supporting schools in the wake of the pandemic?

These issues and other pandemic-related concerns will necessarily be of paramount importance as the nation continues to battle the pandemic. In recognizing that education research can and should play a pivotal role in helping schools and communities address these critical questions, the committee has considered its work and framed its recommendations with the understanding that the aftershocks of the COVID-19 pandemic will bear on the research community for generations to come.

In addition to these broader social and political trends, insights from advances in research across the many fields that study education—education science, the learning sciences, psychology, sociology, anthropology, economics and political science—are providing more nuanced understanding of the processes of learning itself, as well as how education systems function and can be improved (see Chapter 2 for a more in-depth discussion of these advances). These insights are the result, in part, of IES research investments over the past 20 years and they offer guideposts for how IES will need to renew its approach and its portfolio to be relevant for the next 20 years.

For example, there is now wide recognition that learning is a complex cognitive and emotional phenomenon that is situated in specific social and cultural contexts (NASEM, 2018). The experiences that learners have outside of school shape and influence their learning experiences in school. Similarly, there is now a deeper appreciation of the dynamics and challenges of educational improvement and change. Classrooms, schools, and districts are situated within communities and regions across the country that vary on a variety of dimensions. Changes at the school, classroom, or district level need to be understood in context with recognition that a successful program in one setting may not lead to the same outcomes in another setting. There is also increasing recognition of the need to understand and attend to the interlocking elements of the education system. That is, changing what happens in a given classroom for a given student or group of students may be limited in the absence of attention to a broad array of interacting policies and practices that are under the purview of many different actors and decision makers operating at many different levels of the education system.

Crosscutting Themes

In order to make sense of and provide focus to this broad set of contextual issues and take account of advances in the understanding of learning and of education broadly, the committee developed five crosscutting themes: (1) equity in education, (2) changing use of technology, (3) use and usefulness of education research, (4) heterogeneity in education, and (5) implementation and system change. These themes helped the committee to maintain a coherent analysis as we worked through the specific tasks in our charge. Within each task, we have attempted to use these themes as lenses through which to identify salient questions, analyze key issues, and orient our recommendations.

In the chapters that follow, we refer to these five themes to help explain our thinking and contextualize our recommendations, and endeavor to be transparent where it is our judgment of the available evidence undergirding our claims. In the following sections, we describe why we relied on these five crosscutting themes and why they are essential to the ongoing work of IES.

Equity in Education

As the committee's work commenced, issues around equity in education emerged as one of the most urgent, primary factors that must be centered in decisions about the future work of IES. As noted above, exposing inequities in student achievement across lines of race, class, gender, language minority status, and disability status was a central feature of the No Child Left Behind Act, which set the stage for the founding of IES. In this section, we describe why equity is designated as a crosscutting theme in this report, as well as our approach to operationalizing the theme in this document.

As noted above, the student population in the nation's schools has become more racially and ethnically diverse over the past 20 years. Students are more likely to speak a language other than English at home, and there is a higher percentage of students who are immigrants (NASEM, 2020). In addition, rising income inequality has increased residential segregation, as families move to places where they can afford the cost of housing, which frequently leads to areas with high concentrations of poverty (Fry & Taylor, 2012). Black and Latinx children are more likely than White children to live in high-poverty areas (NASEM, 2019b). Specifically,

- The rate of Black children living in high-poverty areas in 2016 was about six times higher than that for White children (30% and 5%, respectively). The rate for Latinx children (22%) was about four times that for non-Latinx White children (Annie E. Casey Foundation, 2018).
- The rate of children living in poverty in 2016 was about three times higher for Black children (34%) than for White children (12%). The rate for Latinx children (28%) was more than double that for White children.

Moreover, Black children (12%) were twice as likely as White children (6%) to live in families in which the head of the household did not have a high school diploma. The rate for Latinx children (32%) was more than five times that for non-Latinx White children (Annie E. Casey Foundation, 2018).

Most school districts reflect the demographic and socioeconomic compositions of their neighborhoods. School assignment policies that send all (or many) children from a high-poverty neighborhood to the same school create schools with high concentrations of children living in poverty. Schools serving children from low-income families tend to have fewer material resources (books, libraries, classrooms, etc.), fewer course offerings, and fewer experienced teachers. The educational opportunities available to students attending these schools are not of the same quality as those in schools in more affluent neighborhoods (Monarrez & Chien, 2021).

These kinds of disparities in access to educational opportunity are deep and enduring characteristics of the American education system. While education is sometimes characterized as the "great equalizer," the country has not found ways to successfully address the adverse effects of socioeconomic circumstances, prejudice, and discrimination (NASEM, 2019b). Recognizing this, the last two reauthorizations of the Elementary and Secondary Education Act have specified that states need to address achievement gaps between different student groups.

The committee noted that the language in ESRA's charge to NCER and NCSER puts equity issues front and center, for example calling on NCER[4]

> ...to sponsor sustained research that will lead to the accumulation of knowledge and understanding of education, to—
> (A) ensure that *all children* have access to a high-quality education;
> (B) improve student academic achievement, including through the use of educational technology;
> (C) *close the achievement gap between high-performing and low-performing students* through the improvement of teaching and learning of reading, writing, mathematics, science, and other academic subjects; and
> (D) improve access to, and opportunity for, postsecondary education;... (ESRA, 2002 emphasis added).

In addition to these federal mandates, the importance of equity also emerges out of decades of research pointing to educational inequity in all facets of the education system. In the committee's view, educational inequity is one of the paramount challenges facing education researchers, and often the problems that IES and education research broadly are trying address are fundamentally problems of equity. When ESRA mandates that NCER ensure that its funded work is in service of "ensur[ing] that all children have access to a high-quality education," NCER is being asked to take on questions of equity. This same logic also applies to work designed to address the achievement gap and the multitude of other problems enumerated under the law.

To frame its thinking on this issue, the committee relied on President Biden's 2021 Executive Order on Advancing Racial Equity and Support for Underserved Communities Through the Federal Government, which outlines in full all federal agencies' responsibilities related to equity. President Biden has declared that this order applies across his administration, and

---

[4]This sentence was modified after release of the report to IES in order to clarify the role of NCER vs. NCSER in addressing equity issues.

because IES (and therefore NCER and NCSER) fall under the purview of the executive order (EO), it seems clear that organizational and programmatic decisions within IES will need to be consistent with the order. The committee has taken this into account in forming its recommendations.

The EO directs several federal actors to take actions to rectify past inequities and also advance a formal equity agenda in all future work. Of note, the EO directs the heads of all agencies to "assess whether underserved communities and their members face systemic barriers in accessing benefits and opportunities" in their respective programs, and to produce a plan for addressing these barriers. As part of that plan, agencies should identify "whether new policies, regulations, or guidance documents may be necessary to advance equity in agency actions and programs." Finally, the EO calls on agencies to "consult with members of communities that have been historically underrepresented in the Federal Government and underserved by, or subject to discrimination in, Federal policies and programs [in order to to] evaluate opportunities, consistent with applicable law, to increase coordination, communication, and engagement with community-based organizations and civil rights organizations" (Executive Order 13985, 2021). These directives, and others, are intended to "better equip agencies to develop policies and programs that deliver resources and benefits equitably to all" (Executive Order 13985, 2021).

Ultimately, the EO's definition of equity and of underserved communities helped focus the committee's understanding of IES's obligations:

> The term "equity" means the consistent and systematic fair, just, and impartial treatment of all individuals, including individuals who belong to underserved communities that have been denied such treatment, such as Black, Latino, and Indigenous and Native American persons, Asian Americans and Pacific Islanders and other persons of color; members of religious minorities; lesbian, gay, bisexual, transgender, and queer (LGBTQ+) persons; persons with disabilities; persons who live in rural areas; and persons otherwise adversely affected by persistent poverty or inequality (Executive Order 13985, 2021).

Throughout this report, the committee has operationalized these definitions of equity and of underserved communities when discussing how equity considerations can and should enter into IES's decisions. When the committee calls for attention to equity in its findings and recommendations, it is calling for treatment of underserved communities that is actively "fair, just, and impartial." In the committee's view, equitable treatment extends beyond diversity goals, though that may be one aim. Indeed, "just" treatment of underserved communities requires active attention to the historic and systemic issues that have perpetuated inequity broadly. As a result, the committee has endeavored to put these shared understandings of the terms equity and underserved communities to work throughout this report.

The committee's interpretation of the text of both ESRA and the executive order point to two primary equity aims for NCER and NCSER. First, NCER and NCSER are obliged to fund research that offers insight into and solutions aimed at addressing the equity challenges outlined in ESRA. To fulfill that obligation, it is incumbent upon IES to encourage research that explores issues related to equity and to support the development of an equitable education research enterprise. This report is intended to assist IES responding to both of those aims.

The urgency of addressing equity in education and understanding how inequities in society interact with inequities in schooling has been made even more salient by the events of the COVID-19 pandemic. The impact of the pandemic has varied widely for different communities with particularly devastating impacts for communities of color and communities experiencing poverty. Understanding how to help students, educators, and communities recover from the devastating effects of the pandemic will require a nuanced and deep understanding of equity.

In sum, the attention to equity issues laid out in both ESRA and Executive Order 13985 is rooted in a wealth of education research that posits that attending to equity is a necessary condition for ensuring that education in the United States lives up to its promise. For these reasons, the committee has used equity in education as a crosscutting theme throughout this report. We have attempted to articulate a set of recommendations that, if operationalized, will allow NCER and NCSER to be responsive to President Biden's commitment to providing the underserved communities defined in his Executive Order with "an ambitious whole-of-government equity agenda" (Executive Order 13985, 2021).

Technology in Education

Though the role that technology plays in education has certainly changed since 2002, it is critical to note that the importance of technology was explicitly included in the ESRA legislation. In fact, ESRA takes care to specify that attending to the role of technology in education (and in particular, the role of technology in supporting student achievement) should be one of the primary foci of IES's work (ESRA, 2002). Given the centrality placed on technology in the legislative language, the committee recognizes that the unprecedented technological leaps that have occurred in the last 20 years are a critical consideration for any future education investments.

The scope of the change in how schools engage with technology is dramatic. Although most public schools in 2002 had access to the Internet (via Ethernet cables with a student-to-computer ratio of approximately 5:1), the vast majority of educational technology offerings were limited and most did not take advantage of the Internet (Wells & Lewis, 2006). Low-cost personal computers did not yet exist, despite discounts offered to schools and educators by many companies. The intervening years have seen robust change not only in the nature of technology used, but also in the modalities in which technology is integrated. Teachers, students, and caregivers now make liberal use of smartphones, tablets, and low-cost laptops, and they leverage an increasing number of related applications and web-based platforms for both communication and educational content (U.S. Department of Education, 2021). New genres of technologies are being used for learning and collaboration, such as games (Plass, Mayer, & Homer, 2020), augmented reality, virtual reality (Weiss et al., 2006), among others, and many schools and districts are endeavoring to productively engage social media platforms (Yamaguchi & Hall, 2017). In addition to the proliferation of student-facing learning management systems such as Google Classroom, teachers, administrators, and other staff are now obliged to engage with a battery of education data systems as part of their jobs. This same phenomenon is true in special education contexts: In the past 20 years, access to adaptive technologies has exploded, enabling exciting new possibilities for learning for special education populations (Zimmerman, 2019). And, as noted later in this chapter, the circumstances surrounding schooling in the COVID-19 pandemic have demanded an exponential increase in teacher, student, and caregiver use of technology-based strategies for supporting remote learning (NASEM, 2021a).

Advances in technology, both in systems to support learning and administrative data systems, have led to an explosion of data on students and schools. How best to leverage these systems to support improved student outcomes, while also respecting privacy and ethical use, are critical issues for education at all levels.

Given this substantial shift, the committee found it prudent to consider not only the speed of change prior to 2022 in adoption of technology, but also the likelihood that future decades will experience continued growth and development. Moreover, ESRA is clear in its direction to IES that technology and its use for and in education needs to play a central role in the work of NCER and NCSER. For this reason, the committee identified the use of technology as a crosscutting theme that must be attended to when addressing the foci in its statement of task.

Use and Usefulness of Education Research

A major goal of IES, as outlined in ESRA, is to facilitate the use of evidence to inform education. The very structure of IES is designed to identify and promote effective approaches that have robust, scientific evidence behind them. Since the founding of IES, however, there have been major advances in understanding how education decision makers and practitioners use evidence in their work and what can make education research more useful.

When IES was established, a common belief in the field was that when interventions were shown to be effective with rigorous scientific testing, they would be discovered and adopted by users in the field (Farley-Ripple et al., 2018; Coburn, Honig, & Stein, 2009). That is, decision makers would immediately turn to the evidence base when they had a problem to solve. Research conducted during the past two decades, however, shows that research use in education rarely works in this linear fashion (Finnigan & Daly, 2014; Best & Holmes, 2010; Davies & Nutley, 2008). Instead, decisions in school systems rely on a variety of factors, only one of which is evidence produced by research (Coburn, Honig, & Stein, 2009). In fact, policy makers and practitioners are unlikely to identify a problem and turn to peer-reviewed literature for a solution (Penuel et al., 2017). Rather, stakeholders are more likely to engage in conceptual use of research: that is, sustained and iterative interaction with a body of work over time, such that it informs how stakeholders ask questions and understand problems (see Chapter 2 for more discussion).

These insights complicate IES's task of conducting and promoting evidence-based approaches in education. Ensuring that the problems being addressed in education research are meaningful and important to educators and education decision makers is a key challenge. This has been particularly evident during the pandemic when schools sought guidance on how to best support students' learning during the crisis, and the education research community had difficulty both identifying existing studies that could provide guidance and mounting new research that could be completed and acted upon in a timely way.

As outlined in ESRA, the functions of IES include obligations to "promote the use, development, and application of knowledge gained from scientifically valid research activities," and "promote the use and application of research and development to improve practice in the classroom." Thus, the committee understands that IES's function is not merely to "disseminate," or inform the public about, research findings, but to take steps to enable their use in practice. As a result, the committee identified use and usefulness of research as a theme that must be consistently addressed. If the research that NCER and NCSER fund is not useful to or used by its intended audience, then it is not meeting the charge mandated under ESRA to effect change in student outcomes. Throughout this report, the committee repeatedly returns to the question of how NCER and NCSER can continue to ensure that the research it funds is both useful and used.

Heterogeneity

In order to fully address the goals laid out for IES in ESRA, education research funded by NCER and NCSER needs to grapple with the wide variation present at every level of the education system. That is, research on how to improve student outcomes will fall short if it does not explicitly address issues of heterogeneity (Bryan et al., 2021; Bryk et al., 2015). This means that "what works, under what conditions, and for whom" (Gutiérrez & Penuel, 2014, p. 22) and why (Cowen, 2019) must be central questions for research. Often, current approaches to determining what is effective for improving student outcomes assume that there is very little to no variation in effect sizes across students, teachers, and schools. However, over the past 20 years, there is mounting evidence that treatment effects vary, sometimes substantially (Weiss et al., 2017).

This concern suggests to instead *begin* with the assumption that treatment effects can and will vary across students, teachers, and schools. Studies need to treat this heterogeneity as a *primary* concern, not secondary. Understanding heterogeneity involves more than merely a statistical exercise in computing and finding variation. Explaining what led to that heterogeneity, and then applying the inferences based on past findings to future settings, requires analyzing how conditions differ and how important those differences are in influencing an observed variation (Provost, 2011; Deming, 1953).

Analyzing variation may also help distinguish between the need for systemic change or for targeted action. Calculating the variability of a process may reveal whether it is stable and predictable, or whether the results emerge from an out-of-control process or from separate systems (Provost & Murray, 2011; Deming, 1953). A stable process producing undesirable results needs to shift the entire system to yield improvement; an unstable process requires systemic improvements to detect and correct issues to bring the process under control. However, high variability emerging from separate systems "raises questions about hidden factors and potential systemic inequities to identify and resolve" (Ming & Kennedy, 2020).

The committee notes that IES has, in fact, made multiple efforts to attend to issues of heterogeneity in its tenure. As we discuss in Chapter 4, IES has called for research that better addresses the "whom, where, and under what conditions" questions embedded in research. As with a number of challenges the committee will describe throughout this report, however, a series of structural issues present in IES guidance creates a funding context in which questions of heterogeneity may be less likely to receive support. For this reason, the committee chose to highlight the importance of these issues in establishing recommendations that build in heterogeneity as an assumption, as well as methods to study and explain heterogeneity more fully.

Implementation and System Change

The portfolio of research funded by both NCER and NCSER makes clear that the success of interventions is driven in large part by their implementation. It is also clear that understanding implementation needs to go beyond simply determining if a given intervention is implemented with fidelity. Rather, there is increasing recognition that the process of implementation itself is worthy of study if education research is to provide educators with sufficient guidance on how to improve student outcomes.

Implementation research "is the scientific study of methods to promote the systematic uptake of research findings and other evidence-based practices into routine practice, and, hence, to improve the quality and effectiveness" of interventions, policies, and practices (Eccles & Mittman 2006, p. 1). This definition distinguishes between *what* is being implemented and *how* to support its implementation, where "what" refers to the intervention, evidence-based practice, innovation, or "the thing," while "how" refers to the implementation strategies or "how to support the thing" (Curran, 2020; Fixsen et al., 2005). Identifying relevant factors influencing implementation, and situating them within a theoretical explanation for their influence, allows stakeholders to identify and develop strategies targeting those factors more effectively, ultimately improving desired outcomes. This shift in framing will also clarify where systemic changes might be needed in order to support a more effective implementation of an intervention.

It is the committee's judgment that if NCER and NCSER are indeed going to support the kind of research outcomes articulated in ESRA, it is critical that funded research engages with issues of implementation. For this reason, the committee considers implementation as a crosscutting theme throughout this report, and endeavors to address how NCER and NCSER might take on implementation and systemic change in support of its stated goals.

AUDIENCES

This report is intended to address the statement of task provided to the committee by its IES sponsors. For this reason, the committee considers IES, specifically NCER and NCSER stakeholders, as the primary audience for this report. However, the committee sees the audience for this report as extending beyond IES: Insofar as NCER and NCSER support a large percentage of the education research community in the United States, this report is intended to reflect that community's needs and concerns. The committee therefore sees the education research community as an additional but important audience for this report. Finally, the committee recognizes that IES's scope is limited both by its governing language in ESRA and by its congressional appropriations. For these reasons, the committee envisions Congress and other relevant policy makers as another audience.

ORGANIZATION OF THIS REPORT

This report is organized to reflect the committee's recommendations on the items listed in our statement of task. Following Chapters 2 and 3, which describe the background and current organizational structure of IES, the committee turns to the substance of its argument. In Chapter 4, we discuss our recommendations for a structure of project types for organizing funding in NCER and NCSER, and in Chapter 5, we make recommendations for new topics of study. Together, Chapters 4 and 5 cover the research goals and topics that IES uses to organize its work, and these chapters constitute our response to the first element of our charge—to identify problems and issues that should be considered for IES funding. We address the second, third, and fourth elements of our charge in Chapter 6, which focuses on methods and measures; Chapter 7, which examines the future of training; and Chapter 8, which offers commentary on how the request for applications process can be organized to support NCER and NCSER's future work. We conclude with a chapter offering our vision for the future of education research in NCER and NCSER.

REFERENCES

An, B.P., and Gamoran, A. (2009). Trends in school racial composition in the era of unitary status. In C.E. Smrekar and E.B. Goldring (Eds.), *From the Courtroom to the Classroom: The Shifting Landscape of School Desegregation* (pp. 19–47). Cambridge, MA: Harvard Education Press.

Annie E. Casey Foundation. (2018). *2018 Kids Count Data Book: State Trends in Child Well-Being*. Baltimore, MD: Author. http:// www.aecf.org.

Beland, L-P., and Kim, D. (2016). The effect of high school shootings on schools and student performance. *Educational Evaluation and Policy Analysis, 38*, 113–126.

Best, A., and Holmes, B. (2010). Systems thinking, knowledge and action: Towards better models and methods. *Evidence & Policy: A Journal of Research, Debate and Practice, 6*, 145–159. https://10.1332/174426410X502284.

Bryan, C.J., Tipton, E., and Yeager, D.S. (2021). Behavioural science is unlikely to change the world without a heterogeneity revolution. *Nature Human Behaviour, 5*, 980–989. https://doi.org/10.1038/s41562-021-01143-3.

Bryk, A.S., Gomez, L.M., Grunow, A., and LeMahieu, P.G. (2015). *Learning to Improve: How America's Schools Can Get Better at Getting Better*. Cambridge, MA: Harvard Education Press.

Coburn, C.E., Honig, M.I., and Stein, M.K. (2009). What's the evidence on districts' use of evidence? In J.D. Bransford, D.J. Stipek, N.J. Vye, L.M. Gomez, and D. Lam (Eds.), *The Role of Research in Educational Improvement* (pp. 67–86). Cambridge, MA: Harvard Education Press.

Cowen, N. (2019). For whom does "what works" work? The political economy of evidence-based education, *Educational Research and Evaluation, 25*(1–2), 81–98. https://doi.org/10.1080/13803611.2019.1617991.

Curran, F.C. (2020). A matter of measurement: How different ways of measuring racial gaps in school discipline can yield drastically different conclusions about racial disparities in discipline. *Educational Researcher, 49*(5), 382–387.

Davies, H., Nutley, S., and Walter, I. (2008). Why 'knowledge transfer' is misconceived for applied social research. *Journal of Health Services Research & Policy, 13*(3), 188–190. https://doi.org/10.1258/jhsrp.2008.008055.

Deming, W.E. (1953). On the distinction between enumerative and analytic surveys. *Journal of the American Statistical Association, 48*(262), 244–255.

Eccles, M.P., and Mittman, B.S. (2006). Welcome to implementation science. *Implementation Science, 1*, 1. https://doi.org/10.1186/1748-5908-1-1.

Education Sciences Reform Act (ESRA). (2002). Title I of P.L. 107-279.

Executive Order 13985, 86 FR 7009 (January 25, 2021).

Farley-Ripple, E., May, H., Karpyn, A., Tilley, K., and McDonough, K. (2018). Rethinking connections between research and practice in education: A conceptual framework. *Educational Researcher, 47*(4), 235–245.

Finnigan, K.S., and Daly, A.J. (Eds). (2014). *Using Research Evidence in Education: From the Schoolhouse Door to Capitol Hill*. Cham, Switzerland: Springer.

Fixsen, D.L., Naoom, S.F., Blase, K.A., Friedman, R.M., and Wallace, F. (2005). *Implementation Research: A Synthesis of the Literature*. FMHI Publication No. 231. Tampa: University of South Florida, Louis de la Parte Florida Mental Health Institute, National Implementation Research Network.

Fry, R., and Taylor, P. (2012). The Rise of Residential Segregation by Income. Pew Charitable Trusts. https://www.pewresearch.org/social-trends/2012/08/01/the-rise-of-residential-segregation-by-income/.

Gamoran, A. (2015). The Future of Educational Inequality: What Went Wrong and How Can We Fix It? New York: William T. Grant Foundation. http://wtgrantfoundation.org/resource/the-future-of-educational-inequality-what-went-wrong-and-how-can-we-fix-it.

Government Accountability Office (GAO). (2018). Discipline Disparities for Black Students, Boys, and Students with Disabilities. Washington, DC: Author.

Gregory, A., Skiba, R.J., and Mediratta, K. (2017). Eliminating disparities in school discipline: A framework for intervention. *Review of Research in Education, 41*, 253–278.

Gutiérrez, K.D., and Penuel, W.R. (2014). Relevance to practice as a criterion for rigor. *Educational Researcher, 43*(1), 19–23. https://doi.org/10.3102/0013189X13520289.

Irwin, V., Zhang, J., Wang, X., Hein, S., Wang, K., Roberts, A., York, C., Barmer, A., Bullock Mann, F., Dilig, R., and Parker, S. (2021). Report on the Condition of Education 2021 (NCES 2021-144). U.S. Department of Education. Washington, DC: National Center for Education Statistics. https://nces.ed.gov/pubsearch/pubsinfo.asp?pubid=2021144.

Kamenetz, A. (2021). A look at the groups supporting school board protesters nationwide. National Public Radio online. https://www.npr.org/2021/10/26/1049078199/a-look-at-the-groups-supporting-school-board-protesters-nationwide.

Ming, N.C., and Kennedy, A.I. (2020). Developing and using indicators for continuous improvement. *Teachers College Record (Yearbook), 122*(14). https://www.tcrecord.org/Content.asp?ContentId=23462.

Monarrez, T., and Chien, C. (2021). Dividing Lines: Racially Unequal School Boundaries in US Public School Systems. Research Report. Center on Education Data and Policy. The Urban Institute.

National Academies of Sciences, Engineering, and Medicine (NASEM). (2018). *How People Learn II: Learners, Contexts, and Cultures*. Washington, DC: The National Academies Press. https://doi.org/10.17226/24783.

———(2019a). *The Promise of Adolescence: Realizing Opportunity for All Youth*. Washington, DC: The National Academies Press. https://doi.org/10.17226/25388.

———(2019b). *Monitoring Educational Equity*. Washington, DC: The National Academies Press. https://doi.org/10.17226/25389.

———(2020). *Changing Expectations for the K–12 Teacher Workforce: Policies, Preservice Education, Professional Development, and the Workplace*. Washington, DC: The National Academies Press. https://doi.org/10.17226/25603.

———(2021a). *COVID-19 and the K–12 Teacher Workforce: Seizing the Moment to Reimagine Education: Proceedings of a Workshop-in-Brief*. Washington, DC: The National Academies Press. https://doi.org/10.17226/26356.

———(2021b). *Back in School: Addressing the Well-Being of Students in the Wake of COVID-19: Proceedings of a Workshop–in Brief*. Washington, DC: The National Academies Press. https://doi.org/10.17226/26296.

Penuel, W.R., Briggs, D.C., Davidson, K.L., Herlihy, C., Sherer, D., Hill, H.C., Farrell, C., and Allen, A. (2017). How school and district leaders access, perceive, and use research. *AERA Open, 3*(2), 1–17.

Plass, J.L., Mayer, R.E., and Homer, B.D. (Eds.) (2020). *Handbook of Game-based Learning*. Cambridge, MA: MIT Press.

Provost, L.P. (2011). Analytical studies: A framework for quality improvement design and analysis. *BMJ Quality & Safety, 20*(Suppl 1), i92–i96.

Provost, L.P., and Murray, S. (2011). *The Health Care Data Guide: Learning from Data for Improvement*. San Francisco, CA: John Wiley & Sons.

Reardon, S.F., and Owens, A. (2014). 60 years after Brown: Trends and consequences of school segregation. *Annual Review of Sociology, 40*, 199–218.

Reardon, S.F., Weathers, E.F., Fahle, E.M., Jang. H., and Kalogrides, D. (2021). Is Separate Still Unequal? New Evidence on School Segregation and Racial Academic Achievement Gaps. CEPA Working Paper No. 19-06. Stanford, CA: Stanford University, Center for Education Policy Analysis.

U.S. Department of Education. (2021). Use of Technology in Teaching and Learning. https://www.ed.gov/oii-news/use-technology-teaching-and-learning.

Weiss, J., Nolan, J., Hunsinger, J., and Trifonas, P. (Eds.). (2006). *The International Handbook of Virtual Learning Environments* (Vol. 14). Dordrecht, Netherlands: Springer.

Weiss, M.J., Bloom, H.S., Verbitsky-Savitz, N., Gupta, H., Vigil, A.E., and Cullinan, D.N. (2017). How much do the effects of education and training programs vary across sites? Evidence from past multisite randomized trials. *Journal of Research on Educational Effectiveness, 10*(4), 843–876. https://doi.org/10.1080/19345747.2017.1300719.

Wells, J., and Lewis, L. (2006). Internet Access in U.S. Public Schools and Classrooms: 1994–2005 (NCES 2007-020). Washington, DC: U.S. Department of Education, National Center for Education Statistics.

Yamaguchi, R., and Hall, A. (2017). Compendium of Education Technology Research Funded by NCER and NCSER: 2002–2014. NCER 2017-0001. Washington, DC: U.S. Department of Education, National Center for Education Research.

Zimmerman, E. (2019). AR/VR in K–12: Schools Use Immersive Technology for Assistive Learning. https://edtechmagazine.com/k12/article/2019/08/arvr-k-12-schools-use-immersive-technology-assistive-learning-perfcon.

2

Background

As introduced in Chapter 1, this committee was tasked with providing guidance to the Institute of Education Sciences (IES) on how it might expand and improve its work consistent with the mandates laid out in its authorizing legislation, the Education Sciences Reform Act (ESRA). To accomplish this objective, the committee's first step was to consider background information about the context in which the National Center for Education Research (NCER) and National Center for Special Education Research (NCSER) operate. In this chapter, the committee expands on the background information provided in Chapter 1 to describe the initial problems that ESRA was trying to solve, identify how NCER and NCSER have sought to address those problems, consider what NCER and NCSER have achieved in their current structure, and examine how the field has changed in the intervening decades since ESRA was enacted.[1] Taken in concert, this background allowed the committee to lay the groundwork for recommendations for how NCER and NCSER might adapt to meet the contemporary and future needs of education research.

EDUCATION RESEARCH IN 2002

When ESRA was authorized at the turn of the 21st century, education research was in the spotlight. In 2001, Congress reauthorized the Elementary and Secondary Education Act as the No Child Left Behind Act (NCLB)

---

[1] We discuss how NCER and NCSER are organized, including approaches to funding and other structural considerations, in Chapter 3.

of 2001, establishing a series of policy priorities and mandating that decisions about schooling flow from "research that involves the application of rigorous, systematic, and objective procedures to obtain reliable and valid knowledge relevant to education activities and programs." The following year, the National Research Council (now the National Academies of Sciences, Engineering, and Medicine) released *Scientific Research in Education,* which noted that the passage of NCLB had "brought a new sense of urgency to understanding the ways in which the basic tenets of science manifest in the study of teaching, learning, and schooling" so that decisions could be informed by that science (NRC, 2002). When Congress authorized the founding of a new federal science agency devoted solely to education research in November 2002, the timing was fortuitous.

Grover "Russ" Whitehurst was selected as the first director of IES. Whitehurst expressed concerns about the state of education research in the United States prior to 2002. Speaking to the American Educational Research Association (AERA) in 2003, he noted that he was unconvinced that education research prior to 2002 would be able to change practice toward improving student outcomes. Whitehurst remarked, "Education hasn't even incorporated into instruction what we know from basic research [in cognitive neuroscience into] practice—and I learned about that in a psychology course I took in 1962" (Whitehurst, 2003). Whitehurst posited that a new IES would focus on applied research: that is, research "that has high consideration of use, that is practical, that is applied, that is relevant to practitioners and policy makers."

In his 2003 comments to AERA, Whitehurst laid out a set of principles to guide IES in pursuing scientific research in education. He asserted that "questions of efficacy and effectiveness, or what works, are causal, and are addressed most rigorously with randomized field trials." These principles, gleaned from scientific research in other fields, served as the conceptual underpinnings of how IES was initially organized and operated. They included the following:

1. Randomized trials are the only sure method for determining the effectiveness of education programs and practices.
2. Randomized trials are not appropriate for all questions.
3. Interpretations of the results of randomized trials can be enhanced with results from other methods.
4. A complete portfolio of federal funding in education will include programs of research that employ a variety of research methods.
5. Questions of what works are paramount for practitioners; hence randomized trials are of high priority at the Institute (Whitehurst, 2003).

So, while methods outside of the randomized controlled trial would be part of IES's portfolio, studies that employed randomized designs would be privileged in IES's funding competitions. In organizing the institute this way, Whitehurst hoped that IES would create a body of knowledge upon which practitioners could draw to make immediate decisions informed by high-quality research. He concluded his presentation to AERA by presenting a vision for the future:

> The people on the front lines of education want research to help them make better decisions in those areas in which they have choices to make, such as curriculum, teacher professional development, assessment, technology, and management.... I have a vision of a day when any educator or policy maker will want to know what the research says before making an important decision. The research will be there. It will be rigorous. It will be relevant. It will be disseminated and accessed through tools that make it useable. The production and dissemination of this research will be in the hands of an education research community that is large, well-trained, and of high prestige (Whitehurst, 2003).

Responses from the education research community to Whitehurst's vision reflected sharply divided perspectives. Many of the most prominent U.S. education researchers were eager to see leadership oriented toward this articulation of scientific rigor. Previewing Whitehurst's plan for IES, Robert Slavin outlined the opportunities for evidence-based policy in education, describing in detail the critical importance as well as the difficulties of employing randomized designs in making claims about what works in education. Despite its challenges, he argued, it is important that education research seize the moment to demonstrate what kind of study is possible in education. Slavin (2002) noted,

> This is a time when it makes sense to concentrate resources and energies on a set of randomized experiments of impeccable quality and clear policy importance to demonstrate that such studies can be done. Over the longer run, I believe that a mix of randomized and rigorous matched experiments evaluating educational interventions would be healthier than a steady diet of randomized experiments, but right now we need to establish the highest possible standard of evidence, on a par with standards in other fields, to demonstrate what educational research can accomplish.

In praising the move toward randomization, Slavin called for using this opening to build capacity and proof of concept. Eventually, he suggested, the field would be able to strategically engage multiple methods toward a robust, comprehensive knowledge base.

Others in the field were less enthusiastic about this approach. Critiques ranged from frustration around codifying "what counts" as knowledge in education to more tactical concerns about the practical capacity of schools and districts to serve as sites for experiments. In a rebuttal to Slavin's claims, Olson (2004) described the limitations of experimental design for building a robust knowledge base. Olson argued,

> Good research is not just a matter of trying out things or even comparing them, but rather a matter of advancing theoretically inspired notions of sufficient merit that they would benefit from being put to strenuous empirical test. We require richer theories than those assuming simple cause-effect relations among treatments (as defined by designers), their construals and implementations by teachers, and their interpretations by learners. The reputation of educational research is tarnished less by the lack of replicable results than by the lack of any deeper theory that would explain why the thousands of experiments that make up the literature of the field appear to have yielded so little.

Other criticisms emerged at that time, as well. Eisenhart and Towne (2003) argued that the definitions of scientifically based research were not coherent across different forms of policy guidance and would benefit from more public input. Others argued that ESRA, NCLB, and *Scientific Research in Education* fundamentally misunderstood the epistemology and practice of qualitative research (Howe, 2003a; Erickson & Gutiérrez, 2002). These critics argued that qualitative research can do more than just investigate "what is happening," but also can generate theory and develop useful interpretations of classroom activity for both research and practice.

Nevertheless, ESRA gave Whitehurst the opportunity to forge ahead with an IES that reflected his interpretation of rigor in scientific research in education. The organizing structures and priorities of NCER and NCSER reflect his vision. In the section that follows, we discuss the substance of NCER and NCSER's work, and describe how this work has altered the shape of education research in the United States.

FUNDING A VISION OF SCIENTIFIC RESEARCH IN EDUCATION

From their outset, both NCER and NCSER (authorized in an amended ESRA in 2004) were organized to support a science of education research that would contribute to "expanding fundamental knowledge and understanding of education from early childhood through postsecondary study" (ESRA, 2002). As established in ESRA, the founding research mission of NCER was to

(1) Sponsor sustained research that will lead to the accumulation of knowledge and understanding of education, to—(A) ensure that all children have access to a high-quality education; (B) improve student academic achievement, including through the use of educational technology; (C) close the achievement gap between high-performing and low-performing students through the improvement of teaching and learning of reading, writing, mathematics, science, and other academic subjects; and (D) improve access to, and opportunity for, postsecondary education.

Correspondingly, NCSER's founding mission included the following: "Sponsor research to expand knowledge and understanding of the needs of infants, toddlers, and children with disabilities in order to improve the developmental, educational, and transitional results of such individuals."

With these missions in mind, NCER and NCSER have operationalized *scientific research in education* as research that both (a) focuses on student outcomes, and (b) prioritizes rigor by emphasizing research designs and methods appropriate to the research question posed. The aim of documenting programs and practices that work to improve student outcomes ultimately calls for impact studies, which bring a particular emphasis on randomized designs with sufficient statistical power to detect anticipated effects. A corresponding goal has been to improve the capacity of education researchers to carry out this new charge.

In the committee's view, the establishment of NCER and NCSER was foundational for elevating scientific research in education. Over the past 20 years, NCER and NCSER have produced valuable knowledge across a broad range of topics, which collectively provide evidence of how to improve academic outcomes for students from infancy to adulthood. The centers' work has rapidly expanded the research tools (including the methodologies, measures, and technologies) necessary to carry out scientific research. Finally, as discussed in depth in Chapter 7, NCER and NCSER's investments in training education researchers have changed the shape of the field. Since their inception, NCER and NCSER's training programs have provided opportunities for specific methodological training experiences and career development opportunities. These programs have been highly popular, and they have allowed for the development of a cadre of researchers who share similar understandings of how to conduct research on particular issues.

These strengths, taken together, have been pivotal to the work of building a coherent field in education research. In the absence of NCER and NCSER's strategic funding and resources, education research in the United States would be a different enterprise than it is today.

CHANGES SINCE 2002

As noted above, IES—and NCER and NCSER—have substantially re-shaped education research since 2002. In the intervening decades, though, the world has changed around IES—in part because of the knowledge base to which NCER and NCSER have contributed. In this section, we consider several changes that have occurred since the founding of IES, and consider what these changes might mean for NCER and NCSER's current portfolio. The committee acknowledges that IES has already taken many steps to respond to changes in the field; for example, in Chapter 5 we discuss IES's changing approach toward the topics it seeks to fund, including the increasingly prominent role of special topics and of large-scale research networks. The question facing IES, however, is whether NCER and NCSER's current structure and priorities can sufficiently address these broader changes in the field or whether more substantial changes are necessary.

Use of Research Evidence in Education

As noted in Chapter 1, the committee found that the structure of IES (as dictated in ESRA) reflects a particular understanding of how research is used in education. Indeed, as stated earlier, IES categorizes dissemination of research findings as the purview of the What Works Clearinghouse in the National Center for Education Evaluation and Regional Assistance, while NCER and NCSER are tasked with funding the *doing* of research.[2] However, contemporary research on evidence use indicates that this view of how stakeholders engage with research and evidence is inconsistent with the realities of evidence use in the education system. Indeed, in the past 20 years, the field has evolved toward much more nuanced understandings, not only of how stakeholders do (and do not) engage with evidence from research, but also of which conditions facilitate and sustain productive use. The inconsistency between assumptions prevalent in 2002 about how educators would come to use research evidence, and what subsequent studies show about how evidence is used in practice, has constrained IES's ability to achieve its legislated function to "promote the use, development, and application of knowledge gained from scientifically valid research activities (Education Sciences Reform Act of 2002, Section 112(3)).

Research on the instrumental use of research evidence—that is, when evidence from research serves as a tool for making policy or pedagogical decisions—indicates that this form of evidence use is less common than researchers would like; specifically, research evidence plays a limited role in

---

[2]The committee notes that NCER and NCSER do both require that applicants propose a dissemination strategy as part of their request for funding, which we discuss in Chapters 4 and 8 of this report.

the decision making of central office staff, local school boards, principals, and teachers (Finnigan & Daly, 2017; Asen et al., 2013, 2011; Farley-Ripple, 2012).[3] Instead, prior research suggests that educators turn to people first and prefer evidence curated by colleagues to inform their decisions (Finnigan & Daly, 2017; Penuel et al., 2017); central office staff prefer publications from professional organizations, conferences, the Internet, and leadership books over peer-reviewed journal articles (Farley-Ripple, 2012); and school board members rely on a variety of evidence (e.g., experience or testimony) in deliberations, rarely using research as evidence in these processes (Asen et al., 2013, 2011). Educators hold a variety of definitions of what counts as evidence as they consider education issues or problems, ranging from empirical studies, to local evaluation reports, to expert opinion, to the popular press (Finnigan, Daly, & Che, 2012). So, while actors throughout the education system acknowledge that evidence from research is important, the extent to which they actually use research (versus other types of evidence) in instrumental ways varies widely.

However, research on this subject over the last decade has shown that conceptual use of research, while not always commonplace, may be occurring in ways that make meaningful differences throughout the system of U.S. education. Stakeholders engage in conceptual use of research when they interact with research in ways that inform how they ask questions and understand problems. Conceptual use may occur slowly, intermittently, and over long periods of time, which makes it a substantially harder phenomenon to study, though no less important to understand.

As Tseng and Nutley (2014) described:

> [Conceptual] use is contingent, interactive, and iterative. It involves people individually and collectively engaging with research over time, bringing their own and their organization's goals, motivations, routines, and political contexts with them. Research also enters the policy process at various times—as problems are defined (and redefined); ideas are generated; solutions are identified; and policies are adopted, implemented, and sometimes stalled.

Importantly, recent research suggests that the use of research evidence in education by policy makers and practitioners can be facilitated by individuals who serve as "research brokers" as well as by intermediary organizations and networks. This finding is important because it helps clarify the ways that researchers connect with policy makers and practitioners indirectly rather than directly. For example, Finnegan and Daly (2014) found that key individuals in school districts served as brokers. Unfor-

---

[3] This section draws on findings synthesized for the committee by Finnigan (2021).

tunately, high levels of churn in these leadership roles meant that the ties relating to research and evidence were constantly being disrupted. Other work has found that staff at county-level school districts played important brokering roles (Neal et al., 2015) and that district staff have filled gaps between producers and users of evidence (Finnigan & Daly, 2014). In these cases, the brokers serve in intermediary positions, but they are internal to the organization, rather than external entities. In all cases, brokers can play a critical role in the flow of ideas and practices because they filter what is known in a given organization about research and evidence.

In the past decade, new groups have emerged to position themselves as the "interpreters" of evidence (Debray et al., 2014; Scott & Jabbar, 2014; Scott et al., 2014). In essence, brokers operate within a type of market, as policy makers and practitioners require information to make decisions and intermediaries respond to this demand (Debray et al., 2014). Intermediaries have taken on important roles in the packaging of research and the management of perceptions to "sell" policy makers or practitioners on sets of findings, as well as to validate whether evidence is credible. Of course, while filling a larger "need" of the system to bridge researcher to user, another "need" was being filled as many of these organizations spent considerable resources moving their own agendas forward, many unchecked (Reckhow, Tompkins-Strange, & Galey-Horn, 2021; Scott & Jabbar, 2014). Intermediary organizations are active in promoting, participating in, or opposing educational policies like charter schools, vouchers, "parent trigger" laws, and merit-pay systems for teachers (Scott et al., 2015).

Use of research evidence occurs in a robust network of interconnected relationships, whether one focuses on the school, district, state, or federal government. Several studies that involved case studies and network analysis found that trust plays a role in use of research and evidence (Penuel et al., 2020; Asen, 2015; Finnigan & Daly, 2014) in that stakeholders make determinations about the evidence based upon the person providing the evidence. In other words, the same type of evidence brought by a trustworthy or untrustworthy source will have a different result in a person's response to that evidence, for example, whether it resonates or whether they are skeptical of it. As such, it is important for the research community to be mindful not only that individuals have social relationships, but also that the quality of relationships between individuals is consequential for use of research and evidence.

Understanding how research evidence is used by stakeholders making decisions in education is a central component of ensuring that IES's investments in research ultimately matter for improving education in the United States. For this reason, and in light of how much the field has grown in the past two decades, the committee brings these perspectives to bear in its recommendations for IES throughout this report.

Attending to Culture and Deficit Ideologies
in Understandings of Learning

Over the past 20 years, the study of human learning has expanded, shifted, and progressed in critically important ways, leading to foundational changes in conceptions of human learning.[4] Among the most important of these advances is the wide recognition of what Arnett (2008) and later Henrich and colleagues (2010) named the "WEIRD (western, educated, industrialized, rich, democratic) people problem" or the deep systemic bias in the social and behavioral sciences, of which educational sciences is an important part. A watershed special publication in *Brain and Behavioral Sciences*, and another in *Nature*, reviewed the accumulation of evidence demonstrating that overly broad claims to understanding human learning and development were dubious at best. The authors in these collections, and many others, called attention to broad-scale sample bias as well as experimental design bias (e.g., Thalmayer, Toscanelli, & Arnett, 2021; Hruschka et al., 2018; Baumard & Sperber, 2010) that reflect field-level flattening of human diversity and cultural variation. To concretize this problem, 96 percent of studies in psychology are conducted with WEIRD samples, which reflects just 12 percent of the world's population, and even in societies that are multiracial like the United States, more than 83 percent of those studies are conducted with predominantly White samples (Henrich et al., 2010). This critique has allowed social scientists to unpack traditions of literature as they apply to complex, plural societies.

The growing body of scholarship demonstrating important cultural variation ranges from foundational processes such as visual and olfactory perception (e.g., Kay, 2005; Gordon, 2004; Levinson, 2003; Roberson, Davies, & Davidoff, 2000; D'Andrade, 1995) and basic cognitive and moral reasoning processes (e.g., Haidt & Graham, 2007; Norenzayan, Choi, & Peng, 2007; Nisbett, 2003; Thirumurthy, 2003; Al-Shehab, 2002; Baek, 2002; Peng & Nisbett, 1999); to core models of self (e.g., Heine, 2008; Fryberg & Markus, 2003; Oyserman, Coon, & Kemmelmeier, 2002; Markus & Kitayama, 1991) and related motivational and decisional processes (e.g., Tanner, Arnett, & Leis, 2009); to dimensions of sociality such as personal choice (e.g., ojalehto, Medin, & García, 2017; Schwartz, 2004; Kahneman & Tversky, 2000; Bandura, 1982), individualism (e.g., Morling & Lamoreaux, 2008; Vohs et al., 2008; Fryberg & Markus, 2003; Nisbett, 2003; Oyserman et al., 2002; Lipset, 1996; Hofstede, 1980); views of punishment and cooperation (e.g., Gächter, Renner, & Sefton, 2008; Herrmann, Thöni, and Gächter, 2008; Fehr & Gächter, 2002); and motivations to conform

---

[4]This section relies on findings articulated in the committee's commissioned paper on evolving conceptions of learning by Vossoughi, Bang, and Marin (2021).

(e.g., Kim & Markus, 1999). In addition, scholars have increasingly demonstrated that there are significant cultural differences in core understandings and reasoning patterns of school-related phenomena such as biology (e.g., Taverna et al., 2020; ojalehto et al., 2017; Washinawatok et al., 2017; Ross et al., 2007; Atran, Medin, & Ross, 2005; Medin & Atran, 2004) and mathematics (e.g., Hu et al., 2018; Saxe, 2015). This groundswell of evidence from multiple disciplinary and methodological traditions has significant consequences for research on learning and education processes, calling to task theoretical and methodological constructs that do not engage cultural variation as fundamental to science (e.g., Brady, Fryberg, & Shoda, 2018). Work that does not carefully engage cultural variation easily participates in the perpetuation of a science based in White middle-class norms projected as universalist claims.

The field's response to the sobering recognition that there is significant work to do to understand human diversity has been varied. Much of the field has looked to tighten methodological rigor (e.g., as a response to the "replication crisis"; see Shrout & Rodgers, 2018; Maxwell, Lau, & Howard, 2015; Open Science Collaboration, 2015), such as through preregistration efforts (e.g., Simmons et al., 2021; see also Pham & Oh, 2021), and to increase sample diversity (e.g., Amir & McAuliffe, 2020). Others, however, are proposing new methodological approaches and applications (e.g., Zirkel, Garcia, & Murphy, 2015) as well as careful reconsideration of what should be observed (e.g. Barrett, 2020).

While the overrepresentation of "WEIRD" individuals in psychological research resulted in universalist theories of cognition based on narrow samples, its overreliance on skewed population samples reproduced conceptions of cultural variation as a deviation from presumed singular pathways of learning (Lee, 2009; Nasir et al., 2006). As a result of lack of diversity in samples and researchers (Medin et al., 2017), scientific instruments and measures of intelligence have often projected deficit conceptions across cultural communities, with Western researchers presuming their own frames of reference as the universal norm (Medin & Bang, 2014). Research within this deficit paradigm has been used "as the underlying warrant for the ideology of white supremacy" (Lee et al., 2020), justifying the subjugation of Indigenous and non-Western peoples whose thought processes were framed as inferior or "primitive" (Bang, 2016; Medin & Bang, 2014), with particular consequence for the education sciences.

This deficit stance typically fails to inquire into external and structural factors: "How schools are organized to prevent learning, inequalities in the political economy of education, and oppressive macro-policies and practices in education are all held exculpatory in understanding school failure" (Valencia, 1997, p. 2). Gutiérrez, Morales, and Martinez (2009) showed how "students themselves come to be known as the problem rather than a population of people who are experiencing problems in the educational system" (Gutiérrez, Morales, & Martinez, 2009, p. 218). Similarly, Nasir and colleagues (2006) described the everyday implications of the cultural deficit stance for youth, who must learn to manage multiple developmental tasks, both the ordinary tasks of life-course development and the tasks that involve managing sources of stress rooted in particular forms of institutional stigmatization due to assumptions regarding race, poverty, language variation, gender, and disability (Spencer, 1999, 1987; Burton, Allison & Obeidallah, 1995). Such stigmatization limits access to opportunities (e.g., schooling, work, etc.) across the life course for certain groups of youth (Nasir et al., 2006, pp. 489–490).

Despite the well-established role of interactional and structural factors in education outcomes, deficit stances typically treat the individual as their unit of analysis and have thus been shown to perpetuate a view of human learning in which outcomes "ultimately depend on [students'] own individual worth and effort (Varenne & McDermott, 1998)" (Artiles, 2009). Marin (2020) conceptualized units of analysis as theoretically informed "containers" or "bundles" of segmented information that "reflect researchers' ideas about what counts in knowledge building and meaning making processes" (p. 285). Conceptions of learning as an individual accomplishment frequently shape low expectations and levels of instruction, leading to unequal outcomes that are then used to confirm artificial deficiencies in students (Diaz & Flores, 2001). As Sengupta-Irving (2021) argued, "The legacy of these discourses is that they compel stratification—they create 'smart' or 'dumb,' 'success' or 'failure,' 'desirable' or 'undesirable'" (p. 188). There is increasing consensus and evidence that challenging deficit stances requires units of analysis that move beyond the individual to include careful attention to the cultural tools, sources of pedagogical and social support, forms of psychological safety and belonging, valued ways of knowing and being, and access to resources and opportunities that mediate students' experiences both within schools and across contexts (Sengupta-Irving, 2021; Marin, 2020; Bang & Vossoughi, 2016; Artiles, 2009; Gutiérrez, Morales, & Martinez, 2009; Nasir et al., 2006; Lee, 2003; Rogoff, 2003; Diaz & Flores, 2001; Cole, 1998; Moll, 1992). Lee, Spencer, and Harpalani (2003) illustrated how the presence or absence of such resources shapes the risks as well as protective factors that all human beings must learn to manage in ways that facilitate positive outcomes across the life course.

This stance brings three important ideas into view:

- "At risk" is not a trait or category of person but a fundamental human experience that is distributed unequally within a racially and economically stratified society.
- Understanding cultural repertoires of resilience and resurgence, particularly within communities sustaining cultural lifeways in the face of oppression and erasure, leads to a more agentive and ad-

equately complex understanding of how youth and families navigate and productively respond to structures of inequity (Bang et
al., 2016; Paris & Alim, 2014; Lee, 2009; Tuck, 2009; Gutiérrez
& Rogoff, 2003).

• Protective factors leading to positive outcomes include opportunities for academic learning that meaningfully connect disciplinary
domains with students' everyday lives, cultural practices, and ways
of knowing (Warren et al., 2020; Lee, 2001).

Thus, expanding the unit of analysis beyond the individual also widens
the focus of intervention from individuals to environments and systems, notions that IES has attempted to address in its topic structure over time (see
Chapter 5). Arguments for widening units of analysis also have important
practice advantages given that education is ultimately an interactional activity. Importantly, equity efforts that eschew overt deficit stances can nevertheless perpetuate similar ideologies through narrow, culturally normative
conceptions of learning goals and processes.

Upon reviewing this body of evidence, the committee identified an important departure from the conceptions of learning that held sway at the
outset of IES. Consistent with the committee's identification of equity as
a crosscutting theme undergirding our analytic work, we determined that
efforts aimed at supporting "fair, just, and impartial" research in education
need also to account for latent deficit framing at all levels (Executive Order
13985, 2021). Consequently, the committee used these updated frameworks
as a guidepost through which to understand how IES can meet its equity
mandates, both in ESRA and in President Biden's Executive Order, while
reflecting the leading edge of scholarship on learning. Throughout this report, the committee brings these scholarly perspectives to bear on existing
challenges and potential responses for IES.

Methods and Approaches to Conducting Research

As noted earlier in this chapter, the key organizing principle for IES
at its formation was the central importance of answering questions of efficacy and effectiveness to elevate student achievement. Consistent with
this organizing principle, the randomized controlled trial has consistently
been the preferred method for studies funded by IES, though other quasi-
experimental methods have also been supported by IES since its inception.
Over time, however, the need for quasi-experimental approaches has only
been made clearer. Further, the rise of mixed methods research has been
a development over the past two decades that can inform the next two
decades of IES initiatives. Mixed methods designs offer powerful tools
for examining complex social phenomena and systems in education. As

Tashakkori and Creswell (2007) argued, mixed methods involve research in which the investigator "collects and analyzes data, integrates the findings, and draws inferences using both qualitative and quantitative approaches or methods in a single study or program of inquiry" (p. 4). DeCuir-Gunby and Schutz (2017) characterized mixed methods research pragmatically as combining approaches and research methods to solve problems.

The power behind mixed methods research lies with integration. For example, qualitative methods can inform the development or refinement of quantitative instruments or interventions, and quantitative data can inform sampling procedures for naturalistic observations, interviews, or case studies (e.g., O'Cathain, Murphy, & Nicholl, 2010). The specific approaches researchers can use to integrate qualitative and quantitative research procedures operate at three levels: at the study design level, methods level, and interpretation and reporting levels (Creswell & Plano Clark, 2018; DeCuir-Gunby & Schutz, 2017; O'Cathain, Murphy, & Nicholl, 2010). At the study design level, integration occurs through three basic mixed methods designs—exploratory sequential, explanatory sequential, and convergent, as well as various combinations of these (Nastasi et al., 2007). Integration at the methods level occurs through linking approaches to the collection and analysis of data. According to Creswell (2013), linking occurs in several ways: (1) connecting—when one type of data links with the other through the sampling frame; (2) building—when results from one data collection procedure inform the data collection approach of the other; (3) merging—when data from qualitative and quantitative collection procedures are brought together into a single database; and (4) embedding—when qualitative data collection and quantitative data collection are recurrently linked at multiple points in time (Creswell et al., 2011). At the interpretation and reporting level, integration occurs through narrative construction, data transformation, and joint display (Creswell & Plano Clark, 2017; Fetters, Curry, & Creswell, 2013).

IES AT 20: NOW WHAT?

When the issues above are considered in relationship to one another, it is clear that the world of education research has changed dramatically in the years since 2002. Educators are facing different, but no less urgent, challenges; researchers are building upon a constantly expanding knowledge base (much of it funded by NCER and NCSER); and the modes by which education stakeholders engage and interact with one another are continuously developing. NCER and NCSER undeniably laid the foundation for much of this growth. One way to think about the role that IES has played, and the challenge now facing it, is through the concept of *knowledge infrastructures* (Hirschman, 2021; Edwards, 2019, 2010). Sociologists have used the idea of knowledge infrastructures to explain how fields produce codified ways of generating and sharing specific kinds of knowledge about the world, often through the collection and analysis of similar kinds of data over time. Knowledge infrastructures have their affordances—allowing concerted effort toward producing new knowledge in a domain and fostering consensus—but they also have their disadvantages. As Hirschman (2021) described, "Past priorities shape existing knowledge infrastructures that in turn channel researcher attention toward some problems and away from others" (p. 742). These initial priorities may become "locked in" and limit the kinds of knowledge that are generated. It is easy to see the parallel to the situation facing IES. Its initial design choices (i.e., focusing on experimental designs, prioritizing academic student outcomes) have fostered tremendous knowledge generation in domains that lend themselves to such parameters. At the same time, the infrastructures that have facilitated rapid knowledge accumulation in some areas have also limited the kinds of questions that have been readily answered over the past 20 years. IES has an opportunity to set a course that continues the tradition it initially established while also broadening the kinds of research that it supports, with the goal of helming a next generation of equitable, useful education research. With several strategic shifts, this committee believes that NCER and NCSER can continue their inimitable leadership role in supporting an education research enterprise that truly meets the needs of students in all their complexity.

In the next chapters, we describe the current structure of NCER and NCSER at IES, detailing how funding competitions are organized and implemented, and how different topics and issues have been funded since 2002. In Chapters 4 and 5, we propose an updated matrix of project types (sometimes referred to as "goals") by research topics, in response to our charge to identify critical problems and issues that IES should address in its research funding. We address the remaining elements of our charge in Chapters 6 through 8, focusing on methods and measures, training, and the request for applications process. We draw together recommendations intended to enable our suggestions to IES in Chapter 9.

REFERENCES

Al-Shehab, A.J. (2002). A cross-sectional examination of levels of moral reasoning in a sample of Kuwait University faculty members. *Social Behavior and Personality: An International Journal, 30*(8), 813–820.

Amir, D., and McAuliffe, K. (2020). Cross-cultural, developmental psychology: Integrating approaches and key insights. *Evolution and Human Behavior, 41.* https://doi.org/10.1016/j.evolhumbehav.2020.06.006.

Arnett, J.J. (2008). The neglected 95%: Why American psychology needs to become less American. *American Psychologist, 63*(7), 602.

Artiles, A.J. (2009). Re-framing disproportionality research: Outline of a cultural-historical paradigm. *Multiple Voices for Ethnically Diverse Exceptional Learners, 11*(2), 24–37.

Asen, R. (2015). *Democracy, Deliberation, and Education*. State College: Pennsylvania State University Press.

Asen, R., Gurke, D., Solomon, R., Conners, P., and Gumm, E. (2011). "The research says": Definitions and uses of a key policy term in federal law and local school board deliberations. *Argumentation and Advocacy, 47*, 195–213.

Asen, R., Gurke, D., Conners, P., Solomon, R., and Gumm, E. (2013). Research evidence and school board deliberations: Lessons from three Wisconsin school districts. *Educational Policy, 27*, 33–63. https://doi.org/10.1177/0895904811429291.

Atran, S., Medin, D.L., and Ross, N.O. (2005). The cultural mind: Environmental decision making and cultural modeling within and across populations. *Psychological Review, 112*(4), 744–776. https://doi.org/10.1037/0033-295X.112.4.744.

Baek, H. (2002). A comparative study of moral development of Korean and British children. *Journal of Moral Education, 31*(4), 373–391. https://doi.org/ 10.1080/0305724022000029626.

Bandura, A. (1982). Self-efficacy mechanism in human agency. *American Psychologist, 37*(2), 122–147. https://doi.org/10.1037/0003-066X.37.2.122.

Bang, M. (2016). Making human-nature relations: Settler-colonialism, indigenous ways of knowing, and socio-cultural theories of learning. In I. Esmonde and A. Booker (Eds.), *Power and Privilege in the Learning Sciences: Critical and Socio-Cultural Theories of Learning*. New York; Routledge.

Bang, M., and Vossoughi, S. (2016). Participatory design research and educational justice: Studying learning and relations within social change making. *Cognition and Instruction, 34*(3), 173–193. https://doi.org/10.1080/07370008.2016.1181879.

Bang, M., Faber, L., Gurneau, J., Marin, A., and Soto, C. (2016). Community-based design research: Learning across generations and strategic transformations of institutional relations toward axiological innovations. *Mind, Culture, and Activity, 23*(1), 1–14.

Barrett, H.C. (2020). Deciding what to observe: Thoughts for a post-WEIRD generation. *Evolution and Human Behavior*. https://doi.org/10.1016/j.evolhumbehav.2020.05.006.

Baumard, N., and Sperber, D. (2010). Weird people, yes, but also weird experiments. *The Behavioral and Brain Sciences, 33*, 84–85. https://doi.org/10.1017/S0140525X10000038.

Brady, L.M., Fryberg, S.A., and Shoda, Y. (2018). Expanding the interpretive power of psychological science by attending to culture. *Proceedings of the National Academy of Sciences of the United States of America, 115*(45), 11406–11413.

Burton, L.M., Allison, K.W., and Obeidallah, D. (1995). Social context and adolescence: Perspectives on development among inner-city African-American teens. In L.J. Crockett and A.C. Crouter (Eds.), *Pathways through Adolescence: Individual Development in Relation to Social Contexts* (pp. 119–138). Mahwah, NJ: Lawrence Erlbaum Associates, Inc.

Cole, M. (1998). Can cultural psychology help us think about diversity? *Mind, Culture and Activity, 5*, 291–304.

Creswell, J.W. (2013). *Qualitative Inquiry & Research Design: Choosing among Five Approaches (3rd ed.)*. Thousand Oaks, CA: SAGE Publications.

Creswell, J.W., and Plano Clark, V.L. (2017). *Designing and Conducting Mixed Methods Research*. Thousand Oaks, CA: SAGE Publications, Inc.

Creswell, J.W., and Plano Clark, V.L. (2018). *Designing and Conducting Mixed Methods Research (3rd ed.)*. Thousand Oaks, CA: SAGE Publications.

Creswell, J.W., Klassen, A.C., Plano Clark, V.L., and Smith, K.C. (2011). Best Practices for Mixed Methods Research in the Health Sciences. Commissioned paper for the Office of Behavioral and Social Sciences Research (OBSSR), National Institutes of Health. https:// obssr.od.nih.gov/research-resources/mixed-methods-research.

Daly, A.J., Finnigan, K.S., Jordan, S., Moolenaar, N.M., and Che, J. (2014). Misalignment and perverse incentives: Examining the role of district leaders as brokers in the use of research evidence. *Educational Policy, 28*(2), 145–174.

D'Andrade, R.G. (1995). *The Development of Cognitive Anthropology.* Cambridge, UK: Cambridge University Press. https://doi.org/10.1017/CBO9781139166645.

Debray, T.P.A., Koffijberg, H., Nieboer, D., Vergouwe, Y., Steyerberg, E.W., et al. (2014). Meta-analysis and aggregation of multiple published prediction models. *Statistics in Medicine, 33,* 2341–2362.

DeCuir-Gunby, J., and Schutz, P. (2017). *Developing a Mixed Methods Proposal: A Practical Guide for Beginning Researchers.* Thousand Oaks, CA: SAGE Publications, https://www.doi.org/10.4135/9781483399980.

Diaz, E., and Flores, B. (2001). Teacher as sociocultural, sociohistorical mediator: Teaching to the potential. In M. Reyes and J. Halcón (Eds.), *The Best for Our Children: Critical Perspectives on Literacy for Latino Students* (pp. 29–47). New York: Teachers College Press.

Education Sciences Reform Act (ESRA). (2002). Title I of P.L. 107-279.

Edwards, P.N. (2019). Knowledge infrastructures under siege: Climate data as memory, truce, and target. In D. Bigo, E. Isin, and E. Ruppert (Eds.), *Data Politics* (pp. 21–42). New York: Routledge.

Edwards, P.N. (2010). *A Vast Machine: Computer Models, Climate Data, and the Politics of Global Warming.* Cambridge, MA: MIT Press.

Eisenhart, M., and Towne, L. (2003). Contestation and change in national policy on "scientifically based education research". *Educational Researcher, 32*(7), 31–38.

Erickson, F. and Gutierrez, K. (2002). Comment: Culture, Rigor, and Science in Educational Research. *Educational Researcher, 31*(8), 21–24. https://doi.org/10.3102/0013189 X031008021.

Farley-Ripple, E.N. (2012). Research use in school district central office decision making: A case study. *Educational Management Administration & Leadership, 40*(6), 786–806. https://doi.org/10.1177/1741143212456912.

Fehr, E., and Gächter, S. (2002). Altruistic punishment in humans. *Nature, 415,* 137–140.

Fetters, M.D., Curry, L.A., and Creswell, J.W. (2013). Achieving integration in mixed methods designs-principles and practices. *Health Services Research, 48*(6, Pt. 2), 2134–2156. https://doi.org/10.1111/1475-6773.12117.

Finnigan, K.S., and Daly, A.J. (Eds.) (2014). *Using Research Evidence in Education: From the Schoolhouse Door to Capitol Hill.* Cham, Switzerland: Springer.

Finnigan, K.S., and Daly, A.J. (2017). The trust gap: Understanding the effects of leadership churn in school districts. *American Educator, 41*(2), 24–29.

Finnigan, K.S., Daly, A.J., and Che, J. (2012, April). The Acquisition and Use of Evidence Districtwide. [Paper presentation]. Annual Meeting of the American Educational Research Association, Vancouver, Canada.

Fryberg, S.A., and Markus, H.R. (2003). On being American Indian: Current and possible selves. *Self and Identity, 2*(4), 325–344. https://doi.org/10.1080/714050251.

Gächter, S., Renner, E., and Sefton, M. (2008). The long-run benefits of punishment. *Science, 322*(5907), 1510.

Gordon, P. (2004). Numerical cognition without words: Evidence from Amazonia. *Science, 306,* 496–499. https://doi.org/10.1126/science.1094492.

Gutiérrez, K., and Rogoff, B. (2003). Cultural ways of learning. *Educational Researcher, 32,* 19–25. https://doi.org/10.3102/0013189X032005019.

Gutiérrez, K.D., Morales, P.Z., and Martinez, D.C. (2009). Re-mediating literacy: Culture, difference, and learning for students from nondominant communities. *Review of Research in Education, 33,* 213–245.

Haidt, J., and Graham, J. (2007). When morality opposes justice: Conservatives have moral intuitions that liberals may not recognize. *Social Justice Research, 20,* 98–116. https://doi.org/10.1007/s11211-007-0034-z.

Heine, S.J. (2008). *Cultural Psychology.* New York: Norton.

Henrich, J., Heine, S., and Norenzayan, A. (2010). The weirdest people in the world? *Behavioral and Brain Sciences, 33*(2–3), 61–83. https://doi.org/10.1017/S0140525X0999152X.

Herrmann, B., Thöni, C., and Gächter, S. (2008). Antisocial punishment across societies. *Science, 319,* 1362–1367. https://doi.org/10.1126/science.1153808.

Hirschman, D. (2021). Rediscovering the 1%: Knowledge infrastructures and the stylized facts of inequality. *American Journal of Sociology, 127*(3), 739–786.

Hofstede, G. (1980). Culture and organizations. *International Studies of Management & Organization, 10*(4), 15–41. https://doi.org/10.1080/00208825.1980.11656300.

Howe, K. (2003). *Closing methodological divides: Toward democratic educational research.* Dordrecht, the Netherlands: Kluwer Academic Press.

Hruschka, D.J., Medin, D.L., Rogoff, B., and Henrich, J. (2018). Pressing questions in the study of psychological and behavioral diversity. *Proceedings of the National Academy of Sciences of the United States of America, 115*(45), 11366–11368. https://doi.org/10.1073/pnas.1814733115.

Hu, X., Gong, Y., Lai, C., and Leung, F.K.S. (2018). The relationship between ICT and student literacy in mathematics, reading, and science across 44 countries: A multilevel analysis. *Computers and Education, 125,* 1–13.

Kahneman, D., and Tversky, A. (Eds.). (2000). *Choices, Values, and Frames.* Cambridge, UK: Cambridge University Press.

Kay, P. (2005). Color categories are not arbitrary. *Cross-Cultural Research, 39*(1), 39–55.

Kim, H., and Markus, H. (1999). Deviance or uniqueness, harmony or conformity? A cultural analysis. *Journal of Personality and Social Psychology, 77,* 785–800. https://doi.org/10.1037/0022-3514.77.4.785.

Lee, C.D. (2009). Cultural influences on learning. In J.A. Banks (Ed.), *The Routledge International Companion to Multicultural Education* (pp. 239–251). New York: Routledge.

Lee, C.D. (2003). Toward a framework for culturally responsive design in multimedia computer environments: Cultural modeling as a case. *Mind, Culture, and Activity, 10*(1), 42–61.

Lee, C.D. (2001). Is October Brown Chinese? A cultural modeling activity system for underachieving students. *American Educational Research Journal, 38*(1), 97–141.

Lee, C., Spencer, M., and Harpalani, V. (2003). "Every shut eye ain't sleep": Studying how people live culturally. *Educational Researcher, 32,* 6–13. https://doi.org/10.3102/0013189X032005006.

Lee, C.D., Nasir, N.S., Pea, R., and McKinney de Royston, M. (2020). Reconceptualizing learning: A critical task for knowledge-building and teaching. In N. Nasir, C. Lee, R. Pea, and M. McKinney de Royston (Eds.), *Handbook of the Cultural Foundations of Learning* (pp. xxvii–xxxv). New York: Taylor & Francis.

Levinson, S.C. (2003). Language and mind: Let's get the issues straight! In D. Gentner and S. Goldin-Meadow (Eds.), *Language in Mind: Advances in the Study of Language and Thought* (pp. 25–46). Cambridge, MA: MIT Press.

Lipset, S.M. (1996). *American Exceptionalism: A Double-Edged Sword.* New York: W.W. Norton.

Marin, A.M. (2020). Ambulatory sequences: Ecologies of learning by attending and observing on the move. *Cognition and Instruction, 38*(3), 281–317. http://doi.org/10.1080/07370008.2020.1767104.

Markus, H.R., and Kitayama, S. (1991). Culture and the self: Implications for cognition, emotion, and motivation. *Psychological Review, 98,* 224–253.

Maxwell, S.E., Lau, M.Y., and Howard, G.S. (2015). Is psychology suffering from a replication crisis? What does "failure to replicate" really mean? *American Psychologist, 70*(6), 487–498. https://doi.org/10.1037/a0039400.

Medin, D.L., and Atran, S. (2004). The native mind: Biological categorization and reasoning in development and across cultures. *Psychological Review, 111*(4), 960–983.

Medin, D.L., and Bang, M. (2014). *Who's Asking?: Native Science, Western Science, and Science Education.* Cambridge, MA: MIT Press.

Medin, D., ojalehto, B., Marin, A., and Bang, M. (2017). Systems of (non-)diversity. *Nature Human Behaviour, 1*, 0088. https://doi.org/10.1038/s41562-017-0088.

Moll, L.C. (1992). Bilingual classroom studies and community analysis: Some recent trends. *Educational Researcher, 21*(2), 20–24. https://doi.org/10.3102/0013189X021002020.

Morling, B., and Lamoreaux, M. (2008). Measuring culture outside the head: A meta-analysis of individualism-collectivism in cultural products. *Personality and Social Psychology Review, 12*, 199–221.

Nasir, N., Rosebery, A.S., Warren, B., and Lee, C.D. (2006). Learning as a cultural process: Achieving equity through diversity. In K. Sawyer (Ed.), *Handbook of the Learning Sciences* (pp. 489–504). Cambridge, UK: Cambridge University Press.

Nastasi, B.K., Hitchcock, J., Sarkar, S., Burkholder, G., Varjas, K., and Jayasena, A. (2007). Mixed methods in intervention research: Theory to adaptation. *Journal of Mixed Methods Research, 1*(2), 164–182.

National Research Council (NRC). (2002). *Scientific Research in Education.* Washington, DC: The National Academies Press. https://doi.org/10.17226/10236.

Neal, J.W., Neal, Z.P., Kornbluh, M., Mills, K.J., and Lawlor, J.A. (2015). Brokering the research-practice gap: A typology. *American Journal of Community Psychology, 56*, 422–435. https://doi.org/ 10.1007/s10464-015-9745-8.

Nisbett, R.E. (2003). *The Geography of Thought: How Asians and Westerners Think Differently ... And Why.* New York: Free Press.

Norenzayan, A., Choi, I., and Peng, K. (2007). Cognition and perception. In S.K.D. Cohen (Ed.), *Handbook of Cultural Psychology* (pp. 569–594). New York: Guilford Press.

O'Cathain, A., Murphy, E., and Nicholl, J. (2010). Three techniques for integrating data in mixed methods studies. *British Medical Journal, 341*, c4587.

ojalehto, B., Medin, D., and García, S. (2017). Conceptualizing agency: Folkpsychological and folkcommunicative perspectives on plants. *Cognition, 162*, 103–123. https://doi.org/10.1016/j.cognition.2017.01.023.

Olson, D.R. (2004). The triumph of hope over experience in the search for "what works": A response to Slavin. *Educational Researcher, 33*(1), 24–26. http://www.jstor.org/stable/3699840.

Open Science Collaboration. (2015). Estimating the reproducibility of psychological science. *Science, 349*(6251), aac4716. https://doi.org/10.1126/science.aac4716.

Oyserman, D., Coon, H.M., and Kemmelmeier, M. (2002). Rethinking individualism and collectivism: Evaluation of theoretical assumptions and meta-analyses. *Psychological Bulletin, 128*, 1773–1775.

Paris, D., and Alim, H.S. (2014). What are we seeking to sustain through culturally sustaining pedagogy? A loving critique forward. *Harvard Educational Review, 84*(1), 85–100. https://doi.org/10.17763/haer.84.1.982l873k2ht16m77.

Peng, K., and Nisbett, R.E. (1999). Culture, dialectics, and reasoning about contradiction. *American Psychologist, 54*(9), 741–754.

Penuel, W.R., Briggs, D.C., Davidson, K.L., Herlihy, C., Sherer, D., Hill, H.C., Farrell, C., and Allen, A.-R. (2017). How school and district leaders access, perceive, and use research. *AERA Open.* https://doi.org/10.1177/2332858417705370.

Penuel, W.R., et al. (2020). A Comparative, Descriptive Study of Three Research-Practice Partnerships. Boulder, CO: The National Center for the Study of Research in Policy and Practice.

Pham, M.T., and Oh, T.T. (2021). Preregistration is neither sufficient, nor necessary for good science. *Journal of Consumer Psychology, 31*(January), 163–176.

Reckhow, S., Tompkins-Stange, M., and Galey-Horn, S. (2021). How the political economy of knowledge production shapes education policy: The case of teacher evaluation in federal policy discourse. *Educational Evaluation and Policy Analysis, 43*(3), 472–494. https://doi.org/10.3102/01623737211003906.

Roberson, D., Davies, I., and Davidoff, J. (2000). Color categories are not universal: Replications and new evidence from a stone-age culture. *Journal of Experimental Psychology: General, 129*(3), 369–398.

Rogoff, B. (2003). *The Cultural Nature of Human Development.* Oxford, UK: Oxford University Press.

Ross, L.A., Saint-Amour, D., Leavitt, V.M., Javitt, D.C., and Foxe, J.J. (2007). Do you see what I am saying? Exploring visual enhancement of speech comprehension in noisy environments. *Cerebral Cortex, 17,* 1147–1153.

Saxe, G. (2015). *Culture and Cognitive Development: Studies in Mathematical Understanding.* New York; London: Psychology Press.

Schwartz, B. (2004). *The Paradox of Choice: Why More Is Less.* New York: Harper-Collins.

Scott, J., and Jabbar, H. (2014). The hub and the spokes: Foundations, intermediary organizations, incentivist reforms, and the politics of research evidence. *Educational Policy, 28*(2), 233–257. https://doi.org/10.1177/0895904813515327.

Scott, J., Jabbar, H., LaLonde, P., DeBray, E., and Lubienski, C. (2015). Evidence use and advocacy coalitions: Intermediary organizations and philanthropies in Denver, Colorado. *Education Policy Analysis Archives, 23*(124). http://epaa.asu.edu/ojs/article/view/2079.

Scott, J., Lubienski, C., DeBray, E., and Jabbar, H. (2014). The intermediary function in evidence production, promotion, and mobilization: The case of educational incentives. In K. Finnigan and A. Daly (Eds.), *Using Research Evidence in Education: From the Schoolhouse Door to Capitol Hill* (pp. 69–90). Cham, Switzerland: Springer.

Sengupta-Irving, T. (2021). Positioning and positioned apart: Mathematics learning as becoming undesirable. *Anthropology and Education Quarterly, 52*(2), 187–208.

Shrout, P.E., and Rodgers, J.L. (2018). Psychology, science, and knowledge construction: Broadening perspectives from the replication crisis. *Annual Review of Psychology, 69*(1), 487–510.

Simmons, J.P., Nelson, L.D., and Simonsohn, U. (2021). Pre-registration: Why and how. *Journal of Consumer Psychology, 31*(1).

Slavin, R. (2002). Evidence-based education policies: Transforming educational practice and research. *Educational Researcher, 31*(7), 15–21.

Spencer, S.M. (1999).The formation of ethnic-American identities: Jewish communities in Boston. In P.P.A. Funari, M. Hall, and S. Jones (Eds.), *Historical Archaeology: Back from the Edge* (pp. 284–307). London: Routledge.

Spencer, S.M. (1987). A survey of domestic reform movement sites in Boston and Cambridge, ca. 1865–1905. *Historical Archaeology, 21*(2), 7–36.

Tanner, J.L., Arnett, J.J., and Leis, J.A. (2009). Emerging adulthood: Learning and development during the first stage of adulthood. In M.C. Smith and N. DeFrates-Densch (Eds.), *Handbook of Research on Adult Learning and Development* (pp. 34–67). New York: Routledge/Taylor & Francis Group.

Tashakkori, A., and Creswell, J.W. (2007). Editorial: Exploring the nature of research questions in mixed methods research. *Journal of Mixed Methods Research, 1*(3), 207–211. https://doi.org/10.1177/1558689807302814.

Taverna, S., Cammarata, G., Colomba, P., Sciarrino, S., Zizzo, C., Francofonte, D., Zora, M., Scalia, S., Brando, C., Curto, A.L., Marsana, E.M., Olivieri, R., Vitale, S., and Duro, G. (2020). Pompe disease: Pathogenesis, molecular genetics and diagnosis. *Aging, 12*(15), 15856–15874. https://doi.org/10.18632/aging.103794.

Thalmayer, A.G., Toscanelli, C., and Arnett, J.J. (2021). The neglected 95% revisited: Is American psychology becoming less American? *American Psychologist, 76*(1), 116–129. https://doi.org/10.1037/amp0000622.

Thirumurthy, V. (2003). Children's cognition of geometry and spatial reasoning: A cultural process. Unpublished doctoral dissertation, State University of New York at Buffalo.

Tseng, V., and Nutley, S.M. (2014). Building the infrastructure to improve the use and usefulness of research in education. In K. Finnegan and A. Daly (Eds.), *Using Research in Education* (pp. 163–175). Cham, Switzerland: Springer.

Tuck, E. (2009). Suspending damage: A letter to communities. *Harvard Educational Review, 79*(3), 409–427. https://doi.org/10.17763/haer.79.3.n0016675661t3n15.

Valencia, R.R. (Ed.). (1997). *The Evolution of Deficit Thinking: Educational Thought and Practice.* New York: The Falmer Press/Taylor & Francis.

Varenne, H., and McDermott, R. (1998). *Successful Failure: The School America Builds.* Boulder, CO: Westview.

Vohs, K.D., Baumeister, R.F., Schmeichel, B.J., Twenge, J.M., Nelson, N., and Tice, D. (2008). Making choices impairs subsequent self-control: A limited-resource account of decision making, self-regulation, and active initiative. *Journal of Personality and Social Psychology, 94*, 883–898.

Vossoughi, S., Marin, A., and Bang, M. (2021). *Foundational Developments in the Science of Human Learning and their Implications for Educational Research.* Paper prepared for the National Academies of Sciences, Engineering, and Medicine, Committee on the Future of Education Research at the Institute of Education Sciences in the U.S. Department of Education.

Warren, B., Vossoughi, S., Rosebery, A.S., Bang, M., and Taylor, E. (2020). Multiple ways of knowing: Re-imagining disciplinary learning. In N. Nasir, C.D. Lee, R. Pea, and M. McKinney de Royston (Eds.), *Handbook of the Cultural Foundations of Learning* (pp. 277–294). New York: Routledge.

Washinawatok, K., Rasmussen, C., Bang, M., Medin, D., Woodring, J., Waxman, S., Marin, A., Gurneau, J., and Faber, L. (2017). Children's play with a forest diorama as a window into ecological cognition. *Journal of Cognition and Development, 18*(5), 617–632. https://doi.org/10.1080/15248372.2017.1392306.

Whitehurst, G. (2003, April 22). The Institute of Education Sciences: New Wine, New Bottles. [Paper presentation]. Annual Meeting of the American Educational Research Association, Chicago, IL.

Zirkel, S., Garcia, J., and Murphy, M. (2015). Experience-sampling research methods and their potential for education research. *Educational Researcher, 44*. https://doi.org/10.3102/0013189X14566879.

3

IES at 20

To offer a coherent set of recommendations that respond to our charge, the committee first needed to understand how the Institute of Education Sciences (IES) and particularly its National Center for Education Research (NCER) and National Center for Special Education Research (NCSER) currently operate. In this chapter, the committee describes IES's operating structure, funding and staffing resources, the centers' project types and topics, and recent policy and programming efforts. We will return to the discussion of how the research centers operate throughout this report, referring to this chapter's content to respond to the questions posed by our statement of task.

OPERATING STRUCTURE

IES's operating structure is articulated in its founding legislation, the Education Sciences Reform Act (ESRA), which specifies the institute's organizing framework as well as the roles and responsibilities of each of its research centers and offices. The committee conceptualized the institute's functions as mandated in the legislation as divided into three separate areas of responsibility: direction, administration, and programming, each of which has multiple offices or centers (see Figure 3-1 for a diagram of IES's operational structure). In the following sections, we discuss the chief functions of each part of IES.

FIGURE 3-1 IES organizational structure.
SOURCE: Adapted from https://ies.ed.gov/help/ieschart.asp.

Programming

The programming work of IES is accomplished through the work of four independent research centers: NCER, the National Center for Education Statistics, the National Center for Education Evaluation and Regional Assistance, and NCSER. As noted in Chapter 1, in accordance with the committee's statement of task, this report is focused on the work of NCER and NCSER, also referred to as "the research centers" of IES. NCER and NCSER support a wide range of research activities with the broad goal of improving the quality of education in the United States. These research activities span from infancy through adulthood and across multiple education settings, depending on the center, and encompass three primary mechanisms: research grants, research and development (R&D Centers), and research networks. Grants for Education Research (including Education Research Grants [305A], Systematic Replication [305R], Special Education Research Grants [324A], and Systematic Replication in Special Education [324R]) comprise the central, continued work of NCER and NCSER. According to the IES website, these investments are intended to "advance our understanding of and practices for teaching, learning, and organizing education systems, and it helps to identify what works, what doesn't, and why. The goal is to improve education programs and, hence, outcomes for all learners, particularly those at a heightened risk of failure" (IES, 2022a). Both NCER and NCSER also fund R&D Centers. At NCER, R&D Centers are intended to "contribute to the production and dissemination of rigorous evidence and products that provide practical solutions to important education problems in the United States. The R&D Centers develop, test, and disseminate new approaches to improve education outcomes" (IES, 2022b). The R&D Centers at NCSER have a similar purview, although their work is more squarely focused on improving child outcomes through enhancements in the special education and early intervention systems (IES, 2022c). Finally, the Research Network program is an effort to marshal the talents and skills of multiple teams of researchers toward addressing complex problems in education. These networks provide a structure for researchers "to share ideas, build knowledge, and strengthen their research and dissemination capacity" (IES, 2022d).

NCER and NCSER also support the development of the next generation of education researchers through various research training programs including, but not limited to, predoctoral, postdoctoral, early career, and research methods training programs. NCER and NCSER fund these activities through a competitive grant process, and the funding to support research and research training programs is provided through annual congressional appropriations.[1]

Administration

IES has two primary functions that are part of the Office of the Director: (1) the Office of Administration and Policy provides ongoing administrative support for the activities of the centers and the Office of the Director and (2) the Office of Science is responsible for scientific issues across IES, including independent scientific peer-review processes of competitively funded research and research training grants, as well as reports conducted or supported by the institute. The deputy director for science serves as the Department of Education's chief science officer. As noted in Chapter 1 of this report, this latter function is necessarily independent from both NCER and NCSER: In order to maintain the integrity of the peer-review process, governance of the scientific peer review of research and research training competitions is managed by an entirely separate IES office. For more discussion on how the Office of Science supports review, see Chapter 8 of this report.

Direction

IES has two primary directive entities: the National Board for Education Sciences (NBES) and the Office of the Director. As per ESRA, the primary responsibilities of NBES include (1) advising and consulting with the IES director on the policies of the institute; (2) considering and approving priorities proposed by the director to guide the work of the institute; (3) reviewing and approving procedures for technical and scientific peer review

---

[1] This sentence was modified after the release of the report to IES to clarify how IES receives its annual appropriations.

of the activities of the institute; and (4) advising and providing recommendations to the IES director in a number of areas related to enhancing the scope and impact of IES-funded activities and enhancing the overall effectiveness of the institute. NBES consists of 15 voting members appointed by the President of the United States. The director of IES, each of the four commissioners of the National Education Centers, the director of the National Institute of Child Health and Human Development, the director of the Census, the commissioner of Labor Statistics, and the director of the National Science Foundation all serve on the board as nonvoting ex officio members. NBES has not met since 2016 due to a lack of quorum of appointed members, signaling that this directorial function has been inactive.[2] President Trump announced his nomination of several additional members to the board shortly before the end of his term, but the board did not meet, and those members were never seated.[3]

The director of IES is appointed by the President and confirmed by the Senate and serves a term of 6 years. ESRA outlines a series of responsibilities for the director specific to the ways that she or he should effectively carry out the mission of IES. The director and NBES share responsibility for setting the institute's agenda and research priorities. Although the board is tasked with approving the director's priorities, the director is offered substantial latitude in setting a course for the institute's investments that is in line with the mission as articulated in ESRA. The committee also notes that, in practice, the director typically works closely with the each of the four IES center commissioners and the deputy directors to establish an agenda and substantive priorities for IES.

FUNDING AND STAFF LEVELS

Given the breadth of what IES is expected to accomplish as mandated in ESRA, its funding for both programmatic activities and staffing has historically been limited in comparison to other federal science, research, and statistical agencies with similar objectives. In 2021, IES received a congressional appropriation of $197 million for Research, Development, and Dissemination, about $172 million of which was available to cover the

---

[2]The most recent NBES meeting was held on November 8, 2016. See https://ies.ed.gov/director/board/minutes/index.asp.

[3]A reviewer of this report who was appointed by President Trump stated that "[President] Biden summarily dismissed the whole Board in 2021 with a one-line email."

entirety of NCER's grantmaking.[4] NCSER,[5] on the other hand, receives far less funding from Congress to perform its core responsibilities. In FY2021, NCSER's appropriation was $58.5 million. For detailed information about funding at NCER and NCSER, see Appendix E for a series of tables provided to the committee by IES.

Although both NCER and NCSER face funding constraints, NCSER's limited budget remains a particular and perpetual challenge. In FY2010, NCSER received more than $71 million, but this amount was cut by Congress by more than $20 million annually in subsequent years. NCSER's current funding is still $27.1 million short of the buying power of its FY2010 funding level after factoring in inflation, an issue that has yielded serious consternation and instability within the special education research community.

In comparison, the Education and Human Resources division of the National Science Foundation operated in FY2020 and FY2021 with a $940 and $968 million budget, respectively. Similarly, funding for the National Institute for Child Health and Human Development—a subagency of the National Institutes of Health with a mandate similar to that of NCSER— has a $1.6 billion budget. The committee notes that these discrepancies in funding are a critical consideration in the recommendations in this report: Limitations in the centers' capacities mean that both NCER and NCSER need to be extremely judicious in how they allocate resources.

Since IES was established in 2002, NCSER, NCER, and the Office of Science have also operated with limited staffing resources. NCER has ranged in its staffing from 13 to 17 full-time employees, while NCSER has ranged in its staffing from 5 to 7 full-time employees, and the Office of Science has ranged in its full-time employees from 6 to 9.

RECENT EFFORTS AND DECISIONS

In recent years, under the leadership of IES Director Mark Schneider, NCER and NCSER have implemented a series of policy and programming initiatives aimed at continuing IES's legacy of funding and communicating robust research in education. In this section, we discuss a few of these efforts. Though the efforts described below are only a subset of the ongoing work at NCER and NCSER, the committee has selected these particular

---

[4]This sentence was modified after the release of the report to IES to reflect the actual 2021 appropriation and to clarify the amount of the appropriation available to NCER for grantmaking.

[5]NCSER was not able to run any of its competitions for FY2022 as the funds appropriated to NCSER were needed to meet outstanding commitments for current awards. The pandemic recovery competitions that NCSER was able to run in FY2022 are supported in their entirety via American Rescue Plan funds appropriated to IES.

examples for discussion here due to their relevance to this study's statement of task.

SEER Principles

In September of 2018, Director Schneider introduced a set of principles designed to define rigor in IES-funded research. Known as the Standards for Excellence in Education Research (or the SEER principles), the principles are comprised of a set of "key domains and core questions" aimed at identifying quality in research proposals and supporting the production of high-quality research (see Box 3-1). As noted on the IES website,

> SEER codifies practices that IES expects—and increasingly requires—to be implemented as part of IES-funded causal impact studies. But note that many standards and associated recommendations are applicable to other types of research and IES increasingly requires applicable standards be followed in those studies as well. IES-funded researchers should consult grant and contract documents for more information about how SEER applies to your project.

X Prize

In March of 2021, Director Schneider introduced a competition designed to stimulate innovation in digital learning. According to his blog (Schneider, 2021), the challenge is

> designed to incentivize developers of digital learning platforms to build, modify, and then test an infrastructure to run rigorous experiments that

---

BOX 3-1
The SEER Principles

SEER encourages researchers to

- Pre-register studies
- Make findings, methods, and data open
- Identify interventions' components
- Document treatment implementation and contrast
- Analyze interventions' costs
- Use high-quality outcome measures
- Facilitate generalization of study findings
- Support scaling of promising interventions

SOURCE: https://ies.ed.gov/seer/index.asp.

can be implemented and replicated faster than traditional on-ground randomized control trials. The long-term goal of the competition is to modernize, accelerate, and improve the ways in which we identify effective learning tools and processes that improve learning outcomes.

The winning team will have demonstrated that their platform can successfully support researchers in conducting rapid, reproducible experiments in formal learning contexts. The winning team will be announced in March 2023 and will receive a $1 million prize.

Research-Practice Partnerships[6]

In 2018, Director Schneider announced that IES would be reviewing its existing commitments to research-practice partnership (RPPs) models for conducting research and building knowledge. Though IES had historically funded RPPs through a number of funding mechanisms outside of NCER and NCSER, NCER began a specific competition solely for RPP models in 2013. This competition became a topic in a new competition focused on NCER's investment in partnership work, Partnership and Collaborations Focused on Problems of Practice of Policies, in 2014. This RFA invited applications under three topics: Researcher-Practitioner Partnerships in Education, Continuous Improvement Research in Education, and Evaluation of State and Local Programs and Policies. The Evaluation topic was competed as a separate topic from 2009 to 2014. The Partnership and Collaborations competition was discontinued in 2019. Director Schneider expressed concern with the extent to which RPP models were focused primarily on "process rather than outcomes," noting that IES would continue to "encourage, support, and prioritize collaboration between researchers and practitioners, but without specifying how that cooperation should be structured" (Schneider, 2020).

Given the identification of usefulness in education research as a cross-cutting theme described in Chapter 1, the committee notes the existence of multiple bodies of research that provide evidence related to the utility and function of research-practice partnerships. While not all RPPs are successful at achieving all intended outcomes, research shows that co-designed interventions from RPPs can positively impact student learning outcomes (e.g., Krajcik et al., 2021; Saavedra et al., 2021; Coburn & Penuel, 2016; Booth et al., 2015; Barab, Greslfi, & Ingram-Goble, 2010; Geier et al., 2008; Snow, Lawrence, & White, 2009), as well as teaching and assessment

---

[6]Although IES uses the convention "researcher-practitioner partnerships" in its work, the committee elected to use the more commonly used to term "research-practice partnerships" throughout this report.

outcomes (DeBarger et al., 2017; Yarnall, Shechtman, & Penuel, 2006). RPPs have supported efforts that resulted in dramatic reductions in high school dropout rates (Allensworth, 2015), and they have enabled partners to make effective use of research to inform their thinking and guide local decision making (Penuel et al., 2020; Henrick, Jackson, & Smith, 2018). Indeed, an evaluation of IES's RPP initiative conducted by the IES-funded National Center for Research in Policy and Practice found that, from the perspective of nearly all grantees, the program was achieving its stated purposes (Farrell et al., 2018).

Though RPPs are no longer a separate topic, NCER continues to fund research that involves partnerships between researchers and practitioners, including awards made under the FY2020 and FY2021 Using Longitudinal Data to Support State Education Policymaking competitions.

DATA COLLECTION

In responding to its charge, one of the committee's chief concerns was understanding the current state of funding in NCER and NCSER: that is, who has been funded through NCER and NCSER competitions over time, and what institutions and research areas have *not* received funding. Given our focus on the importance of attending to equity at every step in the NCER and NCSER funding process, the committee was interested to know how successful IES has been in engaging researchers from multiple disciplines, across institutions, and from a variety of backgrounds.

In its open sessions with IES staff, the committee asked for demographic and institutional information related to funded and unfunded applicants, as well as reviewer panels, and was informed that such information was not available for privacy and statistical reasons. In a post shared to the *Inside IES Blog* on September 16, 2021, IES shared limited demographic data about applicants (see Box 3-2).

The committee notes that the communication of this information is a critical step to helping IES address equity issues both inside and outside the organization. Throughout this report, the committee will discuss how continued sharing of data along these lines can buttress IES's good work in each of the areas of our statement of task.

CONCLUSION

This chapter describes the current state of IES: its current structure and funding levels, as well as recent policy and programming efforts. In the following chapters, the committee will make use of this information in order to address the committee's statement of task.

BOX 3-2
Demographic Data on NCER and
NCSER's Applicants and Awardees

Data indicate that the percentage of applications received from MSIs [Minority Serving Institutions] between 2013 and 2020 was very small—4 percent of applications to NCER and 1 percent to NCSER. Of those applications that were funded, 10 percent of NCER's awards were made to MSIs and none of NCSER's awards was made to an MSI. IES reviewed the demographic information that FY 2021 NCER and NCSER grant applicants and awardees voluntarily submitted, and among those who reported their demographic information, found the following:

- *Gender* (response rate of approximately 82%): The majority of the principal investigators who applied for (62%) and received funding (59%) from IES identified as female.
- *Race* (response rate of approximately 75%): The majority of principal investigators who applied for (78%) and received funding (88%) from IES identified as White, while 22% of applicants and 13% of awardees identified as non-White or multi-racial.
- *Ethnicity* (response rate of approximately 72%): The majority of principal investigators who applied for (95%) and received funding (97%) identified as non-Hispanic.
- *Disability* (response rate of approximately 70%): The majority of principal investigators who applied for (97%) and received funding (96%) identified as not having a disability.

SOURCE: IES (2021).

REFERENCES

Allensworth, E. (2015). The use of ninth-grade early warning indicators to improve Chicago schools. *Journal of Education for Students Placed at Risk, 18*(1-2), 68–83. https://doi.org/10.1080/10824669.2013.745181.

Barab, S.A., Gresalfi, M.S., and Ingram-Goble, A. (2010). Transformational play: Using games to position person, content, and context. *Educational Researcher, 39*(7), 525–536.

Booth, J.L., Cooper, L.A., Donovan, M.S., Huyghe, A., Koedinger, K., and Pare-Blagoev, E.J. (2015). Design-based research within the constraints of practice: AlgebraByExample. *Journal of Education for Students Placed at Risk, 20*(1–2), 79–100. https://doi.org/10.1080/10824669.2014.986674.

Coburn, C.E., and Penuel, W.R. (2016). Research-practice partnerships: Outcomes, dynamics, and open questions. *Educational Researcher, 45*(1), 48–54.

DeBarger, A.H., Penuel, W.R., Boscardin, C.K., Moorthy, S., Beauvineau, Y., Kennedy, C., and Allison, K. (2017). Investigating science curriculum adaptation as a strategy to improve teaching and learning. *Science Education, 101*(1), 66–98. https://doi.org/10.1002/sce.21249.

Farrell, C.C., Davidson, K.L., Repko-Erwin, M., Penuel, W. R., Quantz, M., Wong, H., Riedy, R., and Brink, Z. (2018). *A Descriptive Study of the IES Researcher–Practitioner Partnerships in Education Research Program.* Boulder, CO: National Center for Research in Policy and Practice.

Geier, R., Blumenfeld, P., Marx, R.W., Krajcik, J., Fishman, B.J., and Soloway, E. (2008). Standardized test outcomes for students engaged in inquiry-based science curricula in the context of urban reform. *Journal of Research in Science Teaching, 45*(8), 922–939.

Henrick, E.C., Jackson, K., & Smith, T.M. (2018). Assessing the impact of partnership recommendations on district instructional improvement strategies. In P. Cobb, K. Jackson, E. Henrick, T.M. Smith, and the MIST Team (Eds.), *Systems for Instructional Improvement: Creating Coherence from the Classroom to the District Office* (pp. 209–220). Harvard Education Press.

Institute of Education Sciences (IES). (2022a). Education Research and Method. IES Website, February 2022. https://ies.ed.gov/ncer/research/researchMethods.asp.

—— (2022b). Research and Development Centers. IES Website, February 2022. https://ies.ed.gov/ncer/research/randdCenters.asp.

—— (2022c). Special Education Research and Development Centers. IES Website, February 2022. https://ies.ed.gov/ncser/research/developmentCenters.asp.

—— (2022d). Research Networks. IES Website, February 2022. https://ies.ed.gov/ncer/research/researchNetworks.asp#:~:text=Through%20the%20Research%20Networks%20program,their%20research%20and%20dissemination%20capacity.

—— (2021). Updates on Research Center Efforts to Increase Diversity, Equity, Inclusion, and Accessibility. IES Blog, September 16. https://ies.ed.gov/blogs/research/post/updates-on-research-center-efforts-to-increase-diversity-equity-inclusion-and-accessibility.

Krajcik, J.S., Schneider, B., Miller, E., Chen, I.-C., Bradford, L., Bartz, K., Baker, Q., Palincsar, A., Peek-Brown, D., and Codere, S. (2021). *Assessing the Effect of Project-Based Learning on Science Learning in Elementary Schools.* Michigan State University.

National Center for Education Statistics, Institute of Education Sciences. (n.d.). Survey and Program Areas. https://nces.ed.gov/surveys/.

Penuel, W.R., Farrell, C.C., Anderson, E.R., Coburn, C.E., Allen, A.-R., Bohannon, A.X., Hopkins, M., and Brown, S. (2020). *A Comparative, Descriptive Study of Three Research–Practice Partnerships: Goals, Activities, and Influence on District Policy, Practice, and Decision Making.* National Center for Research in Policy and Practice.

Saavedra, A.R., Liu, Y., Haderlein, S.K., Rapaport, A., Garland, M., Hoepfner, D., Morgan, K. L., and Hu, A. (2021). *Knowledge in Action Efficacy Study over Two Years.* USC Dorsife Center for Economic and Social Research.

Schneider, M. (2021). Compete to win the XPRIZE Digital Learning Challenge. Blog post. March 22. https://ies.ed.gov/director/remarks/3-22-2021.asp.

Schneider, M. (2020). Research-Practice Partnerships, Redux. Blog post. February 4. https://ies.ed.gov/director/remarks/2-4-2020.asp.

Snow, C.E., Lawrence, J., and White, C. (2009). Generating knowledge of academic language among urban middle school students. *Journal of Research on Educational Effectiveness, 2*(4), 325–344. https://doi.org/10.1080/19345740903167042.

Yarnall, L., Shechtman, N., and Penuel, W.R. (2006). Using handheld computers to support improved classroom assessment in science: Results from a field trial. *Journal of Science Education and Technology, 15*(2), 142–158.

4

Project Types for
NCER/NCSER Grants

G rants funded by the National Center for Education Research (NCER) and National Center for Special Education Research (NCSER) use a structure of goals or project types to divide the studies "into stages for both theoretical and practical purposes" (IES RFA, 2018). Since 2002, five such project types have been funded: (1) Exploration, (2) Development and Innovation, (3) Initial Efficacy and Follow-up, (4) Scale-up/Effectiveness/ Systematic Replication,[1] and (5) Measurement.[2] In this chapter, we focus on the first four of the project types; we address Measurement (along with Statistical and Research Methodology projects) in Chapter 6.

We begin our response to the question of new problems and issues that warrant Institute of Education Sciences (IES) research grant funding with a focus on project types for two reasons. First, these project types play an administrative role in IES, as different types of projects result in different request for applications (RFA) requirements and different budgets. Project types thus set the stage for the types of studies that IES would like to see conducted, including the purpose of each study. Second, these project types have from the outset played a *normative* role in education research, reflecting assumptions about the process through which interventions—programs, policies, and practices—*ought* to be developed and evaluated. For

---

[1] Note that in FY2020, 1–3 and 5 have been funded under the Education Research grants competition, whereas 4 is funded under a separate RFA.

[2] Whereas grants submitted to the main research funding competitions of NCER and NCSER enter with a specific project type, applications for Research Networks and Research & Development Centers typically encompass multiple project types.

example, these project types emphasize that randomized controlled trials offer the highest form of evidence regarding the effect of an intervention. Importantly, this normative role is what is often perceived by education researchers as being the core identity of IES.

Based on testimony from numerous speakers and our own analysis of grant patterns, the committee identified a fundamental mismatch between the presumed structure of scientific practice as expressed in the IES project structure and what is required to meet the needs of children, schools, and society. This is not to say that a scientific structure is not needed, but that such a structure should be based upon the realities and contexts found in education from early childhood to adulthood. Based upon this analysis, we articulate a new system of science that is distinctly aligned and attuned to education science. Corresponding to this system, we propose a new project type structure, and recommend its adoption by IES.

PROGRESSION ACROSS PROJECT TYPES

Prior to 2020, what are now referred to as "project types" were called "goals."[3] The numbering of these goals gave the appearance of a linear process, with a possible intervention moving from an idea (Goal 1) to a scalable intervention (Goal 4) that could then reach and impact student outcomes in schools across the nation. While no longer called "goals," this same logic can be found in the descriptions of the project types. In the current system, *Exploration* projects focus on the identification of relationships between learner, educator, school, and policy-level characteristics and student outcomes; in particular, the focus is on identifying characteristics that can be changed via new interventions. Projects that might be funded in this type include small experiments testing if it is possible to change an observed factor, and the identification of associations between possible malleable factors and outcomes using both primary and secondary data. In *Development and Innovation* projects, an intervention is "developed," resulting in a logic model, intervention components, and a pilot study in a handful of schools (or sites). This intervention is then evaluated in an *Initial Efficacy* project. This is an explanatory, proof-of-concept study, focused on establishing that the intervention can produce an effect under "ideal" conditions (i.e., when

---

[3] While Exploration studies and Development and Innovation studies have remained roughly the same over time, project types (3) and (4) have been continually changed. Until 2018, studies of type (3) were called "Efficacy and Replication"; from 2019 onward these were renamed "Initial Efficacy and Follow-up." Until 2012, studies of type (4) were called "Scale-up Evaluations," then 2013 to 2018, they were called "Effectiveness," in 2019, "Replication: Efficacy and Effectiveness," and since 2020, this competition has been removed. In its place, "Systematic Replication" studies are now funded through a separate competition. See Brock and McLaughlin (2018) for more information.

implemented well). Finally, if an efficacy study suggests that an intervention has a positive impact, a *Replication* study may be conducted. In a replication study, the focus is on systematically changing one or more features of the intervention or context, to see if the previous efficacy findings are robust to this change. This replication study can itself be an efficacy study or an effectiveness study. In the latter case, the intervention is evaluated under routine conditions by an independent evaluator, with less researcher control and, likely, more variable implementation.

Notably, this last project type is where most changes have occurred in the past two decades. In the beginning, these fourth project types were referred to as "Scale-up" studies, with a focus on studying the intervention in a larger, broader, and more representative sample of schools. Later, these studies were renamed "Effectiveness" studies, with a focus on "typical" implementation and independent evaluation. This shift from "scale-up" to "effectiveness" on the one hand offered cost savings to IES (since "scale-up" studies were more expensive[4]), while on the other hand they deemphasized the need for interventions to be studied in more heterogeneous settings. At the same time, these changes to the fourth project type led to changes to the third. Initially these were referred to as "Efficacy" studies—which could include replications of previous efficacy studies. When the fourth project type shifted to "Replication," this third type was thus repositioned as "Initial Efficacy" studies instead.

To better understand these project types, Klager and Tipton (2021) analyzed data made available on the IES website about funded grants. These data include grants funded since 2002 and categorize them by project types, as well as program, center, topic area, year, principal investigator (PI), and institution. Since the purpose of this analysis was to understand project types, these analyses included all grants, regardless of funding mechanism. For further details on data coding this analysis, please see Appendix D of this report.

Tables 4-1 and 4-2 provide the total number of all grants and the total dollars spent on grants by NCER (Table 4-1) and NCSER (Table 4-2). The top rows of these tables show the total number of grants awarded in each 5-year time period (with the exception of the last time period, 2017–2020, which only covers 4 years) and overall. The second row shows the total funding awarded in millions of dollars. The next three rows indicate the number of grants, funding, and proportion of the total funding that fall into the Exploration, Development & Innovation, Efficacy, and Replication/Effectiveness categories. The columns depict the proportion of funds distributed in

---

[4] Many researchers now turn to Investing in Innovation (i3, first established with American Recovery and Reinvestment Act funds in 2009, and now called Education Innovation and Research, or EIR) for scaling studies instead.

TABLE 4-1 Proportion of Funding by Project Type and Year—NCER

	2002-2006	2007-2011	2012-2016	2017-2020	Overall
Grants	228	443	421	362	1454
Funding (Millions of $)	466.6	952.2	770.9	649.1	2838.9
Project Grants	174	305	256	240	975
Project Funding	269.3	561.1	508.8	458.2	1797.5
% of Total Funding	58%	59%	66%	71%	63%
Exploration	5%	8%	17%	23%	14%
Development & Innovation	35%	37%	24%	18%	28%
Efficacy	34%	28%	35%	43%	35%
Replication/Effectiveness	25%	27%	24%	15%	23%

SOURCE: Klager & Tipton, 2021 [Commissioned Paper]. Data from https://ies.ed.gov/funding/grantsearch/.
NOTE: Total grants includes all grant types, including Research Networks and R&D Centers. Project grants include those awarded in specific goals or project types.

TABLE 4-2 Proportion of Funding by Project Type and Year—NCSER

	2002-2006	2007-2011	2012-2016	2017-2020	Overall
Grants	39	175	144	149	507
Funding (Millions of $)	86.3	337.6	286.8	245.4	956.1
Project Grants	23	135	108	105	371
Project Funding	41.2	248.5	224.1	205.7	719.5
% of Total Funding	48%	74%	78%	84%	75%
Exploration	1%	5%	7%	12%	7%
Development & Innovation	37%	49%	32%	31%	38%
Efficacy	7%	18%	36%	43%	30%
Replication/Effectiveness	56%	28%	25%	14%	25%

SOURCE: Klager & Tipton, 2021 [Commissioned Paper]. Data from https://ies.ed.gov/funding/grantsearch/.
NOTE: This analysis includes all grant types, including Research Networks and R&D Centers.

each time period to each grant category. Going across a row for each grant category shows how the proportion of funding awarded in each category has changed over time.

These tables indicate that over time, IES has focused an increasing proportion of its funding on these four project types—increasing from 57 percent to 71 percent of the total spending in NCER and from 48 percent to 85 percent in NCSER. Much of this increase can be attributed to the implementation of a more standardized goal structure over time. In the first time period (2002–2006), a large portion of the NCER/NCSER spending went to studies that were "other goals," "no goals," or some combination of goals (e.g., "development and measurement"); for NCSER this included grants already encumbered by the Office of Special Education Programs. Over time the portion of these funds provided to each of the four project types has shifted. For example, both *Exploration* (5%–23% NCER; 1%–12% NCSER) and *Efficacy* (44%–54% NCER; 49%–56% NCSER) projects have increased in share over time, while *Development* (35%–18% NCER; 37%–31% NCSER) and *Replication/Effectiveness* (from 16%–6% NCER; 14%–2% NCSER) have decreased.

Examining Progression of Projects

The committee began by examining whether and how projects progress through and among the project types. To study this, Klager and Tipton (2021) examined the reporting of "related grants" in IES grant abstracts. For each grant, they examined whether there were later grants (of any type) identified as related that were funded. These results are shown in Table 4-3. Importantly, because these data do not indicate whether the "related" studies are of the exact same intervention or are only loosely related, these analyses may overestimate the amount of progression across projects.[5,6]

The analyses presented in Table 4-3 indicate that within IES-funded studies, interventions are not moving across the project types in a connected way from Exploration to Replication/Effectiveness very often. This lack of connection is most prominent for Exploration grants, of which only 16 percent are connected to at least one later IES-funded study. Given the nature of exploratory work, it might be expected that a smaller percentage of these types of studies would progress. In comparison, 30 percent of Development and Innovation grants are later connected to other grants, including 20 percent associated with Efficacy grants and 4 percent with

---

[5]There are no public data available that clearly identify progressions across project types by intervention. To approximate this, this table uses public data on "related grants" as a proxy. Parsing "initial efficacy" versus "replication" studies is also not definitive in these data, and instead the latter are identified by use of the word "replication" in the title or abstract. This results in 47 "Initial Efficacy" studies that are "related to" later "Initial Efficacy" studies, but that do not use the word "replication" in the title or abstract. A cursory read of these studies suggests that many are "related" in that they have the same PI or team members.

[6]While it not possible to tell from these data how studies funded by other agencies (e.g., National Institutes of Health [NIH], National Science Foundation [NSF]) might precede or follow IES-funded studies, it is possible to make some inferences regarding how they might connect. For example, we know that NSF EHR also funds development studies, but that they less often fund efficacy or effectiveness studies. Similarly, we know that NIH (and the National Institute of Child Health and Human Development specifically) funds both the development of interventions and efficacy and effectiveness studies; however, these are focused on a small subset of the education space. Thus, it is more likely that development studies funded by these other agencies funnel *into* IES Efficacy studies than the reverse.

TABLE 4-3 Grants Related to Future Grants by Goal (2002–2017)

Table 7. Grants funded from 2002-2017 that are related to future grants by category

		Related to a future grant in...					
		Exploration	Development & Innovation	Efficacy	Replication / Effectiveness	None in Future	Total Grants
Grants from...	Exploration	17	15	5	3	177	211
	Development & Innovation	9	68	97	19	339	487
	Efficacy	13	19	17	22	184	236
	Replication/Effectiveness	6	16	25	30	119	169

Note. Grants included in the "Grants from..." rows were funded bewteen 2002 and 2017. Grants included in the "Related to a future grant in..." were funded between 2002 and 2020.

SOURCE: Klager & Tipton, 2021 [Commissioned Paper]. Data from https://ies.ed.gov/funding/grantsearch/.

NOTE: Relationship determined from language in abstracts of grants. If the originating study resulted in multiple later studies of the same project type, it is only counted once in this table. However, if the originating study resulted in later studies of different project types, it is counted in both; thus the rows do not sum to the "total." The bolded diagonal numbers indicate multiple grants of the same type related to one another. Those above the bolded diagonal numbers indicate goals that progressed forward (e.g., D&I to Efficacy), while those below the diagonal progressed backward (e.g., Efficacy to D&I).

Replication/Effectiveness grants. (Since a grant many be associated with more than one subsequent grant, some of these may be duplicates.) Perhaps surprisingly, only 9 percent of Initial Efficacy studies are associated with later Replication/Effectiveness grants, while 6 percent are associated with additional Efficacy grants, and another 6 percent with new Development and Innovation grants. Notably, most grants are not associated with any future grants at all.

As early as 2013, in collaboration with NSF, IES noted few interventions were moving across these goals in a direct path. As the IES-NSF Common Evidence Guidelines (p. 10) state, "Knowledge development is not linear. The current of understanding does not flow only in one direction (that is, from basic research to studies of effectiveness). Rather, research generates important feedback loops, with each type of research potentially contributing to an evidence base that can inform and provide justification for other types of research."

Later analyses by Albro and Buckley (2015) supported the highly non-linear and iterative process through which research moved across and within the pipeline. This observation contributed to the decision to change the names from "goals" to "project types" and remove the numbering. The data in Table 4-3 speak to the iterative, nonlinear nature of the development process; for example, many Development and Innovation grants are followed up with new Development and Innovation grants, and Efficacy studies are sometimes also followed up with Development and Innovation grants.

Understanding Project Progression

The committee considered several potential reasons for the lack of consistent progression across project types (Farley-Ripple et al., 2018; Farrell & Coburn, 2017; Greenhalgh et al., 2004). The first is the lack of connections between different researchers or research teams. Nearly 84 percent of Exploration grants and 70 percent of Development and Innovation grants are not associated with *any* later grants. Furthermore, only 24 percent of the Development and Innovation grants were associated with later Efficacy, Effectiveness, or Replication grants. While one interpretation of this could be that the interventions explored and developed simply did not achieve desired ends, another possible explanation is a hand-off problem between project types that leaves promising interventions slipping through the cracks.

This hand-off problem is not hard to imagine, given that a given researcher may be more likely to possess skills and interests that fit into one (or maybe two) project types. For example, relative to those at research firms, university researchers are far more likely to be involved in Development and Innovation studies than Efficacy studies (Klager & Tipton, 2021). This makes sense in many regards, given the complexities of running randomized trials in large, sometimes geographically dispersed sets of schools. But unlike other fields, such as the pharmaceutical industry, researchers who undertake Development and those who undertake Efficacy studies are found in disparate organizations, with limited opportunities for natural connection across skills and interests. Thus, it is possible that one reason some interventions do or do not move from Development and Innovation to Efficacy has less to do with promise and more to do with connections researchers do or do not have across skill sets and organizations.

A second potential reason for lack of progression is related to implementation concerns. How an intervention works in a local context is directly related to how well it can be implemented given the culture, constraints, and resources found in its classrooms, teachers, schools, and districts (Century & Cassata, 2016; Bauer et al., 2015). As a result, most interventions are ultimately adapted to local environments, and some of these adaptations are likely better than others. Highly scripted, packaged programs provide a means to control implementation—which is ideal for teasing apart causality—but these can lead to an entire intervention being discarded when it does not fit well into the school environment. This creates an inherent tension between implementation and usefulness. The interventions most implementable with fidelity are heavily scripted and require specific supports, yet these requirements may not be feasible or desirable in many school environments (Coburn, 2003).

As a result, implementation plays out differently in Development and Innovation grants versus Efficacy and beyond studies. In Development and Innovation studies, implementation can be more tightly controlled: through the selection of schools and teachers into the study, through the small sample size, and through close monitoring by researchers. This degree of selection and monitoring simply cannot continue, however, as sample sizes grow larger in Efficacy studies. Thus, even though Efficacy studies often seek to focus on "high implementation" conditions, these goals are not always achieved.

A third possible reason for lack of progression relates to heterogeneity. The fact that students are inherently nested in classrooms, schools, and school systems is important since classrooms, teachers, and schools vary considerably in a myriad of ways. These factors include student backgrounds and baseline knowledge, classroom composition, teacher characteristics and behaviors, and school policies, practices, and resources (Weiss, Bloom, & Brock, 2014). Indeed, numerous studies in education research show that teachers' experiences of teaching and students' experiences of learning vary considerably across contexts (Nasir et al., 2016).

Furthermore, studies show that treatment effects can vary across these school and contextual factors (e.g., see Weiss et al., 2017). One of the most obvious sources of variation in effects, both across and within studies, has to do with what practice would have been absent the intervention. That is, the comparison condition ("business as usual") in causal studies is rarely doing nothing; rather, these studies are often teaching the same subjects and skills but using different curricula or approaches. It is easy to see, then, that these business-as-usual practices might vary, and as a result, so do impacts of an intervention.

The committee recognizes that NCER and NCSER have been aware of and actively sought to address many of these concerns. Efforts to respond to these challenges are reflected in additional recommendations included in the RFAs. For example, the RFAs include a list of possibilities that could be included for a "strong proposal" in addition to the primary focus on estimation of the average treatment effect. The 2022 RFA for Education Research Grants, for example, recommends that researchers proposing Efficacy and Replication studies "describe the setting and implementation conditions," assess "fidelity of implementation and comparison group practice," collect implementation outcomes, and describe a plan for examining fidelity of implementation.

Similarly, the RFA *requires* proposals to describe their sample and *recommends* that they define a target population. Proposals are encouraged to develop a plan to represent this target population during recruitment and to address concerns with the generalizability of their sample. "[A]lthough not required," the RFA suggests "the analysis of factors that influence the relationship between the intervention and learner outcomes (mediators and moderators)" and notes that when these are included, power analyses for related hypothesis tests should be included.

Regarding the concerns about connecting points between different project types, however, there has been considerably less work. The committee understood that in the original conception of the goal structure, the same researcher or team might develop an intervention over a sequence of studies from Exploration to Effectiveness.[7] In this conception, no connecting points were needed since the same team carried the idea through to completion. Over time, however, it became clear that this model was rarely followed in practice, and that the research process was iterative. But removing the numbering and changing the names did nothing to address this connecting point problem—if different researchers conduct different types of studies, how should interventions be moved along in the system?

Perhaps the closest IES has come to addressing this concern is again through the "dissemination plan" found in the RFA. For example, for Development and Innovation grants, proposals must include dissemination plans that focus on "letting others know about the availability of the new intervention for more rigorous evaluation and further adaptation." This includes activities like journal publications, presentations, and engagement with research networks. Importantly, these activities are focused on individual researchers and their own networks and interests since no repository or database of preliminary findings exists within IES.

CONNECTING RESEARCH AND PRACTICE

The model of education improvement that IES research is built upon assumes that interventions are developed, tested, refined, and tested some more and then ultimately the successful interventions are adopted by school districts, schools, and teachers—thus ultimately improving student learning and reducing disparities at a national scale. Information about successful interventions is made accessible to decision makers through a variety of dissemination activities and especially through the What Works Clearinghouse (WWC), which is housed in the National Center for Educational Evaluation and Regional Assistance. To this end, the WWC developed and maintains a database of intervention effects that can be accessed online, as well as practice guides. The WWC also develops and maintains a Standards Handbook that provides rules regarding different designations that studies

---

[7]This sentence was modified after release of the report to IES to indicate that this statement is part of the committee's judgment.

can receive. As a result, most Efficacy, Effectiveness, and Replication grants at NCER and NCSER strive to meet these standards so that their results can ultimately contribute to this knowledge base and make it to schools and decision makers.

A continued question at IES is whether the research produced by IES grants is used in schools and educational contexts for decision making. To date, however, it has been difficult to answer this question since there are little data available to understand the outputs of the IES research system. For example, simple online searches of interventions studied via IES grants often result in project or intervention websites, but without any clear indicator of how often the program is adopted. Research on knowledge mobilization suggests that only 17 percent of school and district leaders report accessing research from the WWC "often" (13%) or "all the time" (4%) (Penuel et al., 2017). Yet at the same time, some individual researchers have made considerable headway in getting their curricula and/or interventions into classrooms.

As noted in Chapter 1, however, there is now a deeper understanding of how educators and education decision makers access and use research evidence to inform practice and policy. These insights suggest that traditional models of dissemination are insufficient for connecting the education policy and practice communities with the evidence produced by research. The complexity of decision making in education raises several possible explanations for why a given intervention may not be identified or adopted by education decision makers even when it is accessible through the WWC.

First, decision makers may be facing problems other than those being addressed by IES-funded educational interventions. Adoption decisions are one of many decisions that educational leaders make, and some research suggests that these decisions are relatively rare (Penuel et al., 2018; Coburn, Toure, & Yamashita, 2009). Put another way, researcher foci and school and district needs may be out of sync. This disconnect could occur because the current project structure does not prioritize understanding and connecting with decision makers regarding their needs and current practice, or because IES's preferred study types and methods are not well suited to investigating the issues that schools and districts are facing. There may be whole classes of interventions or approaches that are not being studied by IES-funded research but that are of interest to education organizations. These might include issues that are difficult to study using randomized controlled trials (e.g., student assignment algorithms, school funding approaches, teacher hiring practices, course de-tracking policies, or meal subsidy policies) or that are not directly focused on student achievement (e.g., approaches to school discipline, social-emotional learning, or school-community collaborations related to health, safety, and wellness).

A second possible explanation is that even if an intervention or approach addresses a "real" problem faced by teachers, schools, and school districts and is potentially implementable, it may not be available for schools and school districts to use. That is, the intervention may not be marketed and distributed in the same way as commercial curricula, leaving most schools and districts unaware that the intervention even exists. Or it may be that even if marketed and available, it is not packaged and supported in the same way that other curricula and programs are. This suggests that there may be a need for approaches that bring together and incentivize partnerships between researchers, communities, education technology companies, publishers, and nonprofits that focus on selling curricula and professional development to schools. Through these partnerships, researchers can take advantage of the scale and reach of these organizations, thus getting "best practices" out to schools more efficiently.

Third, interventions developed by researchers may not be readily adaptable, implementable, and sustainable in schools and districts: that is, the results are not useful because they are difficult to use. For example, a brief, 9-week science program may be effective and yet, if compared to a full-year science program, may be difficult to implement (since curricula for the remaining weeks of the year then need to be selected, too). Other barriers may arise around training personnel, freeing up staff time from competing demands, or aligning programs to related initiatives.

Furthermore, in many instances, schools and districts may not be interested in packaged programs as much as developing their own, locale-specific programs based upon best practices found in research. This suggests a need also for research evaluating approaches developed by practitioners, strategies for developing locale-specific interventions (e.g., for districts), and identification of core components of interventions.

Again, the concerns the committee raised above are not unfamiliar to IES. Indeed, over time IES has responded to concerns of this type via various revisions to both the WWC and to RFAs and requirements for grants. Perhaps one of the most concerted efforts can be found in the requirements for dissemination plans for Efficacy and Replication grant proposals. The RFA notes that "IES considers all types of findings from these projects be potentially useful to researchers, policymakers, and practitioners…" and that researchers who create interventions "are expected to make these products available for research purposes or … for general use." In practice, these efforts often include workshops or trainings for the districts and schools involved in the study, for other districts or schools, or the development of a website for the intervention. The success of these plans, however, is difficult to monitor since they occur in the last year of the grant funding for a study.

More broadly, though, research shows that dissemination by itself is not sufficient for enacting research in practice (Rabin & Brownson, 2012; Greenhalgh et al., 2005). Decision making occurs through relational dynamics within larger systems (Best & Holmes, 2010; Boswell & Smith, 2007), where policy makers engage with multiple actors around multiple forms of knowledge (Farrell & Coburn, 2017; Greenhalgh et al., 2004). Furthermore, packaging, scaling, and marketing interventions are far beyond the skill set of most academic researchers. To have substantive impact, dissemination and engagement activities require time and resources that go beyond what can be conducted in the last year of a grant, as educators also need continued support beyond the adoption decision to train, implement, and adapt new practices within their local contexts (Dearing & Kee, 2012). While the challenges are clear, much remains to be learned about robust strategies for ensuring that findings from education research reverberate in the decisions of educational leaders and practitioners (Conaway, 2021).

This speaks to a need to better understand *knowledge mobilization*, including how schools and decision makers identify problems and develop solutions; which interventions, curricula, and programs are currently used in schools; how to get promising evidence into their hands; how education leaders harness that evidence to guide action; and what conditions support education leaders to use research more centrally and substantively in their decision making (Farley-Ripple et al., 2018). Improving understanding of the processes of knowledge mobilization would help develop better mechanisms for determining what research would be useful for education policy makers and practitioners, as well as identifying strategies for supporting them in using that research when it is available (Jackson, 2021).

A REVISED SCIENTIFIC STRUCTURE IS NEEDED

As the committee showed in the previous section, the existing IES project structure has encountered and addressed a variety of problems over the previous 20 years. These include problems moving interventions from Exploration to Efficacy and from Efficacy to scale and practice. In the face of each of these concerns, IES has reflected on and acknowledged these shortcomings, each time attempting to address concerns with new additions, including new names, new requirements, and new trainings. But at the core, this project structure has remained the same.

This project structure was developed around assumptions that seemed reasonable 20 years ago: that the challenges facing schools could be addressed by developing and testing interventions that could be easily packaged (and thus randomized) and that would uniformly increase student achievement. Twenty years into this science, however, it is clear that this model does not map onto the reality of education science and U.S. schools, that changing practice is harder than simply providing evidence, and that changing school environments and reducing inequity is difficult work.

For these reasons, the committee argues that now is the time for IES to rejuvenate and revise its project type structure. Unlike the previous project structure, which followed a pattern that is familiar from other scientific fields such as biomedical research, the new structure is grounded in the specific challenges of education today, and thus is uniquely designed to support a robust and cumulative science of education. To develop this new project structure, we begin with the charge, often repeated in RFAs and reports that the goal of research supported by IES is to determine "what works, *for whom*, and *under what conditions*." This framing puts the users of evidence at the center: the school districts, schools, teachers, and students. This charge is echoed in the mission statement for IES:

> Our mission is to provide **scientific evidence** on which to ground education practice and policy and to share this information in formats that are **useful and accessible** to educators, parents, policymakers, researchers, and the public [emphasis added].

As we articulated in previous chapters, an overarching goal of this science of education should be to reduce inequities in schooling and society. From the No Child Left Behind Act, to the Every Student Succeeds Act, to President Biden's Executive Order on Racial Equity, a bipartisan sequence of Presidents and other policy makers has placed equity at the heart of the national goals for education. It is time for the research enterprise to do the same (Jackson, 2021; Farrell et al., 2021).

Drawing on both the five themes introduced in Chapter 1, and on the previous analysis of how and why interventions may or may not be progressing through the existing project types, the committee identified a set of framing principles for education research that inform the revised project structure.

1. One of the major purposes of education research is to identify and intervene on inequities in schools and society. This purpose pushes beyond understanding what works simply for the sake of science toward identifying the most promising ways to improve schools. It targets the nation's greatest educational challenge: to eliminate pervasive and persisting disparities among groups such as those defined by race, ethnicity, gender, income, disability, and language minority status, as called for in repeated enactments of the Elementary and Secondary Education Act, the Higher Education Act, the Education Sciences Reform Act, and President Biden's Executive Order.

2. The effects of interventions will vary given the complexities of school contexts, cultures, resources, learners, and existing practices (Bryan, Tipton,

& Yeager, 2021; Joyce & Cartwright, 2010). Contextual conditions, such as the social, economic, political, and resource structures in which education operates, shape the needs of actors in the education system, the feasibility of implementation, and the effects of interventions. Greater attention to contextual differences is also essential to make progress toward advancing equity through education research. Decision makers are rarely interested in the average impact of an intervention; instead, they want to understand the projected effect in *their* local context, often for a specific student population. This suggests that the primary focus on "the effect" of an intervention—at any stage of research—is likely inappropriate.

   3. **Interventions will be adapted differently in different environments, thus contributing to the heterogeneity of effects.** This implies that it is important to both develop *and* evaluate interventions in the realistic conditions found in schools and school systems. Given concerns with implementation, adaptation is an inherent part of the adoption of new interventions in schools. For this reason, decision makers need information regarding which adaptations are responsive versus unresponsive to local contexts, which barriers and facilitators may affect implementation, and which supports are needed (McLeod et al., 2017; Abry, Hulleman, & Rimm-Kaufman, 2015; Nilsen, 2015; Powell et al., 2015; Waltz et al., 2014; Michie, van Stralen, & West, 2011; Damschroder et al., 2009).

   4. **Decision makers obtain information on educational interventions from a variety of sources.** Decision makers are inundated with potential interventions and professional development services, in addition to frequently adapting and creating their own, and would benefit from guidance on how to efficiently surface and weigh evidence to compare different options. Altogether, this speaks to a need to better understand *knowledge mobilization*, including how schools and decision makers identify problems and develop solutions; which interventions, curricula, and programs are currently used in schools; how to get promising evidence into their hands; how educational leaders harness that evidence to guide action; and what conditions support educational leaders to use research more centrally and substantively in their decision making. Improving understanding of the processes of knowledge mobilization would help develop better mechanisms for determining what research would be useful for education policy makers and practitioners, as well as identifying strategies for supporting them in using that research when it is available.

   5. **The most promising interventions will not necessarily find their way through the research structure and into educational settings.** Infrastructure is needed to both support research (e.g., to disseminate knowledge across project types, to surface promising interventions, to encourage evaluations of these interventions) and to connect researchers with users (e.g., to develop networks, identify knowledge brokers). There are many potential

forms for this infrastructure, but at the core, they need to be about building systems to integrate research with practice.

Beginning with these principles makes clear that issues of equity, implementation, heterogeneity, and usefulness need to be addressed from the very beginning of the research and development process, not at the end. The research process needs to begin in the field—in schools and other educational settings—and should involve exploring what current constraints, resources, and needs teachers, schools, and school systems face; the range of practices and policies they have already been developing and exploring; and the variety of contexts found in schools nationwide. The development of new interventions, including policies, practices, supports, and organizational approaches, needs to, from the beginning, account for issues of adaptation, implementation, and heterogeneity that arise in this diversity of contexts, when researchers are not nearby. Studies evaluating these interventions need to focus not only on estimating the average effect, but also on understanding variation in effects, and helping to guide decision makers where, under what conditions, and for whom such an intervention may be promising.

Finally, infrastructure is needed that continually synthesizes and updates what is known—for each project type—and uses this infrastructure to connect with and direct research in other project types. Importantly, this means systematic reviews of not only efficacy studies and those that meet WWC standards intended for decision makers, but also of exploration and development studies intended for researchers. This interstitial work might surface, for example, promising interventions that have been developed and that need to be evaluated. This could be the work of IES directly or commissioned to be carried out by others. These syntheses—and the ability to understand gaps—are essential to creating the feedback loops necessary to move the field forward.

In more practical terms, this means revising the underlying project structure. Like the current structure, we envision four project types, each of which can be crossed with a topic area. However, these project types would differ in focus and content from their current versions. Importantly, these changes should not be seen as in opposition to the current structure so much as an outgrowth and evolution of this structure—and of the knowledge we, as a field, have accumulated over the past two decades. The committee notes that these proposed project types would encompass research that currently exists in the IES grant system but would expand beyond and address some of the limitations, thus making space for new research. (A fifth project type, for measurement studies, is discussed in Chapter 6.) These project types pertain to both NCER and NCSER.

1. Discovery and Needs Assessment

Current: In the original goal structure, the intervention pipeline was assumed to begin in the research "lab." This meant early studies would focus on identifying "malleable factors" associated with educational outcomes (IES RFA, 2019). Many current Exploration studies continue to focus on establishing the relationships between pre-determined "malleable" factors and pre-determined "outcomes." In this way, Exploration studies are often less "exploratory" and more "confirmatory" in nature, focused on determining if theories developed in the laboratory can be confirmed to hold in schools.

Over time, Exploration studies have expanded to include a broader range of study types. As Table 4-4 indicates, more than one-third (35% NCER; 13% NCSER) of these studies have been focused on questions of causality, with some addressed via strong quasi-experimental methods (11%; e.g., regression discontinuity designs) and others using small experiments (22%). Here is it notable that studies focused on causal questions—answered with quasi-experimental methods and secondary data—are considered "exploratory." Calling these exploratory indicates that even findings from high-quality quasi-experiments are not to be taken as serious evidence.

Finally, to date 6 percent (4% NCER; 7% NCSER) of these Exploration studies have been systematic reviews and meta-analyses. In examining the abstracts of these reviews, nearly all of them focus on synthesizing the results of randomized trials and high-quality quasi-experiments. Yet in the current structure, while they summarize a broad base of causal research, the research itself is considered "exploratory."

New: If, as a field, we are to develop and refine interventions that can successfully improve educational outcomes for students, then it is imperative that these interventions consider the diversity of the educational

TABLE 4-4 Current Exploration Study Types

	NCER		NCSER		
	Primary Data	Secondary Data	Primary Data	Secondary Data	Total
(Any) Meta-Analysis	0	12	0	4	16
(Only) Correlational	97	36	21	22	176
(Only) Quasi-experiment	10	19	0	3	32
(Any) Experiment	56	6	4	0	66
Total	163	73	25	29	290

Note. When grants included multiple data sources and/or studies, primary data collection supercedes secondary data collection. Likewise, meta-analysis supercedes experiments which supercede quasi-experiments.

SOURCE: Klager & Tipton, 2021 [Commissioned Paper]. Data from https://ies.ed.gov/funding/grantsearch/.

contexts found in this nation. For this reason, the committee proposes that schools, districts, and out-of-school learning spaces should actively be the breeding ground of scientific theories themselves. To highlight this anchoring in educational context, we call this new project type *Discovery and Needs Assessment*. These studies would begin in authentic learning environments, with a focus on observing, measuring, and understanding the varieties of practices and processes *on the ground* and determining gaps between "what is" and "what could be."

By emphasizing the need for situating work in authentic school environments, we are also highlighting the need for a broad range of descriptive work that involves primary data collection. Qualitative data might include deep descriptions of processes and problems, identifying the ways in which these processes and problems might contribute to persistent inequality and surfacing potential barriers, facilitators, and implementation strategies. Quantitative data might include descriptive or correlational analysis of surveys of current practices—including curricula used and time allocations—as well as the problems faced by teachers, schools, and school systems. Of course, this is also a place in which new sources of data, such as big data and administrative data, could be examined to better describe educational contexts and trajectories.

The language of *Needs Assessment* makes clear that the factors under study would shift from a primary focus on students to also consider classrooms, teachers, schools, and systems. This means shifting toward landscape analyses and diagnostic work, with the goal of understanding the social, economic, political, and resource structures in which schools operate; current business-as-usual practices; considerations for implementation of new practices; and possibilities and levers available for intervening. Importantly, this also means soliciting and understanding the problems education organizations care about and are searching to solve. This is not to say that this research needs to *only* respond to the immediate, stated concerns of decision makers; certainly science can have a longer and broader vision of what is possible than what is immediate. But without this information—without understanding the needs of the actors involved in the system—moving toward this broader vision is not possible.

This project type would allow IES to continue its current stance to "encourage, support, and prioritize collaboration between researchers and practitioners, but without specifying how that cooperation should be structured" (Schneider, 2020). However, the research literature suggests that research-practice partnerships, which are increasingly found in large school districts across the country as well as many states and regional collaborations,[8] would provide an especially hospitable context for discovery and needs assessment research. As Turley and Stevens (2015) explained, by jointly developing a research agenda, researchers are more likely to ask questions whose answers matter to educational decision makers. The partnership also enables researchers to understand the context more deeply, and to interpret their findings in light of local conditions. Meanwhile, educators benefit from the chance to have their questions addressed in the most pertinent context of all, their own district, state, or region. Both needs assessment and discovery of responses to those needs may be enhanced when undertaken in the context of a sustained partnership that embodies trust, a diverse range of expertise, and opportunities for many actors to have a voice in the questions pursued and the interpretation of findings (Farrell et al., 2021).

This new framing of *Discovery and Needs Assessment* studies is responsive to the general mission of IES as laid out in the Education Sciences Reform Act (ESRA), Section 111(b)(1): "to provide national leadership in expanding fundamental knowledge and understanding of education from early childhood through postsecondary study, in order to provide parents, educators, students, researchers, policymakers, and the general public with reliable information" about the condition of education; practices that support access, learning, and achievement; and program effectiveness. By beginning in the field instead of in the laboratory, IES-sponsored research will be better positioned to uncover new knowledge and understanding that responds to the need to improve outcomes and advance equity in U.S. education.

2. Development and Adaptation

Current: In the current project structure, Development and Innovation grants focus on iteratively developing or refining new interventions for use in schools. These studies are encouraged to identify how their innovation differs from current practice, how much such an intervention would cost, and how the sample of schools in which it is piloted represent a (narrow) target population that might use the intervention (IES RFA, 2022). Here we focus on two issues.

Pilot studies often include only a small sample of schools (e.g., less than 10) and involve a high degree of researcher control. This means that the intervention is developed in an optimal condition: that is, one where implementation is highly monitored so that high fidelity is achieved. In the short run, this focus on optimal implementation is ideal, as it allows for

---

[8]The National Network of Education Research–Practice Partnerships now includes 57 members across the United States; see https://nnerpp.rice.edu/.

the causal effect to be isolated in the best-case scenario. In the long run, this can be far from optimal, as it means that problems of implementation and adaptation are not discovered until later studies with larger samples (Farley-Ripple et al., 2018; Finnigan & Daly, 2014).

The current project structure also has not sufficiently addressed heterogeneity. Development studies are encouraged to identify a target population that is "narrow," and in practice—given the smaller resources found in these grants relative to Efficacy studies—this can mean a population that is local to the researcher and somewhat homogenous. Again, in the short run, this may be optimal, as reduced variation can improve statistical precision. But this pushes questions of heterogeneity to later studies. To see why, note that "narrow" target populations may not represent well schools elsewhere in terms of resources, practices, organizational conditions, students, or business-as-usual curricula and teaching practices. As a result, the intervention has only been developed and refined in one, particular population, delaying questions of contextual variation and the feasibility and fit elsewhere until later studies.

New: In contrast, we propose that researchers need to—from the outset—consider the types of heterogeneous environments that an intervention may be implemented within and focus on determining barriers and facilitators (Tabak et al., 2012) and effective implementation strategies. We include the word *Adaptation* in the title to clarify that adaptations to local contexts *will* occur and that it is incumbent on researchers to develop their interventions with this in mind. The language of *adaptation* recognizes that by adapting to local conditions, an intervention may be more likely to be adopted, supported, and sustained, thus improving educational outcomes. As Joyce and Cartwright (2020, pp. 1048–1049) explained, research on local conditions that support or impede program success requires information that goes well beyond impact assessment.

The kinds of research that can produce the requisite information, locally or more generally, often in coproduction, require a mix of methods well beyond those listed in current evidence hierarchies. The standard reasons for mixing methods in evidence-based education are to aid implementation (Gorard, See, & Siddiqui, 2017) and to make general effectiveness claims more reliable (Connolly et al., 2017; Bryk, 2015). We, by contrast, encourage mixed methods because reliable and useful effectiveness predictions require a variety of different kinds of information relevant to determining how an intervention will perform in a specific setting that different kinds of research help uncover. These different modes of research allow the development of interventions that not only work in one, narrow population, but that are robust and potentially effective in a broad range of school contexts.

Importantly, while planning for adaptation does require greater heterogeneity in the samples included in pilot studies, it does not necessarily mean that larger samples are required. For example, it is possible to include a small sample that is even more heterogeneous than a population simply by carefully and purposively including schools that differ in a myriad of ways during the design process (see Tipton, 2021). Collecting both quantitative and qualitative data would allow information on supports and derailers to be studied, and for the intervention itself to be robustly developed quickly.

By positioning adaptation and heterogeneity as central to the development of interventions, we also highlight the potential for new approaches to intervention development entirely. Often, development is a researcher-led activity, one in which a person from the outside brings in new ideas and approaches. But if the goal is for an intervention to be implementable and adaptable, it may mean that starting with existing practices and programs and refining these to be more evidence based may ultimately be more scalable. This framing, too, allows for consideration of who designs, for what purposes, and how design will take place (Philip et al., 2018; Bang & Vossoughi, 2016).

Finally, taken together, this call for focusing on adaptation and heterogeneity in design has important consequences for the goals and purpose of the pilot study in Development and Adaptation studies. Certainly, this increased variation will make it more difficult to estimate a statistically significant average treatment effect in a pilot study. But many scholars in both medicine and education research have already argued that the focus of pilot studies should *not* be on estimation of the average treatment effect or on testing null hypotheses (e.g., see Westlund & Stuart, 2017). Instead, these studies should be focused on the preparations needed to ensure success in later efficacy studies—and being able to anticipate adaptations across a wide range of contexts is essential to this work. This means that requirements for later efficacy, effectiveness, and replication studies would not be focused primarily on an estimated effect size or hypothesis test, but should consider them in tandem with the logic model for the intervention, proximal measures, and the ability to implement and adapt to a range of contexts.

This new conception of *Development and Adaptation* studies is no less responsive than current practice to ESRA's call for "scientifically valid research activities, including basic and applied research, statistics activities, scientifically valid education evaluation, development, and widespread dissemination" (Section 112(1)). Indeed, if it leads to greater identification of programs and practices that, because they are responsive to real needs and attend to implementation challenges, can actually be implemented and are in fact implemented, the new conception will meet the law's requirements with even greater force than the present system.

3. Impact and Heterogeneity

Current: In the current goal structure, interventions are tested first in "some" population (often considered "ideal," often "narrow") via an "initial" efficacy study, later in another context (or version of the intervention) via an efficacy "replication" study, and, rarely, in a broad population, via an "effectiveness" replication study. In the best-case scenario, this results in *over a decade* of evaluation before the intervention is considered ready for marketing to schools. By this time, both current practices in schools and the intervention itself may have shifted, making the direct evidence from these studies out of date. And in the interim, the average effect from each of these studies may still be considered evidence for school decision making (e.g., via the WWC), albeit based on evidence from a small fraction of school environments that may not at all represent the schools that might benefit from the intervention.

In the current framework, the focus is on ensuring high internal validity—the ability to detect cause-and-effect relationships—at the expense of external validity. This can be seen in the fact that considerations of heterogeneity and implementation are pushed later and later in the process. Initial efficacy trials are *not required* to focus on either, leaving these for replication grants (efficacy or effectiveness), which are rarely conducted. Studies of existing research practices indicate that the samples included in efficacy studies have not historically represented either national or state populations of schools well and are vastly less heterogeneous than these populations (Tipton, 2021; Tipton, et al., 2021; Stuart et al., 2017). Thus, understanding heterogeneity is saved for replication studies, which are to systematically vary "at least one aspect" of a prior study, in order to determine "the conditions under which [interventions] work and for whom" (IES RFA, 2021). Importantly, these aspects could include the version of the intervention itself (a "conceptual" replication), thus not necessarily addressing the heterogeneity found in business-as-usual conditions across education contexts.

This prioritization of internal validity can also be seen in the predominance of randomized trials in both efficacy and effectiveness studies.[9] The fact that randomization to treatment provides clear identification of a cause-and-effect relationship is not to be disputed. But not all interventions can *feasibly* be randomized, particularly those involving school and system interventions, both because of the large commitment required by schools and budget limitations. Even when randomization is possible, attrition before outcomes are measured, particularly in long-term interventions, can

---

[9]This section has been modified after release of the report to IES to clarify research design types permitted for Efficacy, Effectiveness, and Replication projects, as well as for Exploration projects.

undermine the benefits of randomization. Thus, it is not surprising that the interventions studied via Initial Efficacy and Replication studies largely focus on student-level interventions, while teacher, school, and system interventions are largely found in quasi-experiments.

Finally, while IES focuses strongly on internal validity, new research suggests that policy makers appear mainly concerned with external validity when accessing and using research. This point is driven home by a recent experimental study that found that while policy makers do not exhibit a preference for experimental over observational findings, they are more likely to be drawn to evidence from larger studies and from contexts like their own than to smaller studies and contexts that differ from their own settings (Nakajima, 2021). Likewise, a recent national survey of education leaders found that when asked to identify specific examples of research that informed their practice, respondents most commonly pointed to books covering broad topics, and they rarely identified research studies that would meet the top tier of evidence in the Every Student Succeeds Act (Farrell, Penuel, & Davidson, 2022). These studies point to a disconnect between the priorities of researchers and decision makers when considering what makes evidence useful for practice.

New: In contrast, we call for combining all studies focused on determining causal effects of interventions into a single project type referred to as *Impact and Heterogeneity* studies. This includes quasi-experimental studies (currently most commonly funded via *Exploration* studies), as well as all types of efficacy and effectiveness studies. Combining these type of studies under a single project highlights that the question and purpose is the same in each—to estimate causal effects—while allowing variation in the approaches used depending upon the population, context, and intervention. Furthermore, a single project type for causal questions, which includes both efficacy and effectiveness studies and addresses heterogeneity as well as the average impact, will elevate matters of external validity to be considered on par with the matters of internal validity.

The inclusion of quasi-experiments in this category is of particular importance, as some interventions may simply not be able to be studied using randomized trials. For example, we know that it is difficult to recruit schools into trials, in general, and particularly in trials with intensive interventions. Interventions focused on changing school policies, leadership, and structures may be particularly difficult to randomize. This means that focusing only on the inclusion of randomized trials as "evidence" of a causal impact severely narrows the types of interventions that can be studied and evaluated. Here, we are calling to elevate the ability to use high-quality quasi-experimental designs when conducting a randomized trial would be infeasible. High-quality quasi-experimental designs might include regression discontinuity, instrumental variables, (comparative) difference-in-difference, and propensity score methods. (Importantly, studies of this type would not be possible without the methodological developments for quasi-experiments funded by IES Statistical and Research Methods grants over the past two decades.) By elevating these methodologies, the focus becomes clearly on determining the best evidence for the interventions that schools need, instead of on finding interventions that fit the best methods of evidence.

Within randomized trials, combining efficacy and effectiveness studies into a single project type also removes what can be arbitrary distinctions between the two. In medicine, it has long been noted, for example, that very few studies are fully either efficacy or effectiveness trials, with most operating on a continuum between these (e.g., the PRECIS-2 tool; see Loudon et al., 2017). Our assessment as a committee is that in education, it is hard if not impossible to fully "control" the school environment in ways that are typical in efficacy trials in medicine. For example, in education, the comparison condition is very often a business-as-usual condition (effectiveness language) instead of a researcher-determined comparison (efficacy language). Similarly, even when the intervention is highly scripted, it is often very difficult to highly control how it is both delivered and how well its implementation matches what is intended (efficacy language); instead, very often the intervention is adapted to local conditions (effectiveness language). Similarly, the line between a "conceptual replication" study—in which an intervention that exists is changed systematically in some way—and a new "efficacy" study—based on a "new" intervention—can also be an arbitrary distinction. The point here is that this is not an either-or, that most studies fall on the spectrum of efficacy-effectiveness, and that the current language reifies a distinction that is often false.

Furthermore, combining Initial Efficacy and Replication studies (of both types) into a single project type makes clear that heterogeneity and implementation should be front and center in *any* impact analysis (Bryan, Tipton, & Yeager, 2021). For some interventions, this may mean condensing what would have been several studies—Initial efficacy, Efficacy replication, another Efficacy replication, and perhaps others—into a single large study focused on testing theories about the mechanism of the intervention (via moderator and mediation analyses), questions of impact variation, and questions about the local conditions under which the intervention may be effective. Certainly, a study of this type would be more expensive (and require more schools) than a single efficacy trial. Yet, it may be *less* expensive (and require fewer schools) when compared to the multiple trials necessary to produce this evidence in the current approach.

For other interventions, this may mean that a series of smaller studies, closer to the prototypical "efficacy" study, may be necessary. For example, this may be the case for a high-dosage, focused intervention funded by NCSER. The distinction is that while the studies may be conducted sequentially, the planning of the studies would need to consider the broader set of studies and what the contribution of a particular study is to answer theoretical questions about mechanism and heterogeneity. Instead of a wait-and-see approach, researchers would design a series of studies (what may currently be considered replication studies) in advance, to develop what might be called a "prospective meta-analysis" and to argue clearly for how these studies in combination will answer the questions posed.

Taken together, this combination of experimental and quasi-experimental, efficacy and effectiveness studies into a single project type means that decisions regarding the methods, scale, and purpose of the study would need to be aligned clearly with the intervention proposed, the population in need, and the state of knowledge in the field. With these considerations in mind, a study would need to articulate *why this research design* is the best possible design for the intervention studied. It may be, for example, that for a structural intervention affecting school district organization—in a literature in which there are no previous causal studies—a well-done quasi-experimental design would provide the best evidence possible at this time. At the same time, arguing for this design in a study focused on a student-level intervention in which there are several previous studies using randomized designs may be much harder. Again, this framing allows researchers to center the needs of schools and gaps in the research base, instead of the choice of study design.

Finally, we note that this new conception of *Impact and Heterogeneity* is grounded in IES's longstanding commitment to assessing causal impact using designs that warrant such inferences. As stated in ESRA Section 102(19)(D), a "scientifically valid education evaluation" is one that "employs experimental designs using random assignment, *when feasible*, and other research methodologies that allow for the *strongest possible* causal inferences when random assignment is not feasible [emphasis added]." The revision we are recommending fulfills ESRA's promise to ensure that education research meets the standards of science, but with sufficient nuance to be implemented in real schools in a timely way.

4. Knowledge Mobilization

Current: The current project structure is built upon the assumption that decision makers will act upon evidence once it is available. In fact, very few school and district leaders regularly consult the WWC as a way to learn about research (Penuel et al., 2016). More generally, education leaders do not regularly incorporate examination of research findings in an instrumental way when making decisions about programs or policies (Finnigan & Daly, 2014; Coburn, Honig, & Stein, 2009). In recent years, IES has increased requirements for dissemination from grants. These dissemination plans focus on increasing and diversifying the number of *outputs* that researchers produce; for example, this might include publishing in both scholarly journals and practitioner journals. These dissemination plans also encourage researchers to make their intervention available (e.g., via websites) and to provide findings to the schools involved in the research. Based on available research, however, these specific dissemination plans, however well intended, are unlikely to greatly influence education decision makers at the early childhood, K–12, and postsecondary levels, because reporting research evidence, even when it is timely, relevant, and accessible, does not necessarily lead to the use of evidence (Finnigan & Daly, 2014).

While IES's operating assumption is that educational leaders need high-quality evidence about interventions, research shows that educational leaders and practitioners in fact face a glut of information of varying quality (e.g., Tseng, 2012; Honig & Coburn, 2008). It is not clear how decision makers weigh the evidence produced by IES-funded research versus other sources, including research that is less rigorous. This suggests that the problem is not simply one of providing evidence to those in need. Instead, it is about understanding how school and district leaders are making decisions about improving student outcomes, how research makes its way into these deliberations, and the conditions and supports that enable them to use this research evidence in productive ways. Conceiving of the problem of evidence use in this way makes it clear that the same sorts of questions that IES fosters about evidence *production* also warrant asking about evidence *use*.

Further, even if education decision makers consult research to adopt interventions, implementation requires practitioners to integrate and adapt the interventions in a new setting (Joyce & Cartwright, 2020; Nilsen, 2015; Dearing & Kee, 2012; Rabin et al., 2012; Greenhalgh et al., 2005). That adaptation process may then result in practices that no longer align to the original evidence (e.g., Cohen, 1990). Conversely, studying interventions developed in practice may enable more systematic spread of success (LeMahieu et al., 2017; Spreitzer & Sonenshein, 2004). For these reasons, we propose that strategies to mobilize knowledge be studied directly, not merely as another stage of the project to implement the findings in practice, but rather as a research enterprise in itself.

New: We propose a new project type focused on *Knowledge Mobilization*. We propose the term "knowledge mobilization" rather than "knowledge utilization" or "research evidence use" because we incorporate into this project type the organization and synthesis of bodies of evidence as well as improvement of the use of research evidence in real-world settings. This project type would encompass a range of activities and would, in many ways, serve as the central engine of the research infrastructure.

These projects would focus on studies of the conditions that foster research use in a range of contexts from early childhood to postsecondary, synthesizing bodies of evidence to arrive at generalizable conclusions (about *"what works, for whom, and under what conditions"*), developing and testing robust strategies to foster the use of research in varied contexts, and studies to support the development of robust measures of research use. As Conaway (2021) argued,

> In its role as a funder of basic research, IES should prioritize research on research use itself. We need to know how to measure research use, because if we can't measure it, then we can't tell if it's happening, let alone increasing. We need to know more about the conditions, mechanisms, and strategies for increasing research use, so that we can understand when, how, and why it works best. And we need to better understand the role of boundary-spanners—people who sit between researchers and practitioners and enable them to work effectively together.[10]

Consistent with the view that evidence use demands the same type of attention as that given to evidence production, we propose that projects of this type might include descriptive, synthesis, intervention, or measurement focus, which we describe below. Given this range of possible study foci, the committee deliberated on whether it would be more appropriate for Knowledge Mobilization to be a topic or a project type. We ultimately decided that by positioning Knowledge Mobilization as a project type, we emphasize that *the entire field of education research* needs to develop and study the success of these strategies to integrate research with practice. Establishing Knowledge Mobilization as a project type that cuts across multiple topics, rather than as a standalone topic, also recognizes that due to heterogeneity in populations, interventions, implementation, adaptation, and contexts, *successful mobilization strategies likely differ by topic.* They vary not just by domain (e.g., language and literacy, math, socioemotional learning, or technology use), but also by sector (e.g., early childhood, postsecondary education, or special education), given different structures, accountability requirements, staffing pipelines, family partnership roles, and cultural norms. Thus, by designating it as a project type, the responsibility for understanding how to mobilize knowledge lies *within* existing topic areas (e.g., literacy), not as a separate body of research that can be ignored.

4a. Descriptive studies on Knowledge Mobilization would include research on the ways that system leaders draw on (or do not use) research evidence in their ongoing decision making, including but not limited to the factors influencing development, adoption, and adaptation of policies and practices. Other studies might examine the organizational, social, and political conditions that enhance or inhibit research engagement in school

---

[10]For a discussion of these and other terms for evidence use, see Nelson and Campbell (2019).

systems, including how existing power structures maintain and reproduce inequities in knowledge use. Yet others might explore how publishers update materials when new research emerges, how education technology companies incorporate current research, how the media portray and report on research, and the networks via which educational decision makers share knowledge. Some studies of this type might focus on the broader research enterprise, including whose knowledge is valued, who gets to decide on the implications of knowledge, and who is benefited or harmed by the production or use of that knowledge.

Another critical set of questions could explore circumstances leading to inequitable or harmful consequences of knowledge mobilization, particularly research which devalues lived experience or perpetuates deficit narratives (Chicago Beyond, 2019; Doucet, 2019; Kirkland, 2019; Tuck & Yang, 2014). Importantly, these studies would need to identify ways in which the system could be changed or intervened upon to increase productive and equitable research use. Finally, because studies of the social, political, and organizational conditions that foster decision making have largely been done in the context of K–12 education and, more specifically in K–12 general education, descriptive studies are needed that focus on early childhood settings, postsecondary, and special education at every level for the birth–grade 16 system.

4b. Synthesis studies would take stock of both current practices in schools as well as interventions studied to date, indicating *across* interventions the types of program features that are effective and which are not. At the same time, and just as importantly, these syntheses would identify gaps in the evidence base—places where decision makers need evidence and where such evidence does not yet exist. In this way, these syntheses would both provide evidence (ultimately to be "mobilized") for schools and decision makers *and* for the research community regarding priorities for the future.

This information for the research community could also include interstitial work between project areas, helping summarize and disseminate important research regarding current practices and contexts in schools (to those that develop interventions), and locating and elevating promising new interventions (to those that conduct impact studies). Notably, this would mean moving meta-analyses from Exploration studies (current) to Knowledge Mobilization (new).

4c. Intervention studies in Knowledge Mobilization would focus on the development and evaluation of strategies for mobilizing knowledge; developing and investigating tools to support incorporating evidence in decision making; partnerships between intervention developers and vendors; and partnerships between researchers and practitioners. Indeed, more research on the effectiveness of research-practice partnerships is needed to

contribute to improved understanding about whether and how these structures for connecting research and practice not only provide a context for
the emergence of trusting relationships, but also affect decisions made by
educational leaders and outcomes for students (Penuel et al., 2020; Schneider, 2020). However, interventions should not only target the instrumental
use that IES has long prized: that is, situations where research is applied
to inform a specific decision, usually after weighing the relative costs and
benefits of various options (Weiss & Bucuvalas, 1980). In light of research
that suggests the power and importance of conceptual use in educational
decision making at the K–12 and postsecondary level (Penuel et al., 2017;
Finnigan & Daly, 2014; Farley-Ripple, 2012)—that is, situations where
individuals change how they view a problem or possible solutions via engagement with research, often outside of a specific decision—interventions
designed to foster such use should also be a priority. Finally, intervention
research should be especially attentive to fostering knowledge mobilization
strategies that are most likely to address structural and systemic inequality,
as there is a long and unfortunate history of research reinforcing rather than
interrupting inequality (Kirkland, 2019; Saini, 2019).

Intervention studies related to knowledge mobilization should be
rooted in existing research on the nature of decision making in specific
contexts, such as those discussed above. Specific knowledge mobilization
strategies may differ in the way they affect the production as well as the use
of evidence. For example, community-engaged scholarship may strengthen
the relevance and rigor of the research produced, through refining the questions and methods to better fit the local context (Balazs & Morello-Frosch,
2013). In contrast, intermediaries and networks may be especially valuable
for facilitating conceptual research use, through increasing connections to
research knowledge and enabling dialogue with trusted colleagues about
implications (Penuel et al., 2020; Neal et al., 2015; Finnigan & Daly, 2014).
Understanding these distinct mechanisms and outcomes could help elucidate how best to mobilize knowledge across research and practice.

4d. Measurement studies would also be necessary to develop valid and
reliable measures of knowledge mobilization. Gitomer and Crouse (2019)
provide a reference guide to such measurement work, and Penuel and colleagues (2016) provide an example from IES-funded research. In developing these measures, it will be important to attend to the variety of ways in
which research evidence may be used. Measuring conceptual use of research
is notoriously difficult and thus should be a priority for measurement studies. Likewise, developing reliable measures of research use and the varied
contributions of multiple stakeholders to the generation, use, and impact
of high-quality research will help the field build a common understanding
of success.

Finally, we note that ESRA specifically charges IES with disseminating its work "in forms that are understandable, easily accessible, and usable, or adaptable for use in the improvement of educational practice by teachers, administrators, librarians, other practitioners, researchers, parents, policy-makers, and the public..." (Section 102(10)). ESRA also asks, as part of the mission of the Research Center, for IES to "support the synthesis, and as appropriate, the integration of education research" (Section 131(b)(1) (D)) and to "synthesize and disseminate, through the National Center for Education Evaluation and Regional Assistance, the findings and results of education research conducted or supported by the Research Center" (Section 133(a)(7)). A project type for Knowledge Mobilization would be newly responsive to these elements of the IES mandate.

CONCLUSION

Throughout this chapter, we have argued that it is time for a structure of science that embraces and builds upon the past 20 years of knowledge generated by IES. We have focused here on project types both since they structure the types of studies that can be funded by the agency and since they serve a normative role, identifying clearly to the field what "IES research" is about. We have argued that this new system needs to be focused around the end goal—to improve student outcomes and reduce disparities—and around the decision makers who ultimately mediate this process. This new system needs to be built upon five principles: equity, heterogeneity, implementation, usefulness, and infrastructure. These principles result in four new project types that are uniquely suited to the science of education: Discovery and Needs Assessment, Development and Adaptation, Impact and Heterogeneity, and Knowledge Mobilization. In sum, the committee recommends:

RECOMMENDATION 4.1:
IES should adopt new categories for types of research that will be more responsive to the needs, structures, resources, and constraints found in education. The revised types of research should include
- **Discovery and Needs Assessment**
- **Development and Adaptation**
- **Impact and Heterogeneity**
- **Knowledge Mobilization**
- **Measurement**

The committee envisions a model of research that would have multiple parts working simultaneously for educational change. Since this new structure assumes that different researchers will play different roles, focusing on different types of studies, this system cannot depend upon individual researchers to move interventions along the research-to-practice process. For this reason, Knowledge Mobilization sits at the center, serving as the engine of this structure. These studies fit at the interstitial spaces, connecting research of one type with researchers focused on another, researchers with practitioners, and synthesizing and integrating knowledge (see Figure 4-1). Each of the other three project types interface both with one another and with this central engine.

The committee expects that this revised project structure will facilitate research that will be more useful and better used in practice. First, shining an equity lens across the entire research portfolio demands a broader examination of systems and practices, as well as a deeper analysis of the mechanisms by which inequities emerge and persist. Elevating the use of descriptive and quasi-experimental methods enables unraveling the many contextual factors and systemic processes that perpetuate or disrupt inequitable opportunities. Second, the need to anticipate and examine heterogeneity requires prioritizing these important questions immediately, facilitating faster discovery of and response to the many differences which exist across populations and contexts. Third, planning for implementation from the beginning requires researchers to ensure that their proposed strategies and interventions are usable, emphasizing the need to study phenomena in real-life settings, not just in the laboratory, and to study adaptations throughout the process. Finally, more fluid movement and more rapid iteration across project types accelerates the production of useful and actionable research, not just theoretically interesting findings that await further study before yielding relevant implications. With these changes, research will be better

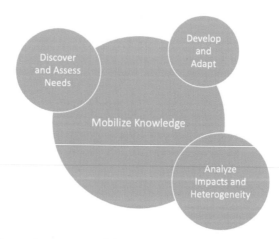

FIGURE 4-1 New project types in collaboration.

positioned to address urgent questions for policy and practice through providing more useful knowledge. We provide an overview of this new structure in Table 4-5, describing the possible questions that might emerge when examining crosscutting themes (heterogeneity, implementation, and equity) within each of our proposed project types.

Connecting all of these parts is the new project type of Knowledge Mobilization, which highlights the need to systematically study and improve both research usefulness and research use. Such inquiry may unearth processes of knowledge exchange that would enable researchers to develop a richer understanding of the kinds of research that would be useful for educational practice. Further, knowledge mobilization explicitly studies the conditions and processes that promote more systematic, sustained, and reliable use of research. Positioning knowledge mobilization in the center of the engine creates greater opportunities for sharing and applying knowledge across all stages of the research enterprise. Embedding these revised expectations within IES's RFAs would direct the education research community to prioritize these needs in how they conceptualize and conduct research.

Reorganizing project types in the way we have described will allow IES to fund research that more closely addresses the needs of the field. In the following chapter, we turn to a discussion of topic areas, and offer insight into how IES might continue this reorganization toward better meeting its stated goals.

TABLE 4-5 Proposed Project Type Structure and Crosscutting Themes

Project Type	Equity	Heterogeneity	Implementation
1. Discovery and Needs Assessment	Not sufficient merely to characterize inequitable outcomes. Explore systems, inputs, and practices that create, reproduce, or interrupt inequity. Examine assets, not just deficits. Identify possible levers of change. May need smaller samples or oversampling to represent minoritized populations. Need methods to explore and explain mechanisms.	Examine diverse school contexts, seeking to understand variation in business-as-usual practices and the ability to intervene across school structures and cultures. Build theoretical explanations of how heterogeneity affects practices and outcomes.	Apply appropriate models, theories, or frameworks to examine how characteristics of the individuals, the intervention, and the context affect implementation. Examine influences across multiple levels of system. Identify barriers and facilitators to implementation, as well as potentially promising strategies.
2. Development and Adaptation	Build on assets within populations and communities of interest to develop strategies aligned to local context. Develop solutions to improve structures and processes enacted by adults in the system, not to "fix" the students. Address systemic barriers and upstream causes of inequities. Create high-leverage, multicomponent strategies to address inequities within and across schools.	Develop interventions in a wide range of purposively selected contexts, so as to develop a robust intervention (or clearly delineate under what conditions it should or should not be selected).	Design, develop, and iterate on potential interventions and implementation strategies together. Identify core components of intervention; explore likely adaptations. Develop implementation strategies that preserve core components and allow for productive adaptations. Develop strategies that build on supports and address derailers.

3. Impact and Heterogeneity	Define success not just as overall improvements, but as a decrease in equity gaps. Be driven by the potential for impact, not the ability to conduct a randomized controlled trial. In some situations, the best design may be a quasi-experimental design (QED). Report continuous measures of effects in order to capture variation and reveal potentially promising interventions. Report effects for focal populations of interest. Attend closely to inclusion, exclusion, and attrition.	Test interventions in heterogeneous and generalizable samples across a diverse range of contexts representing the groups and places of interest. Examine differential effects by setting and population. Estimate not only an average treatment effect, but also provide information necessary for local predictions.	Encourage hybrid evaluation designs which examine effectiveness of the intervention along with the implementation strategy. Account for effects due to differences in implementation. Analyze effects relative to implementation costs. Characterize benefits and harms of alternatives.
4. Knowledge Mobilization	Focus on supporting knowledge production and use in systems and schools facing large inequities. Attend to inequities in whose knowledge is valued, who gets to decide on the implications of the knowledge, who takes action on that knowledge, and who is benefited or harmed by the production or use of that knowledge. Examine how existing power structures maintain and reproduce inequities in knowledge production and use.	Explore and integrate knowledge across interventions (systematic reviews), accounting for different designs, populations, interventions, and measures. Develop and test approaches to improve knowledge production and use in diverse settings. Tailor strategies to individuals with different roles and backgrounds; adapt strategies to different topics and contexts. Investigate existing pathways of knowledge mobilization.	Articulate how knowledge flows across different roles, levels, offices, and sites in the system. Examine and compare different processes for cultivating and sharing knowledge about implementation. Develop and test strategies for addressing barriers and facilitators and for supporting productive adaptation. Investigate best practices for implementation and adaptation. Examine how structures and systems contribute to sustainment, spread, and scale of successful implementation.

continued

TABLE 4-5 Continued

Project Type	Equity	Heterogeneity	Implementation
5. Measurement	Explore and develop measures of equity beyond achievement tests. Develop valid measures of inequities (gaps and variation). Develop measures of educational opportunity. Refine system-level measures of diversity and heterogeneity (e.g., student and staff composition, resource allocation).	Be validated in generalizable and heterogeneous samples.	Ensure measures can be implemented in a broad range of contexts. Develop common measures for core components of interventions. Develop measures to assess intervention fidelity, adaptation, and enhancement. Develop measures of implementation strategies, implementation outcomes, and service delivery outcomes. Develop measures of partnership, engagement, and collaboration.
Methods (Stand Alone Panel)	Develop standards and methods for QEDs that can be useful when studying structural interventions. Develop methods for evaluating interventions on rare subgroups. Refine methods for examining structural inequities and intersectionality by race, gender, language background, socioeconomic class, and ability status.	Develop methods for understanding treatment effect heterogeneity, moderators of effects, and local predictions. Develop approaches that focus on a "total error" framework beyond internal validity.	Explore designs that allow for identifying and testing implementation strategies, including SMART, single case, factorial, hybrid, stepped-wedge, and other designs. Refine methods for specifying implementation strategies, studying causal mechanisms of change, and evaluating implementation in education.

REFERENCES

Abry, T., Hulleman, C.S., and Rimm-Kaufman, S.E. (2015). Using indices of fidelity to intervention core components to identify program active ingredients. *American Journal of Evaluation, 36*(3), 320–338. https://doi.org/10.1177/1098214014557009.

Albro, E., and Buckley, J. (2015). Strategic questions about the IES goal structure pipeline. Discussion paper prepared for the National Board for Education Sciences. Washington, DC: Institute of Education Sciences.

Balazs, C.L., and Morello-Frosch, R. (2013). The three R's: How community based participatory research strengthens the rigor, relevance and reach of science. *Environmental Justice (Print), 6*(1). http://doi.org/10.1089/env.2012.0017.

Bang, M. and Vossoughi, S. (2016). Participatory Design Research and Educational Justice: Studying Learning and Relations Within Social Change Making. *Cognition and Instruction, 34*:3, 173-193.

Bauer, M.S., Damschroder, L., Hagedorn, H., Smith, J., and Kilbourne, A.M. (2015). An introduction to implementation science for the non-specialist. *BMC Psychology, 3*, 32. https://doi.org/10.1186/s40359-015-0089-9.

Best, A., and Holmes, B. (2010). Systems thinking, knowledge and action: Towards better models and methods. *Evidence & Policy: A Journal of Research, Debate and Practice, 6*, 145–159. https://doi.org/10.1332/174426410X502284.

Boswell, C., and Smith, K. (2007). Rethinking policy 'impact': Four models of research-policy relations. *Palgrave Communications, 3*, 44. https://doi.org/10.1057/s41599-017-0042-z.

Brock, T., and McLaughlin, J. (2018). Building evidence: Changes to the IES Goal Structure for FY 2019. Inside IES Research Blog. https://ies.ed.gov/blogs/research/post/building-evidence-changes-to-the-ies-goal-structure-for-fy-2019U.

Bryan, C.J., Tipton, E., and Yeager, D.S. (2021). Behavioural science is unlikely to change the world without a heterogeneity revolution. *Nature Human Behaviour, 5*(8), 980–989. https://doi.org/10.1038/s41562-021-01143-3.

Bryk, A.S. (2015). 2014 AERA distinguished lecture: Accelerating how we learn to improve. *Educational Researcher, 44*, 467–477.

Century, J., and Cassata, A. (2016). Implementation research: Finding common ground on what, how, why, where, and who. *Review of Research in Education, 40*(1), 169–215. https://doi.org/10.3102/0091732X16665332.

Chicago Beyond. (2018). Why am I always being researched? A guide for community organizations, researchers, and funders to help us get from insufficient understanding to more authentic truth. *Chicago Beyond Equity Series, Volume 1.*

Coburn, C.E. (2003). Rethinking scale: Moving beyond numbers to deep and lasting change. *Educational Researcher, 32*(6), 3–12.

Coburn, C.E., Honig, M.I., and Stein, M.K. (2009). What's the evidence on districts' use of evidence? In J.D. Bransford, D.J. Stipek, N.J. Vye, L.M. Gomez, and D. Lam (Eds.), *The Role of Research in Educational Improvement* (pp. 67–86). Cambridge, MA: Harvard Education Press.

Coburn, C.E., Toure, J., and Yamashita, M. (2009). Evidence, interpretation, and persuasion: Instructional decision making at the district central office. *Teachers College Record, 111*(4), 1115–1161.

Cohen, J. (1990). Things I have learned (so far). *American Psychologist, 45*(12), 1304–1312. https://doi.org/10.1037/0003-066X.45.12.1304.

Conaway, C. (2021). Funding Research That Is Useful and Used. Blog post. https://www.education-next.org/funding-research-that-is-useful-and-used-20-years-institute-education-sciences/.

Connolly, P., Biggart, A., Miller, S., O'Hare, L., and Thurston, A. (2017). *Using Randomised Controlled Trials in Education*. Thousand Oaks, CA: SAGE Publications.

Damschroder, L.J., Aron, D.C., Keith, R.E., Kirsh, S.R., Alexander, J.A., and Lowery, J.C. (2009). Fostering implementation of health services research findings into practice: A consolidated framework for advancing implementation science. *Implementation Science*, 4, 50. https://doi.org/10.1186/1748-5908-4-50.

Dearing, J.W., and Kee, K.F. (2012). Historical roots of dissemination and implementation science. In R.W. Brownson, G.A. Colditz, and E.K. Proctor (Eds.), *Dissemination and Implementation in Health: Translating Science to Practice* (pp. 47–62). New York: Oxford University Press.

Doucet, F. (2019). *Centering the Margins: (Re)defining Useful Research Evidence Through Critical Perspectives*. New York: William T. Grant Foundation.

Farley-Ripple, E.N. (2012). Research use in school district central office decision making: A case study. *Educational Management Administration & Leadership*, 40(6), 786–806. https://doi.org/10.1177/1741143212456912.

Farley-Ripple, E., May, H., Karpyn, A., Tilley, K., and McDonough, K. (2018). Rethinking connections between research and practice in education: A conceptual framework. *Educational Researcher*, 47(4), 235–245.

Farrell, C.C., and Coburn, C.E. (2017). Absorptive capacity: A conceptual framework for understanding district central office learning. *Journal of Educational Change, 18*, 135–159.

Farrell, C.C., Penuel, W.R., and Davidson, K. (2022). "What Counts" as research? Comparing policy guidelines to the evidence education leaders report as useful. *AERA Open, 8(1)*, 1–17.

Farrell, C.C., Penuel, W.R., Coburn, C., Daniel, J., and Steup, L. (2021). Research-Practice Partnerships in Education: The State of the Field. New York: William T. Grant Foundation. http://wtgrantfoundation.org/library/uploads/2021/07/RPP_State-of-the-Field_2021.pdf.

Finnigan, K.S., and Daly, A.J. (Eds.) (2014). *Using Research Evidence in Education: From the Schoolhouse Door to Capitol Hill*. Cham, Switzerland: Springer.

Gartlehner, G., Hansen, R.A., Nissman, D., et al. (2006). Criteria for Distinguishing Effectiveness from Efficacy Trials in Systematic Reviews. Technical Reviews, No. 12. Rockville, MD: Agency for Healthcare Research and Quality. https://www.ncbi.nlm.nih.gov/books/NBK44024/.

Gitomer, D.H., and Crouse, K. (2019). *Studying the Use of Research Evidence: A Review of Methods*. New York: William T. Grant Foundation.

Gorard, S., See, B.H., and Siddiqui, N. (2017). *The Trials of Evidence-Based Education: The Promises, Opportunities, and Problems of Trials in Education*. New York: Routledge.

Greenhalgh, T., Robert, G., Bate, P., Kyriakidou, O., Macfarlane, F., and Peacock, R. (2005). *Diffusion of Innovations in Health Service Organisations: A Systematic Literature Review*. Oxford, UK: Blackwell.

Greenhalgh, T., Robert, G., Macfarlane, F., Bate, P., and Kyriakidou, O. (2004). Diffusion of innovations in service organizations: Systematic review and recommendations. *The Milbank Quarterly, 82*, 581–629. https://doi.org/10.1111/j.0887-378X.2004.00325.x.

Honig, M.I., and Coburn, C. (2008). Evidence-based decision making in school district central offices toward a policy and research agenda. *Educational Policy, 22*, 578–608. https://doi.org/10.1177/0895904807307067.

Institute of Education Sciences (IES) Request for Applications (RFA). (2018). Education Research Grants Program Request for Applications.

——— (2022). Education Research Grants Program Request for Applications.

——— (2021). Education Research Grants Program Request for Applications.

——— (2019). Education Research Grants Program Request for Applications.

Institute of Education Sciences and National Science Foundation (2013). *Common Guidelines for Education Research and Development.* https://ies.ed.gov/pdf/CommonGuidelines.pdf.

Jackson, C. (2021). Democratizing the development of evidence. *Educational Researcher, 49.*

Joyce, K.E., and Cartwright, N. (2020). Bridging the gap between research and practice: Predicting what will work locally. *American Educational Research Journal, 57*, 1045–1082.

Kirkland, D.E. (2019). *No Small Matters: Reimagining the Use of Research Evidence from a Racial Justice Perspective.* New York: William T. Grant Foundation.

Klager, C.R., and Tipton, E.L. (2021). *Commissioned Paper on the Summary of IES Funded Topics.* Paper prepared for the National Academies of Sciences, Engineering, and Medicine, Committee on the Future of Education Research at the Institute of Education Sciences in the U.S. Department of Education. https://nap.nationalacademies.org/resource/26428/READY-KlagerTipton_IES_Topic_Analysis_Jan2022v4.pdf.

LeMahieu, P.G., Grunow, A., Baker, L., Nordstrum, L.E., and Gomez, L.M. (2017). Networked improvement communities: The discipline of improvement science meets the power of networks. *Quality Assurance in Education, 25*(1), 5–25.

Loudon, K., Treweek, S., Sullivan, F., Donnan, P., Thorpe, K.E., and Zwarenstein, M. (2015). The PRECIS-2 tool: Designing trials that are fit for purpose. *BMJ, 350*, h2147. https://doi.org/10.1136/bmj.h2147.

McLeod, S., Verdon, S., and International Expert Panel on Multilingual Children's Speech. (2017). Tutorial: Speech assessment for multilingual children who do not speak the same language(s) as the speech-language pathologist. *American Journal of Speech-Language Pathology, 26*(3), 691–708.

Michie, S., van Stralen, M.M., and West, R. (2011). The behaviour change wheel: A new method for characterising and designing behaviour change interventions. *Implementation Science, 6*(42). https://doi.org/10.1186/1748-5908-6-42.

Nakajima, N. (2021). Evidence-Based Decisions and Education Policymakers. Unpublished paper. Cambridge, MA: Harvard University.

Nasir, N.S., Scott, J., Trujillo, T., and Hernandez, L.E. (2016). The sociopolitical context of teaching. In D. Gitomer and C. Bell (Eds.), *The Handbook of Research on Teaching* (pp. 349–390). Washington, DC: American Educational Research Association.

Neal, J.W., Neal, Z.P., Kornbluh, M., Mills, K.J., and Lawlor, J.A. (2015). Brokering the research-practice gap: A typology. *American Journal of Community Psychology, 56*, 422–435. https://doi.org/10.1007/s10464-015-9745-8.

Nelson, J., and Campbell, C. (2019). Using evidence in education. In A. Boaz, H. Davies, A. Fraser, and S. Nutley (Eds.), *What Works Now? Evidence-Informed Policy and Practice* (pp. 131–149). Bristol, UK: Policy Press.

Nilsen, P. (2015). Making sense of implementation theories, models and frameworks. *Implementation Science, 10*, 53. https://doi.org/10.1186/s13012-015-0242-0.

Penuel, W.R., Farrell, C.C., Anderson, E.R., Coburn, C.E., Allen, A.-R., Bohannon, A.X., Hopkins, M., and Brown, S. (2020). A Comparative, Descriptive Study of Three Research-Practice Partnerships: Goals, Activities, and Influence on District Policy, Practice, and Decision Making. Technical Report 4. Boulder, CO: National Center for Research in Policy and Practice.

Penuel, W.R., Farrell, C.C., Allen, A.R., Toyama, Y., and Coburn, C.E. (2018). What research district leaders find useful. *Educational Policy, 32*(4), 540–568. https://doi.org/10.1177/0895904816673580.

Penuel, W.R., Briggs, D.C., Davidson, K.L., Herlihy, C., Sherer, D., Hill, H.C., Farrell, C., and Allen, A.-R. (2017). How school and district leaders access, perceive, and use research. *AERA Open.* https://doi.org/10.1177/2332858417705370.

Penuel, W.R., Briggs, D.C., Davidson, K., Herlihy, C., Sherer, D., Hill, H.C., Farrell, C., and Allen, A.-R. (2016). Findings from a National Study of Research Use among School and District Leaders. Technical Report No. 1. Boulder, CO: National Center for Research in Policy and Practice.

Philip, T.M., Bang, M., and Jackson, K. (2018). Articulating the "How," the "For What," the "For Whom," and the "With Whom" in Concert: A Call to Broaden the Benchmarks of our Scholarship. *Cognition and Instruction, 36*:2, 83–88.

Powell, B.J., Waltz, T.J., Chinman, M.J., Damschroder, L.J., Smith, J.L., Matthieu, M.M., Procter, E.K., and Kirchner, J.E. (2015). A refined compilation of implementation strategies: Results from the Expert Recommendations for Implementing Change (ERIC) project. *Implementation Science, 10,* 21. https://doi.org/10.1186/s13012-015-0209-1.

Rabin, B., and Brownson, R. (2012). Developing the terminology for dissemination and implementation research. In R.C. Brownson, G.A. Colditz, and E.K. Proctor (Eds.), *Dissemination and Implementation Research in Health: Translating Science to Practice* (Chapter 2). New York: Oxford University Press.

Rabin, B.A., Purcell, P., Naveed, S., Moser, R.P., Henton, M.D., Proctor, E.K., Brownson, R.C., and Glasgow, R.E. (2012). Advancing the application, quality and harmonization of implementation science measures. *Implementation Science, 7,* 119. https://doi.org/10.1186/1748-5908-7-119.

Schneider, M. (2020). Research-Practice Partnerships, Redux [Blog post]. https://ies.ed.gov/director/remarks/2-4-2020.asp.

Saini, A. (2019). *Superior: The Return of Race Science.* Boston, MA: Beacon Press.

Spreitzer, G.M., and Sonenshein, S. (2004). Toward the construct definition of positive deviance. *American Behavioral Scientist, 47*(6), 828–847. https://doi.org/10.1177/0002764203260212.

Stuart, E.A., Bell, S.H., Ebnesajjad, C., Olsen, R.B., and Orr, L.L. (2017). Characteristics of school districts that participate in rigorous national educational evaluations. *Journal of Research on Educational Effectiveness, 10,* 168–206.

Tabak, R.G., Khoong, E.C., Chambers, D.A., and Brownson, R.C. (2012). Bridging research and practice: Models for dissemination and implementation research. *American Journal of Preventive Medicine, 43*(3), 337–350. https://doi.org/10.1016/j.amepre.2012.05.024.

Tipton, E. (2021). Beyond generalization of the ATE: Designing randomized trials to understand treatment effect heterogeneity. *Journal of the Royal Statistical Society: Series A (Statistics in Society), 184*(2), 504–521.

Tipton, E., Spybrook, J., Fitzgerald, K.G., Wang, Q., and Davidson, C. (2021). Toward a system of evidence for all: Current practices and future opportunities in 37 randomized trials. *Educational Researcher, 50*(3), 145–156. https://doi.org/10.3102/0013189X20960686.

Tseng, V. (2012). The uses of research in policy and practice and commentaries. *Social Policy Report, 26,* 1–24. https://doi.org/10.1002/j.2379-3988.2012.tb00071.x.

Tuck, E., and Yang, K.W. (2014). R-words: Refusing research. In D. Paris and M.T. Winn (Eds.), *Humanizing Research: Decolonizing Qualitative Inquiry with Youth and Communities* (pp. 223–247). Thousand Oaks, CA: SAGE Publications.

Turley, R.N.L., and Stevens, C. (2015). Lessons from a school district–university research partnership: The Houston Education Research Consortium. *Educational Evaluation and Policy Analysis, 37,* 6S–15S.

Waltz, T.J., Powell, B.J., Chinman, M.J., Smith, J.L., Matthieu, M.M., Proctor, E.K., Damschroder, L.J., and Kirchner, J.E. (2014). Expert recommendations for implementing change (ERIC): Protocol for a mixed methods study. *Implementation Science, 9,* 39. https://doi.org/10.1186/1748-5908-9-39.

Weiss, M.J., Bloom, H.S., and Brock, T. (2014). A conceptual framework for studying the sources of variation in program effects. *Journal of Policy Analysis and Management, 33,* 778–808.

Weiss, C.H., and Bucuvalas, M.J. (1980). *Social Science Research and Decision Making*. New York: Columbia University Press.

Weiss, M.J., Bloom, H.S., Verbitsky-Savitz, N., Gupta, H., Vigil, A.E., and Cullinan, D.N. (2017). How much do the effects of education and training programs vary across sites? Evidence from past multisite randomized trials. *Journal of Research on Educational Effectiveness, 10*(4), 843–876. https://doi.org/10.1080/19345747.2017.1300719.

Westlund, E., and Stuart, E.A. (2017). The nonuse, misuse, and proper use of pilot studies in experimental evaluation research. *American Journal of Evaluation, 38*(2), 246–261. https://doi.org/10.1177/1098214016651489.

5

Research Topics for NCER
and NCSER Grants

The first charge of this committee was to identify critical problems or issues on which new research is needed. We began our response to this charge in Chapter 4 with a discussion of project types (or goals) of studies supported by the Institute of Education Sciences (IES). In this chapter we continue our response to the first charge by considering the other axis of the IES "matrix," asking what new topics should be addressed by IES-funded research. To inform this question, we heard testimony from a variety of education researchers, practitioners, and other stakeholders across the landscape. We examined data on investments by the National Center for Education Research (NCER) and National Center for Special Education Research (NCSER) in research across topics over time. We also drew on the committee's diverse and extensive expertise. However, when sitting down to identify new topics for NCER and NCSER to invest in, the committee struggled to identify a clear set of issues that were not already technically "fundable" in IES's current structure and organization. At almost every suggestion, the committee found a place in the topic structure where a hypothetical study *could technically* fit. And yet, it is undeniable that IES has accumulated research evidence in some areas far more than in others.

In this chapter, we describe the nature of this challenge. We begin with an overview of how NCER and NCSER use topics to organize their funding opportunities. We then outline barriers within the existing topic structure that prioritize some forms of research at the expense of others. Next, we provide considerations for how NCER and NCSER might develop a mechanism for revisiting these issues in the future to ensure that the development of research is dynamic, cumulative, and responsive to changing times. We conclude the chapter by identifying a small set of topics that are of critical, immediate importance.

OVERVIEW OF TOPICS

NCER and NCSER use topic areas to communicate research needs and to help manage applications that come in through their grant competitions (see, for example, p. 2 of the FY2021 NCER Education Research Grants request for applications [RFA] and p. 9 of the FY2021 NCSER Special Education Research Grants RFA for a discussion of how they use research topics). Additionally, topic areas allow the research centers to distribute applications across program officers to provide targeted feedback throughout the application process and to efficiently assign applications to peer reviewers with the appropriate expertise.

In FY2021, there were 11 topics supported by NCER and 9 supported by NCSER (see Table 5-1 for the list of topics).

Across all topics in the Education Research and Special Education Research Grants competitions, applicants are invited to submit proposals to any of IES's five project types: Exploration, Development and Innovation, Initial Efficacy and Follow-up, Replication/Effectiveness,[1] and Measurement. (See Chapter 4 for our proposed revision to these project types.) Jointly, the intersection of types and topics forms a kind of matrix which serves as an organizational framework for the Education Research Grants and the Special Education Research Grants competitions (Schneider, 2021).[2]

In theory, grouping research into these topics allows NCER and NCSER to be responsive to changes in the field: they can take stock of what has been learned and diagnose where further research is necessary. The committee saw evidence of this in practice. NCER and NCSER routinely add or remove topics based on emerging or changing needs. In FY2021, NCER added a new standing topic focused on *Civics Education and Social Studies*, which had previously been competed as a special topic in FY2019 and FY2020. NCER and NCSER also removed *Education Technology* and *Technology for Special Education* as standalone topics, with the rationale that education technology plays a central role across *all* topic areas. NCER and NCSER have also at times changed the names of topics to reflect

---

[1] For consistency, we include (4) "replication" here, as this is how it has been discussed in Chapter 4. However, more accurately, this project type does not exist in the most recent RFA. Instead, replication studies have a separate RFA altogether.

[2] Other research grant competitions supported by NCER and NCSER do not rely on this matrix structure.

TABLE 5-1 FY2021 NCER and NCSER Topics

NCER	NCSER
Cognition and Student Learning	Cognition and Student Learning
Literacy	Reading, Writing, and Language
Science, Technology, Engineering, and Mathematics (STEM) Education	Science, Technology, Engineering, and Mathematics (STEM)
Civics Education and Social Studies	
Social and Behavioral Context for Academic Learning	Social, Emotional, and Behavioral Competence
English Learners	
Early Learning Programs and Policies	Early Intervention and Early Learning
Career and Technical Education	Transition to Postsecondary Education, Career, and/or Independent Living
Postsecondary and Adult Education	
	Families of Children with Disabilities
Effective Instruction	Educators and School-Based Service Providers
Improving Education Systems	Systems, Policy, and Finance

SOURCE: Committee generated; adapted from Request for Applications (IES, 2021).

changes in conventions in the field or to signal to a broader set of scholars that their research is welcome within a given topic area.

NCER and NCSER also use their annual RFAs as a way to provide broad descriptions of its topics and to indicate areas of "Needed Research." For example, in the FY2021 NCER RFA, the *Cognition and Student Learning* topic highlighted the need for "Exploratory research to guide the development and testing of education technology products that can personalize instruction." One tension the research centers face in providing such descriptions is that investigators who do not see their research interests explicitly named in the topic description may choose to modify the goals of their work. Or worse, they may choose to forego applying to IES entirely. As a result, NCSER has in recent years aimed to broaden the kinds of research it supports by removing language that specifies needed research.[3]

Finally, in addition to their lists of standing topics, NCER and NCSER also include special topics within the Education Research Grants and Special Education Research Grants competitions to respond to pressing issues in the field, or to jumpstart research in areas that have not received

---

[3]This sentence was modified after release of the report to IES to correct information about the actions that NCSER has taken to broaden the kinds of research it supports.

adequate attention. For example, in FY2019, NCSER opened a special topic focused on *Career and Technical Education for Students with Disabilities* that continued into FY2020. In FY2020, it included a special topic on *English Learners with Disabilities*. These special topics, in theory, allow the research centers to adapt to the changing landscape.

THE CHALLENGE OF TOPICS

Overall, the committee agreed that IES's matrix of possible research areas, organized by topics and project types, corresponded well to the broad network of educational research (again, see our proposal for a revised set of project types in Chapter 4). The challenge for the field is how research has accumulated across this matrix. Some of this is to be expected: Knowledge will naturally accumulate at varying rates across IES's project types and topics. For a field as diverse as education, it is understandable that researchers would gravitate toward certain programs of research. But in its review of which topics actually receive funding, the committee noted that, in reality, a series of barriers exist both internal and external to IES that hamper the potential for funding for a set of critically important topics.

Our committee's key takeaway is that the challenge of topics is situated not within the topics themselves. The current set of topics do a good job representing the field. Instead, the committee determined, the challenge lies in how these topics intersect with the present project type structure. Under the existing structure, studies designed toward certain project types lend themselves to demonstrating rigor as described and prioritized by IES (see Chapter 2). In practice, this means that topic areas that can be more readily studied with these methods (i.e., large samples, randomized interventions) are more competitive with reviewers. Further, NCER and NCSER's focus on student outcomes means that studies that would focus on other outcomes in the system are less likely to receive funding. If investigators focused on outcomes other than those at the level of students are to make their proposals competitive, it means they likely have to change their research questions to focus on students and/or divert project resources to ensure they are meeting IES requirements. The committee's concern is not that measuring other outcomes is discouraged, but that the requirement to measure students' academic outcomes takes the focus away from outcomes at other levels, especially for system-level studies.[4]

---

[4]In their analysis of public data on NCER- and NCSER-funded projects, Klager and Tipton (2021) reported that in Development and Innovation, Efficacy, Effectiveness, and Replication studies, 71% of NCER-funded and 72% of NCSER-funded studies focused on student factors as malleable conditions, whereas only 18% of NCER-funded and 20% of NCSER-funded studies focused on teachers and even fewer on classroom, school, or system factors (12% NCER, 8% NCSER).

The Case of Teacher Education

To illustrate this challenge, we use the example of research on teacher education—although we acknowledge that the challenges described can easily be applied to many other areas, a point we return to later in this chapter. There are many reasons IES might want to invest in research on teacher education. There is widespread evidence that teachers play a critical role in improving student outcomes (e.g., Hanushek & Rivkin, 2006), so initial preparation could serve as a key learning opportunity for future educators (e.g., Theobald et al., 2021; Brownell et al., 2019; Ronfeldt et al., 2018). Further, for an organization such as IES, teacher education could play a complementary role to its existing program of research, ensuring, for example, that future educators are equipped with knowledge on effective academic and behavioral interventions for students. Finally, the field of teacher education would benefit a great deal from the investment. Teacher education remains highly localized, with little consistency in how teachers are prepared across programs (CRMSE, 2010; Wilson, Floden, & Ferrini-Mundy, 2001). And causal evidence in teacher education is exceedingly rare (Hill, Mancenido, & Loeb, 2020).

Yet, across 20 years, NCER and NCSER have funded only a handful of studies explicitly focused on teacher education. This is an area of research where there is a clear need, where the challenges have been longstanding, and where the research centers have simply not made much headway. The topic structure does not seem to be the source of the problem. NCER has always maintained a topic focused on *Effective Teaching* (previously known as *Effective Instruction*), and the studies on teacher education that have been funded have most commonly fallen under this topic (e.g., Grant #R305M060065 (2006), #R305A180023 (2018)). Grantees have also found a home for teacher education research under *Systems, Finance and Policy* (#R324A170016), and *Researcher-Practitioner Partnerships* (#R305H170025), among others. In recent RFAs, NCSER has even expressly called for a concerted focus on teacher education research.

So, while the current topic structure looks as though it *could* fund this work, in practice, teacher education research has largely gone unfunded. The challenge, it seems, relates to the project type structure employed by NCER and NCSER as well as their study requirements. Notably, we could find no teacher education projects that have been funded under the Initial Efficacy and Follow-Up project type (nor the Measurement project type for that matter). All of this work has been either Exploratory or Development studies. The lack of efficacy trials in teacher education may reflect the challenge in applying research designs developed for other contexts (such as K–12 settings) in preservice teaching programs. Efficacy or Effectiveness studies would require a sufficient number of students within a teacher education program as well as a sufficient number of programs. Such cross-site coordination rarely occurs. Nor has teacher education research exhibited substantial progress in methodological development (Hill et al., 2020).

A second challenge is the NCER and NCSER requirement that funded studies focus on and include measures of student outcomes. Researchers who study teacher education face problematic constraints in tailoring their research for IES funding. Eventual student outcomes (once preservice teachers transition into their first teaching jobs) are both distal and often secondary to the target of an intervention. More proximal student outcome options are limited, restricted to the progress made by the students of teacher-candidates during the clinical teaching placement, which is only partially attributable to the candidates themselves. Teacher education is certainly not the only area of research subject to these limitations. Studies that would address subject areas that are not tested for accountability purposes, such as science or social studies, have historically run up against similar challenges.

In sum, we argue that the lack of research on teacher education is not one that could be fixed through the mechanism of topics alone. NCER and NCSER could explicitly call out the need for teacher education research—which may be a good idea in its own right—but without making broader changes to their project type structure and to the outcomes they prioritize, it is unlikely that things would change much beyond the current situation.

Teacher education is just one of the many topics that is likely to face challenges like these. Similar claims could be made about research on changing systems or policy effects, where NCER and NCSER have funded considerably fewer projects than other areas, or on improving teacher or administrator quality through professional development. When problems of research do not naturally lend themselves to randomized controlled trials, or when the direct focus of change is on stakeholders other than students, the pathways to funding at IES's research centers can be prohibitive.

A SYSTEM FOR UPDATING TOPICS
AND RESEARCH PRIORITIES

NCER and NCSER have used a number of mechanisms over the years to modify topics included in their grant competitions, whether by adding, combining, or removing standing topics; changing the names of topics; changing descriptions of topics; or holding occasional special topics or topically focused competitions. While our committee acknowledges that these steps have allowed the research centers to adapt over time, we note that in order to truly respond to the field, IES will need to go a step further. A more systematic, transparent process would strengthen IES's responsiveness to the needs of the education research community. Such a mechanism could be used to both (1) assess demand for and awareness of research by key stakeholders, and (2) identify where the supply of research is lacking, inconclusive, or contradictory. Such information can then guide efforts in production, curation, or dissemination of research. Where demand exceeds awareness, IES might then promote greater engagement with existing research products. Where supply exists but not in a usable format to satisfy demand, IES might create more usable practice guides or commission syntheses with plain-language recommendations. Where supply and demand are not aligned, IES can then adapt its research portfolio by adjusting its topic by project type matrix, as well as the questions embedded within those topics and project types.

Although research priority setting is a complex process lacking consensus on best practices, some common themes emerge, such as inclusive stakeholder engagement, relevant criteria and methods for deciding on priorities, and transparency (Viergever et al., 2010; Sibbald, et al., 2009). Numerous methods have been tested in health research, with a summary and critique of their strengths and weaknesses described by the World Health Organization (2020). This publication identifies three categories of criteria: public benefit, scientific feasibility, and cost. It also identifies two types of methods for deciding between priorities: consensus-based approaches and metric-based approaches. Consensus approaches (e.g., Ghaffar et al., 2009) allow for values to drive priorities, but should be balanced by methods that account for diverging perspectives, such as deliberative dialogues (McDonald et al., 2009). Metric-based approaches (e.g., Rudan et al., 2008; Dalkey & Helmer, 1963) aggregate perspectives across a broader audience to generate a list of top priorities, which may then be published or undergo further deliberation (e.g., through the James Lind Alliance).

To expand and strengthen IES's current processes for identifying new research priorities, we highlight key themes rather than suggest the adoption of a specific method to inform research priorities. In particular, we emphasize the important roles for diverse and equitable stakeholder engagement, evidence synthesis, and greater visibility and transparency.

First, engaging with a broader range of stakeholders (policy makers, practitioners, and other community members, as well as researchers) would build a richer picture of where they perceive needs for better research knowledge. While policy makers, practitioners, and the general public would provide key insights about relevance and benefit, researchers would be better positioned to comment on scientific feasibility, as well as where there are unresolved conflicts or gaps in the research base. Both may offer important perspectives on cost, with the former addressing the cost of implementing potential strategies and the latter addressing the cost of conducting the research. Enlisting existing networks, such as the Regional Comprehensive Centers, Regional Education Laboratories, and professional associations, can help expand IES's reach. When analyzing stakeholders' different roles in the research enterprise (e.g., Brugha & Varvasovszky, 2000; Haddaway et al., 2017), applying an equity lens will be critical for rectifying imbalances in values, opportunities, and impacts (Nasser et al., 2013).

Second, tighter coordination between the priority-setting and evidence synthesis processes would further build understanding of how the evidence base compares to the questions being asked. This could help to identify which topics and questions (1) have existing syntheses which need better dissemination, (2) have existing research which needs to be synthesized, or (3) need more research to be produced. Both NCER and NCSER could work with the National Center for Education Evaluation and Regional Assistance (NCEE) to commission practice guides, syntheses, or evidence gap maps in response to emerging demand. In Chapter 4, we also discussed the import of funding research syntheses within a new Knowledge Mobilization project type. Conducting these syntheses across the different goals could illuminate gaps or surpluses in the progression of research. Specifically, they could reveal where there are needs or potential practices (identified during Discovery and Needs Assessment) that lack adequate intervention development, and where promising interventions (from Development and Adaptation) have not yet been adequately evaluated for effectiveness across the range of populations and contexts needed. Alternately, they could reveal where interventions and programs are proliferating, instead of converging on core components. They could reveal where mismatches between research and practice may motivate further study of knowledge mobilization strategies. They could also reveal where new measures are needed or where common measures are needed.

Third, increasing the visibility and transparency of these processes can engage a wider audience in the research enterprise, helping to build awareness, interest, and trust in both existing and emerging research. With clear routines and timelines for engagement, multiple groups of stakeholders would be able to anticipate when and how to provide input and learn about the perspectives of others in the field.

Some potential instantiations of these themes may be to engage in the following activities at routine intervals, such as every 3 years:

- Form an equity committee that releases data and issues equity reports, documenting areas where research is needed, and reporting who has gotten funded;
- In collaboration with NCEE, provide mechanisms for broad community input through an online suggestion form, surveys, and focus groups embedded within existing networks (e.g., professional associations);

- Hold NCER and NCSER researcher panels and community panels for deeper engagement, chaired by a researcher and an IES program officer, who collaborate to identify issues that both the research and practice community see as important unanswered questions in the field;
- On an ongoing and rotating basis, conduct research syntheses based on existing topics, identifying gaps in the research knowledge. Researchers can apply for the (small) contract to complete the synthesis;
- Delineate and document these processes and outcomes transparently, so that stakeholders understand opportunities for input and how their input is being used.

NEW TOPICS

Implementing the above procedures would provide IES with ongoing information about urgent and emerging needs within the field. But given the current circumstances—including both an unprecedented global pandemic and necessary racial reckoning for continued acts of prejudice and violence against historically marginalized groups in this country—the committee would be remiss if it did not provide specific guidance surrounding topics that likely demand immediate action. The field cannot wait for IES to update its processes for integrating new information from more systematic processes if education is to meet the challenge these historical circumstances demand. Thus, drawing on testimony, commissioned papers, our committee's collective expertise, and the crosscutting themes identified in this report, we nominate a small number of topics that merit a concerted investment in the coming years. These nominations should not be taken as an exhaustive or restrictive list; rather, they are examples of areas of potential study that emerge when the field is engaged in a process of assessing its needs.

Civil Rights Policy and Practices

Education researchers have produced valuable empirical and conceptual studies on the context of equity in education over the past 20 years. From this literature, it is clear that U.S. schools are more diverse racially and ethnically, but also more segregated and unequal. This paradox is due, in part, to historical legacies of policies related to housing, zoning, and employment, all of which are affected by racial injustice. More recently, in the past two decades, the courts have moved away from desegregation as a remedy for state-sponsored segregation, even as schools continue to be marked by deepening stratification (Gamoran, Collares, & Barfels, 2016).

Economic inequality is also at historic highs (Gamoran, 2015), and the relationship between racial and economic inequality is deeply intertwined and expressed in housing, labor, health, and educational opportunities (Reardon et al., 2021). The COVID-19 pandemic, the opioid crisis, and the struggles to find and maintain reliable housing, food, and health care have deep implications for educational institutions, educational interventions, and the study and measurement of both. For too long, researchers have been trained to elide these contexts in their examinations of educational innovations, and as a result, missed opportunities to build the field's understanding of the importance of the intimate linkages between the context of schooling and learning and achievement.

IES, through NCER and NCSER, has an opportunity to help build our understanding of how interventions and approaches to teaching, learning, and school processes are informed by these contextual factors for the range of students being educated. In addition, there are important understandings of the within-school practices related to racial and socioeconomic inequality that could be enriched by further robust research (Horsford, 2011). For example, Black, Latinx, and Native American students are far more likely to experience discipline in schools that leads to suspension or expulsion (Losen et al., 2016; Okonofua & Eberhardt, 2015). Also important, students whose identities exist at intersections, such as Black, LGBTQIA, disabled, and/or multilingual children and adolescents, are especially vulnerable to being targeted for harsh discipline that harms their opportunities to learn and predicts greater likelihood for disassociating from school, dropping out, and becoming part of the carceral system as they are referred to police and the courts for behavioral infractions, or simply failing to reach their potential as learners (Scott et al., 2017; Shedd, 2016; Skiba et al., 2011).

Given the challenges within K–12 schooling and for students with disabilities from preschool through age 21, along with the deepening and persistent inequalities that shape school systems, the teaching force, and the learning conditions within and across schools, it is imperative to support and strengthen different epistemological and methodological approaches for investigating issues at the intersection of education and civil rights. As Johnson (2021) argued, IES is not yet equipped with the expertise and systemic data collection and databases to answer questions about racialized mechanisms that shape learning opportunities, experiences with racism and violence in and out of school, and the effects of carceral policies within and out of school. IES could help to support the development of robust metrics to understand race, racialization, and racism in schools and systems; support interventions to remedy inequality; and identify cases that have made progress towards equitable outcomes (Scott et al., 2020).

Consistent with the committee's focus on equity as a crosscutting theme, and in line with President Biden's Executive Order on Racial Equity (EO

13985), the committee sees a need for the future of IES-funded research to be purposively oriented toward addressing the needs of underserved communities. To these ends, IES could better support research on equity and civil rights policies by funding research that responds to the education field's knowledge of how racial injustice in the structures, processes, and practices of schools and systems have an impact on learning and lifetime outcomes by supporting new research on what schools and other education settings can do to mitigate these effects. This might include, for example, research on

- School discipline: Disparities in discipline are well documented, and schools are engaged in a variety of strategies intended to reduce or eliminate these disparities. IES-funded researchers would find willing partners in states and school systems committed to better understanding the conditions that give rise to disparities and the diverse impacts of efforts (such as restorative approaches) to mitigate them.
- Services and supports for students with disabilities: Students with disabilities are likely to have experienced considerable challenges to receiving appropriate supports and services, and considerations for effective mechanisms for engaging students in productive ways educationally are needed.
- COVID-19 and orphans: Over 160,000 children in the United States and 1.5 million worldwide have lost a parent or caregiver. With these numbers likely to grow given unequal access to health care, and with Black, Latinx, and Native American children more likely to have experienced such loss, it is necessary to know how the practice of education can be made responsive to the trauma inflicted by the pandemic on educational opportunities and student well-being, learning, and educational attainment (Cluver, 2021; Imperial College of London, 2021; Treglia et al., 2021).
- Bullying and violence prevention: School violence and bullying pose serious problems, especially for students with intersectional identities based on race, ethnicity, disability, sexual orientation, and gender identity (Esplenage, 2015). Research is needed to identify programs that may work, in specific contexts, to eliminate violence and bullying, with a focus on structural conditions as the source of the problem and the student experience, rather than achievement as the outcome.
- School racial composition: Ongoing research indicates that racial segregation exacerbates inequality because it concentrates Black and Latinx students in high-poverty schools, which tend to be less effective than low-poverty schools (Reardon et al., 2021). Research is needed to examine voluntary and mandatory policies to break

the link between segregation and concentrated poverty and to ensure high-quality learning opportunities for all children.

Teaching Quality and the Teacher Workforce

Teachers (in both general and special education) serve as the primary interface between students and education in the United States, and yet improving the quality of the teacher workforce represents a notably understudied part of NCER and NCSER's portfolio. To be clear, many IES-funded studies have relied on teachers, often as the ones who carry out academic or behavioral interventions. Less common are studies that focus specifically on changing the knowledge, skills, practices, and dispositions of the teacher workforce. As described previously in this chapter, many of the reasons for this go beyond the question of topics. With IES's strong focus on student outcomes, researchers have had fewer avenues for exploring interventions where teacher outcomes are the focus. As we note later in Chapter 6, there has been minimal investment in measurement studies focused on teacher outcomes. The field lacks both IES-funded studies that have focused explicitly on teachers as well as suitable tools for measuring the effects of interventions targeting teachers.[5]

The committee identified research on improving the teaching workforce as a pressing need within both NCER and NCSER. Improving the workforce is a longstanding need but one that has intensified in response to changes in the educational landscape. As articulated in the recent National Academies' report on the teacher workforce: "Teachers are called on to educate an increasingly diverse student body, to enact culturally responsive pedagogies, and to have a deeper understanding of their students' socio-emotional growth. Integrating these various, layered expectations places substantially new demands on teachers" (NASEM, 2020, p. 187) as educators are tasked with supporting students in the wake of COVID-19.

The committee recognized the need for research addressing teacher education (TEd) and professional development (PD). Although there is substantial empirical evidence about the critical importance of teachers for promoting students' academic and long-term success (e.g., Chetty, Friedman, & Rockoff, 2014; Aaronson, Barrow, & Sander, 2007; Clotfelter, Ladd, & Vigdor, 2007; Rivkin, Hanushek, & Kain, 2005; Darling-Hammond, 2000), there are sizable knowledge gaps about the initial preparation and

---

[5]The committee wishes to note that school leaders and other professional leaders clearly deserve the same scholarly attention as teachers, and are similarly overlooked in IES's portfolio for the reasons highlighted in this chapter. Though teachers play a particular role in supporting student achievement because of their direct proximity to students, it is also critically important to understand the impact and potential of other professionals in the school building and throughout the education system.

PD of teachers (Hill, Manciendo, & Loeb, 2021; Phelps & Sykes, 2020; Fryer, 2017; Waitoller & Artiles, 2013; Sindelar, Brownell, & Billingsley, 2010). Research on TEd in this field has been described as "scattered and thin" (Sindelar et al., 2010, p. 13). Reviews of the literature have consistently described the research foundation in these domains as "weak" and identified limitations in the quality and focus of this scholarship (Ronfeldt, 2021; Brownell et al., 2019; National Research Council, 2010; Sindelar et al., 2010; Cochran-Smith & Zeichner, 2009; Wilson et al., 2001). Research on pedagogical practices has been emphasized in the past two decades, but "knowledge accumulation on teacher education ... has been uneven and in many areas, sparse" (Brownell et al., 2019, p. 35). Greater support for research on the initial and continuing education of teachers will improve the design and impact of these programs and interventions, improve teacher quality, and ultimately influence the quality of services provided to students. Specific considerations for additional research are as follows:

- Systematically investing in a range of kinds of research studies to bolster knowledge of effective systems of teacher professional learning that better prepares teachers to effectively meet the needs of a range of learners including those with disabilities. For example, in the case of teacher education, this might look like (a) effectiveness studies to establish teacher education practices resulting in improved candidate outcomes, (b) qualitative studies to explore promising practices and underlying mechanisms, and (c) descriptive studies linking program features to long-term candidate and student outcomes. This will contribute to the advancement of a knowledge base that is rich in explanatory and contextualized models.
- Identifying effective approaches for preparing educators for the complexities of the student population, changing professional roles, and the improvement of outcomes for all students.
- Substantiating research programs on teacher learning with a close attention to theory. Scholars have noted the lack of a sustained and coherent approach in the study of TEd and PD (Billingsley & Bettini, 2019; Brownell et al., 2019; Kennedy, 2019).
- Exploring research designs that support causal inferences in the contexts of TEd and PD research.
- Developing measures that are proximal to the goals of teacher education and professional development. As an example, recent advances have been made in measuring teacher content knowledge and establishing parameters for using teacher content knowledge as an outcome measure in cluster randomized trials (e.g., Kelcey et al., 2017; Phelps et al., 2016). Similar lines of research are necessary to

develop validated, useable measures of teachers' practice that might complement existing observation tools.

- Studying the broader workforce issues that impact the success of TEd and PD opportunities, including ongoing issues related to teacher supply. Issues of teacher supply are particularly relevant in special education where teacher shortages have existed for decades. In the past 20 years, the landscape of teacher licensure has changed dramatically, with the proliferation of a variety of programs and pathways into the classroom (NASEM, 2020). Researchers have begun to look generally at how licensure pathways shape the teaching workforce (Ronfeldt, 2021), but further work is necessary. In particular, we need further research on how best to support schools in staffing the hardest areas to fill (special education, science, technology, engineering, and math).

- Understanding the intersection between education technology and teacher learning in both TEd and PD. This may include, for example, examining the effectiveness of new online TEd or PD programs. Or, it may involve technology to supplement existing learning opportunities, such as the use of simulations in teacher education or providing automated feedback to educators based on videos of classroom instruction.

- Increasing synergies and complementarities in TEd and PD research in general and special education. Increasing awareness of the complexities of student needs complicates the initial preparation and PD of teachers. Teachers are expected to provide quality instruction and social-emotional learning supports to the range of learners in their classrooms. These expectations include how to differentiate instruction and build trusting relationships to provide genuine support that the range of learners (e.g., gifted, students with disabilities, learners from low-resourced families, culturally and linguistically diverse students) require in today's schools. These requirements and expectations are inadequately addressed in TEd and PD scholarship. General education teachers get minimal preparation on how to educate students with disabilities. A complicating factor is that TEd and PD in general and special education operate with disparate conceptions of teaching and learning with little cross-pollinations. These systemic barriers disadvantage general and special education teachers while the expectations for coordinated collaborative work continue to increase (e.g., Response to Intervention and Multi-tiered system of supports models). Research in TEd and PD is urgently needed to address these gaps.

Education Technology

Education technology is the use of digital technologies and related software with the goal to enhance learning. A report commissioned by IES, *A Compendium of Education Technology Research Funded by NCER and NCSER: 2002–2014* (Yamaguchi & Hall, 2017), defines the uses of technology as support for student learning, support of teachers and instructional practice, and support of research and school improvement. The compendium recognizes that education technology can support the development of metacognitive and social strategies, support learners with special needs, support collaborative learning, extend learning beyond traditional boundaries of the classroom, connect learners who are geographically dispersed, and expand learning beyond formal environments into informal settings such as museums, cultural institutions, and learners' homes. Similarly, technology has the potential to transform teacher instruction, teacher professional development, and teacher practice. Additionally, schools and their leaders use technology for a range of administrative tasks, to support data-driven decision making, and help devise strategies to increase equity.

IES competed Education Technology as a separate topic from 2008 to 2020 but not in 2021 or 2022. The RFA for the 2022 competition calls for related research in three of the topics: It lists the "development and testing of interventions designed to support all learners in becoming digitally literate citizens in the 21st century, including those which integrate new forms of technology within social studies programs, such as social media, multiuser virtual environments, virtual and augmented reality, and wearables" (p. 13) under the Civics Education and Social Studies topic; "Exploratory research to guide the development and testing of education technology products that can personalize instruction" (p. 14) in the Cognition and Student Learning topic; and calls for researchers to investigate how "technology be leveraged for more effective reading and writing instruction" (p. 19) under the Literacy topic.

The committee expressed concerns about the decision not to separately compete Education Technology at this historic moment in time because the COVID-19 pandemic has shown the critical importance of education technology to support continuity in formal schooling and informal learning (Schwartz et al., 2020). The pandemic has also revealed deep inequities in access to educational technologies across the country. Where education technology was available, the experience of remote learning forced by the pandemic in 2020 and 2021 has shown the deep limitations of current education technology infrastructure, products, practices, and research (Consortium for School Networking, 2021; Sahni et al., 2021; Education Endowment Foundation, 2020; Gallagher & Cottingham, 2020). As a nation, we now also recognize that inequity, lack of diversity, and lack of inclusion is not only unjust, but also it prevents us from unlocking the full potential of the next generations. Even though the committee recognized that ultimately, education technology needs to serve the specific topics taught in schools, it has become clearer than ever that more research is needed to guide the design of the next generation of education technology tools, and that this research involves many issues that are broader than the specific topics for which IES provides research support. Recent analyses have estimated, for example, that the education technology market will grow by $112.39 billion from 2020 to 2025 (Technavio, 2021). Among the drivers of this growth are artificial intelligence applications, including machine learning, and game-based learning (PRNewswire, 2021). The use of these technologies in the classroom requires a significant, dedicated investment into rigorous research that informs their design to ensure they serve the needs of the learners.

The committee therefore believes that Education Technology proposals should be invited that investigate these broader topics, and that these proposals should be reviewed by a dedicated Education Technology panel. The committee expressed a sense of urgency for this kind of education technology research, as the recognition of the importance of education technology as a result of remote schooling during the pandemic has already begun to result in the development of many new digital tools for learning, support of teachers, and support of schools, which would benefit from this kind of research.

Further, additional research is warranted to more fully explore the relationships between technology and the broader learning environments in which the technology is used. This plays out in two corresponding ways. First, education technology research must examine the ways in which biases become embedded in the design of technology (Scardamalia & Bereiter, 2008). For example, this requires opening up the "black box" of the algorithms for greater transparency in how user profiles and predictive analytics are used to constrain or expand learning opportunities for students based on prior experiences and characteristics (Rospigliosi, 2021). Second, education technology research should examine how technology is embedded within learning environments, or how technology is designed for real-life contexts, social interactions, and cultural influences. This includes how students, teachers, and families use and augment the technology; the role of the "digital divide" in access to resources, including broadband Internet as well as various technological devices; and the moderating influence of peers on students' use and engagement with technology (van Dijk, 2020; Zheng et al., 2017; Jeong & Hmelo-Silver, 2016).

The above concerns highlight the importance for education technology research to have a strong grounding in the theoretical mechanisms of learning under investigation, to guard against research and technology that perpetuate bias and inequity. Theoretical transparency will be essential when building and testing new technologies. The kinds of predictive modeling used to personalize instruction for students often depends on a massive amount of student data, demanding close attention to questions about whether the available data are appropriate for the questions being explored, the conditions under which the data were collected, who and what may be missing from the data, how to balance the information gained from the data with the need to protect privacy, and what additional measures may be worth developing (Schwabish & Feng, 2021; Regan & Jesse, 2019). Given inequitable access to education technology, including variation in how schools deploy technology for students across different achievement levels (Lee et al., 2021), ensuring that such research is not extractive and has relevance across a broad range of populations and contexts takes on even greater importance.

Questions that should be addressed in research on Education Technology supported by NCER and NCSER include, but are not limited to

- Development of new pedagogies and theoretical approaches addressing diversity, equity, and inclusion in education technology;
- Ethically aligned design processes for education technology that benefit from knowledge mobilization and focus on diversity, equity, and inclusion;
- Meaningful integration of responsible, accountable, and transparent analytics in learning environments;
- Approaches to personalization, adaptivity, and adaptability that incorporate diversity, equity, and inclusion; focus on transparency; and go beyond learning progressions and adapting for learners' current level of knowledge;
- Use of artificial intelligence-based approaches for novel education technology solutions, including personalization, adaptivity, and adaptability;
- Measurement approaches for learning outcomes, as well as learner state and learner trait variables, using longitudinal log data from education technology environments;
- Approaches to reliably measuring accountability/attendance versus engagement versus competency in remote learning, and the relative value of each of these outcomes;
- Designing methods of efficacy and effectiveness research harnessing user logs from widely available education technology environments;
- Development of standards for user logging and policies for data collection, storage, and ownership in education technology environments; and

- Effective strategies for the commercialization of successful research prototypes of education technology solutions.

Additional questions that should be addressed in research on Education Technology supported by NCSER could include strategies for use of assistive technology for simulations, games, virtual reality, mixed reality, augmented reality, and similar advanced technologies.

SPECIAL CONSIDERATIONS FOR NCSER

While the current moment motivates the need for further research on specific topics across IES, the committee encourages IES to give specific consideration to pressing challenges facing the field of special education. What makes the re-examination of NCSER's topics so urgent? Among all groups of students affected by COVID-19, it is becoming increasingly clear that the consequences have been particularly pronounced among students with disabilities. The lack of access to specialized instruction during remote instruction (GAO, 2020), coupled with the fact that students too often lost out on legally mandated services throughout the pandemic (Morris, 2021), presents the very real threat of a further widening of academic and career outcomes between students with and without disabilities. Additionally, as the United States grapples with the consequences of structural racism throughout its institutions, it cannot be overlooked that disability identification is racially stratified, and a better understanding is needed on how special education interventions and other programs function for different subpopulations of students. Finally, key policy shifts in recent years have established an even stronger warrant for the quality of special education practice. The 2017 Supreme Court case *Endrew F. v. Douglas County School District* established the responsibility that a school district's special education services produce "appropriate progress" for a given student's needs (Kauffman et al., 2021; Lemons et al., 2018). In other words, schools are to be held accountable for ensuring that the instruction they provide results in academic and behavioral gains in line with what is established in a child's Individualized Education Program. This precedent warrants a close investigation into the totality of services students receive. In the next section, we offer several opportunities for enhancing the knowledge base in special education. These are provided as examples only of possible directions.

Expanding a Focus Beyond Identifying Effective Programs

Identifying the programs that are effective for individuals with disabilities and their families has been an important and necessary focus of IES through NCSER. In addition to program efficacy/effectiveness, it is critical to better understand the teaching practices and instructional contexts in which students with disabilities are provided opportunities for accessing beneficial educational outcomes, both academically and behaviorally. Most of the teaching that teachers do throughout the day is not derived directly from a "program." They design, implement, and evaluate teaching by taking in resources (curricula, professional development, texts, materials), filtering these resources through their own knowledge and perceived needs of their students while navigating institutional affordances and constraints (e.g., district curricular policies, instructional reform mandates, school assessment initiatives), and then co-constructing teaching-learning processes and outcomes. With this in mind, it is critically important to support programs of research that document the multifaceted processes and contingencies that surround the complex work of teachers.

For example, much has been learned in the past two decades about how people learn (as described in Chapter 2 of this report), although much of that work has been conducted outside of special education contexts. IES, through NCSER, is ideally suited to support work that further extends the learning science work to individuals with disabilities and special education teachers. For example, outside of special education, scholarship in content-area instruction (e.g., mathematics, science, history and civics) has shifted increasingly toward inquiry-oriented approaches to instruction; how do these practices affect the learning outcomes of individuals with disabilities? To what extent are students with disabilities engaged in activities and provided opportunities to access learning with their general education classmates? Pedagogies that vary between general and special education may have real consequences for students with disabilities, because neither field has provided suitable guidance on how to support this population as they navigate activity-based classroom work. How can teachers scaffold these learning activities to ensure that students are developing foundational skills as well as higher-order skills and concepts?

Understanding How School Contexts and Structures Support Inclusion and Access to Improved Outcomes for Students with Disabilities

Perhaps one of the most persistent themes in education for students with disabilities is the provision of access to the general education classroom—for whom, under what conditions, and the instructional arrangements associated with positive outcomes within these arrangements. In light of the standards for special education established through *Endrew F.*, the field must tackle the question of how educators, collectively, can work to ensure that students make appropriate academic progress. Most educators would agree that inclusion in the general education classroom is a goal for students with disabilities, but researchers have largely ignored the question of whether specific inclusion policies are associated with improved student outcomes. For example, despite the widespread use of co-teaching (where a general educator and special educator provide instruction in the same classroom) as a service delivery model, there is virtually no causal evidence supporting whether the practice actually leads to improved student outcomes (Jones & Winters, 2020; Solis et al., 2012). NCSER is ideally suited to support research that will better inform educators about inclusive practices and models that yield beneficial outcomes for students and their families.

A related area where expanded research is necessary is in better understanding how other contextual factors outside of classroom teachers can positively impact students with disabilities. These factors include professionals (e.g., school psychologists, physical therapists, speech and language therapists); for example, Mulhern (2020) provided causal evidence that school counselors can affect student attainment at levels approaching typical teacher effects. It will also be important to continue expanding research on the role of families in supporting outcomes among students with disabilities. In addition, research on the mediating effects of organizational factors, the layering of multiple (often contradictory) policies, and sociohistorical legacies (e.g., community and school racial segregation) in the implementation and outcomes of inclusive models is urgently needed.

RECOMMENDATIONS

In this chapter, the committee describes its finding that a series of barriers exists both internal and external to IES that hampers the potential for funding for a set of critically important topics. While the current set of topics does a good job representing the field, these constraints limit the extent to which IES can fund research in areas that are pivotal in efforts toward improving student achievement. Ultimately, reimagining the project types alone (as we have recommended in Chapter 4 of this report) will not address the numerous ways that topics, although technically fundable, are unlikely to get funded in the current topic structure. The committee recognizes that without attention to how the Education Sciences Reform Act (ESRA) is enacted in RFA requirements, as well as the review process, it will be difficult to fund research that looks at interventions targeting teachers or systems in particular. Further, as we describe in Chapter 4, fealty to the methodological rigor associated with experimental design has also limited the use of alternative methods for deep understanding of the context in which interventions work (or do not). Finally, the committee recognizes that there are a set of factors (e.g., teacher knowledge and practice, school and district organizational contexts) that matter for supporting student outcomes; it is essential that these factors are attended to in the design and development of studies.

RECOMMENDATION 5.1:

Existing constraints or priorities in the RFA structure and review process have narrowed the kinds of studies within topics that are proposed and successfully funded. In order to expand the kinds of studies that are proposed and successfully funded in NCER and NCSER, IES should consider the following:

- Allowing use of outcomes beyond the student level (classroom, school, institution, district) as the primary outcome
- Expanding the choice of research designs for addressing research questions that focus on why, how, and for whom interventions work

In advance of these structural changes, however, the committee recognizes that the current moment of racial reckoning and responding to COVID-19 require immediate scholarly attention. Given the issues in education that are emerging at breakneck pace and the subsequent demand for assistance from the field, the committee thinks that designating separate competitions for certain topics is warranted in order to signal their importance even though these topics might technically be "fundable" in existing competitions.

RECOMMENDATION 5.2:

Within each of its existing and future topic area competitions, IES should emphasize the need for research focused on equity.

RECOMMENDATION 5.3:

In order to encourage research in areas that are responsive to current needs and are relatively neglected in the current funding portfolio, NCER and NCSER should add the following topics:

- Civil rights policy and practice
- Teacher education and education workforce development
- Education technology and learning analytics

RECOMMENDATION 5.4:

IES should offer new research competitions under NCSER around these topics:

- Teaching practices associated with improved outcomes for students with disabilities
- Classroom and school contexts and structures that support access and inclusion for improved outcomes for students with disabilities
- Issues specific to low-incidence populations

The topics listed above represent priorities identified by the committee based on our understanding of the current state of education research. This list is not intended to be exhaustive or restrictive; rather, these topics are examples of the types of topics that emerge through consistent, focused engagement with the field. Indeed, the committee recognizes that education research is perennially evolving in response to both the production of knowledge as well as the circumstances in the world. For this reason, the committee advises that the list of topics funded by the centers should also evolve in order to remain responsive to the needs of the field. This responsiveness is a necessary component of fulfilling the obligations laid out in ESRA: In order to "sponsor sustained research that will lead to the accumulation of knowledge and understanding of education," it is important to fully understand not only what knowledge has accumulated, but also where the existing gaps are.

RECOMMENDATION 5.5:

IES should implement a systematic, periodic, and transparent process for analyzing the state of the field and adding or removing topics as appropriate. These procedures should incorporate

- Mechanisms for engaging with a broad range of stakeholders to identify needs
- Systematic approaches to identifying areas where research is lacking by conducting syntheses of research, creating evidence gap maps, and obtaining input from both practitioners and researchers
- Public-facing and transparent communication about how priority topics are being identified

The committee expects that these recommendations, implemented in concert with one another, will allow NCER and NCSER to support research that meets the immediate needs of the field while simultaneously ensuring that it can nimbly adapt to shifting priorities as they inevitably emerge. In the following chapter, we turn to a discussion of how NCER and NCSER might update its work in the area of methods and measures.

REFERENCES

Aaronson, D., Barrow, L., and Sander, W. (2007). Teachers and student achievement in the Chicago public high schools. *Journal of Labor Economics, 25*(1), 95–135.

Billingsley, B., and Bettini, E. (2019). Special education teacher attrition and retention: A review of the literature. *Review of Educational Research, 89*, 697–744.

Brownell, M.T., Jones, N.D., Sohn, H., and Stark, K. (2019). Improving teaching quality for students with disabilities: Establishing a warrant for teacher education practice. *Teacher Education and Special Education, 43*(1), 28–44.

Brugha, R., and Varvasovszky, Z. (2000). Stakeholder analysis: A review. *Health Policy and Planning, 15*(3), 239–246. https://doi.org/10.1093/heapol/15.3.239.

Center for Research in Mathematics and Science Education (CRMSE). (2010). *Breaking the Cycle: An International Comparison of U.S. Mathematics Teacher Preparation.* East Lansing: Michigan State University.

Chetty, R., Friedman, J.N., and Rockoff. J.E. (2014). Measuring the impacts of teachers II: Teacher value-added and student outcomes in adulthood. *American Economic Review, 104*(9), 2633–2679.

Clotfelter, C.T., Ladd, H.F., and Vigdor, J.L. (2007). Teacher credentials and student achievement: Longitudinal analysis with student fixed effects. *Economics of Education Review, Elsevier, 26*(6), 673–682.

Cluver, L. (2021, July 20). COVID has created a scale of family loss not seen since AIDS. Guest essay. *New York Times.* https://www.nytimes.com/2021/07/20/opinion/covid-19-orphans.html.

Cochran-Smith, M., and Zeichner, K.M. (2009). *Studying Teacher Education: The Report of the AERA Panel on Research and Teacher Education.* Mahwah, NJ: Lawrence Erlbaum Associates.

Consortium for School Networking (2021). *EdTech Trends 2021: Members Share their Experience.* https://emma-assets.s3.amazonaws.com/paqab/a7a51dcc643bace61c838465c156ffaa/CoSN_EdTech_Trends_Survey_Report_2021.pdf.

Dalkey, N., and Helmer, O. (1963). An experimental application of the Delphi method to the use of experts. *Management Science, 9*(3), 458–467. http://www.jstor.org/stable/2627117.

Darling-Hammond, L. (2000). Teacher quality and student achievement: A review of state policy evidence. *Education Policy Analysis Archives, 8*(1). https://doi.org/10.14507/epaa.v8n1.2000.

Education Endowment Foundation (2020). *Remote Learning, Rapid Evidence Assessment.* London: Author. https://educationendowmentfoundation.org.uk/public/files/Remote_Learning_Rapid_Evidence_Assessment.pdf.

Espelage, D.L. (2015). Emerging issues in school bullying research & prevention science. In E.T. Emmer and E. Sabornie (Eds.), *Handbook of Classroom Management: Research, Practice, and Contemporary Issues* (pp. 76–93). New York: Taylor & Francis.

Fryer, R.G. (2017). The production of human capital in developed countries: Evidence from 196 randomized field experiments. In A.V. Banerjee and E. Duflo (Eds.), *Handbook of Economic Field Experiments, Volume 2* (pp. 95–322). Amsterdam: North-Holland.

Gallagher, H.A., and Cottingham, B. (2020). Improving the Quality of Distance and Blended Learning. Brief No. 8. EdResearch for Recovery Project. https://annenberg.brown.edu/sites/default/files/EdResearch_for_Recovery_Brief_8.pdf.

Gamoran, A. (2015). *The Future of Educational Inequality: What Went Wrong and How Can We Fix It?* New York: William T. Grant Foundation. http://wtgrantfoundation.org/resource/the-future-of-educational-inequality-what-went-wrong-and-how-can-we-fix-it.

Gamoran, A., Collares, A.C., and Barfels, S. (2016). Does racial isolation in school lead to long-term disadvantages? Labor market consequences of high school racial composition. *American Journal of Sociology, 121,* 1116–1167.

Ghaffar, A., Collins, T., Matlin, S.A., and Olifson S. (2009). The 3D Combined Approach Matrix: An Improved Tool for Setting Priorities in Research for Health. Global Forum for Health Research. http://www.bvs.hn/Honduras/PIS/MEC3DEnglish.pdf.

Government Accountability Office (GAO). (2020). *Distance Learning: Challenges Providing Services to K–12 English Learners and Students with Disabilities during COVID-19.* GAO Publication No. 21-43. Washington, DC: Government Printing Office.

Haddaway, N.R., Kohl, C., da Silva, N.R., Schiemann, J., Spök, A., Stewart, R., Sweet, J.B., and Wilhelm, R. (2017). A framework for stakeholder engagement during systematic reviews and maps in environmental management. *Environmental Evidence, 6*(1), 1–14.

Hanushek, E.A., and Rivkin, S.G. (2006). Teacher quality. In E.A. Hanushek and F. Welch (Eds.), *Handbook of the Economics of Education, Volume 2* (pp. 1052–1078). Amsterdam: North Holland.

Hill, H., Mancenido, Z., and Loeb, S. (2021). Effectiveness Research for Teacher Education (EdWorkingPaper: 20-252). Annenberg Institute at Brown University. https://doi.org/10.26300/zhhb-j781.

Hill, H., Mancenido, Z., and Loeb, S. (2020). New Research for Teacher Education (EdWorkingPaper: 20–252). Annenberg Institute at Brown University. https://doi.org/10.26300/zhhb-j781.

Horsford, S.D. (2011). *Learning in a Burning House: Educational Inequality, Ideology, and (Dis)Integration.* New York: Teachers College Press.

Imperial College of London. (2021). COVID-19 and orphanhood. Orphanhood estimates: United States of America. https://imperialcollegelondon.github.io/orphanhood_calculator/#/country/United%20States%20of%20America.

Institute of Education Sciences (IES) Request for Applications (RFA). (2021). Education Research Grants Program Request for Applications.

Jeong, H., and Hmelo-Silver, C.E. (2016). Seven affordances of computer-supported collaborative learning: How to support collaborative learning? How can technologies help? *Educational Psychologist, 51*(2), 247–265. https://doi.org/10.1080/00461520.2016.1158654.

Johnson, O. (2021). Future of Methods and Measures in the Field of Education Research. PowerPoint slides. https://www.nationalacademies.org/event/07-07-2021/docs/D63472D5D54F4445CC0761E6392B9E600401A620466B.

Jones, N., and Winters, M. (2021). Are Two Teachers Better Than One? The Effect of Co-Teaching on Students With and Without Disabilities. 2020 APPAM Fall Research Conference.

Kauffman, J.M., Ahrbeck, B., Anastasiou, D., Badar, J., Felder, M., and Hallenbeck, B.A. (2021). Special education policy prospects: Lessons from social policies past. *Exceptionality, 29*(1), 16–28. https://doi.org/10.1080/09362835.2020.1727326.

Kelcey, B., Spybrook, J., Phelps, G., Jones, N., and Zhang, J. (2017). Designing large-scale multisite and cluster-randomized studies of professional development. *The Journal of Experimental Education, 85*(3), 389–410.

Kennedy, M.M. (2019). How we learn about teacher learning. *Review of Research in Education, 43*(1), 138–162. https://doi.org/10.3102/0091732X19838970.

Klager, C.R., and Tipton, E.L. (2021). *Commissioned Paper on the Summary of IES Funded Topics.* Paper prepared for the National Academies of Sciences, Engineering, and Medicine, Committee on the Future of Education Research at the Institute of Education Sciences in the U.S. Department of Education. https://nap.nationalacademies.org/resource/26428/READY-KlagerTipton_IES_Topic_Analysis_Jan2022v4.pdf.

Lee, D., Huh, Y., Lin, C.Y., Reigeluth, C.M., and Lee, E. (2021). Differences in personalized learning practice and technology use in high- and low-performing learner-centered schools in the United States. *Educational Technology Research and Development, 69*(2), 1221–1245. https://doi.org/10.1007/s11423-021-09937-y.

Lemons, C.J., Allor, J.H., Al Otaiba, S., and LeJeune, L.M. (2018). 10 research-based tips for enhancing literacy instruction for students with intellectual disability. *TEACHING Exceptional Children, 50*(4), 220–232. https://doi.org/10.1177/0040059918758162.

Losen, D.J., Keith, M.A., Hobson, C.L., and Martinez, T.E. (2016). *Charter Schools, Civil Rights and School Discipline: A Comprehensive Review.* Los Angeles: The Civil Rights Project/Proyecto Derechos Civiles.

McDonald, D., Bammer, G., and Deane, P. (2009). *Research Integration Using Dialogue Methods.* Canberra: ANU E Press. https://press.anu.edu.au/publications/research-integration-using-dialogue-methods.

Morris, A. (2021, September). Parents of students with disabilities try to make up for lost year. *The New York Times.* https://www.nytimes.com/2021/09/17/nyregion/special-needs-children-coronavirus-pandemic.html.

Mulhern, C. (2020). Beyond Teachers: Estimating Individual Guidance Counselors' Effects on Educational Attainment. Working paper. http://papers.cmulhern.com/Counselors_Mulhern.pdf.

Nasser, M., Ueffing, E., Welch, V., and Tugwell, P. (2013). An equity lens can ensure an equity-oriented approach to agenda setting and priority setting of Cochrane Reviews. *Journal of Clinical Epidemiology, 66*(5), 511–521.

National Academies of Sciences, Engineering, and Medicine (NASEM). (2020). *Changing Expectations for the K–12 Teacher Workforce: Policies, Preservice Education, Professional Development, and the Workplace.* Washington, DC: The National Academies Press. https://doi.org/10.17226/25603.

National Research Council. (2010). *Preparing Teachers: Building Evidence for Sound Policy.* Washington, DC: The National Academies Press. https://doi.org/10.17226/12882.

Okonofua, J.A., and Eberhardt, J.L. (2015). Two strikes: Race and the disciplining of young students. *Psychological Science, 26*(5), 617–624. https://doi.org/10.1177/0956797615570365.

Phelps, G., and Sykes, G. (2020). The practice of licensure, the licensure of practice. *Phi Delta Kappan, 101*(6), 19–23. https://doi.org/10.1177/0031721720909582.

Phelps, G., Kelcey, B., Jones, N., and Liu, S. (2016). Informing estimates of program effects for studies of mathematics professional development using teacher content knowledge outcomes. *Evaluation Review, 40*(5), 383–409.

PRNewswire. (2021). Edtech Market to grow by USD 112.39 bn from 2020 to 2025. https://www.prnewswire.com/news-releases/edtech-market-to-grow-by-usd-112-39-bn-from-2020-to-2025evolving-opportunities-with-alphabet-inc--blackboard-inc17000-technavio-reports-301412825.html.

Reardon, S.F., Weathers, E.S., Fahle, E.M., Jang, H., and Kalogrides, D. (2021). Is Separate Still Unequal? New Evidence on School Segregation and Racial Academic Achievement Gaps. CEPA Working Paper. Center for Education Policy Analysis, Stanford University.

Regan, P.M., and Jesse, J. (2019). Ethical challenges of edtech, big data and personalized learning: Twenty-first century student sorting and tracking. *Ethics and Information Technology, 21*(3), 167–179. doi:10.1007/s10676-018-9492-2.

Rivkin, S.G., Hanushek, E.A., and Kain, J.F. (2005). Teachers, schools, and academic achievement. *Econometrica, 73,* 417–458. https://doi.org/10.1111/j.1468-0262.2005.00584.x.

Ronfeldt, M. (2021). Links among teacher preparation, retention, and teaching effectiveness. National Academy of Education Committee on Evaluating and Improving Teacher Preparation Programs. National Academy of Education.

Ronfeldt, M., Brockman, S.L., and Campbell, S.L. (2018). Does cooperating teachers' instructional effectiveness improve preservice teachers' future performance? *Educational Researcher, 47*(7), 405–418. https://doi.org/10.3102/0013189X18782906.

Rospigliosi, P.A. (2021). The risk of algorithmic injustice for interactive learning environments. *Interactive Learning Environments, 29*(4), 523–526. https://doi.org/10.1080/1049482.2021.1940485.

Rudan, I., Boschi-Pinto, C., Biloglav, Z., Mulholland, K., and Campbell, H. (2008). Epidemiology and etiology of childhood pneumonia. *Bulletin of the World Health Organization, 86*(5), 408–416. https://doi.org/10.2471/blt.07.048769.

Sahni, S.D., Polanin, J.R., Zhang, Q., Michaelson, L.E., Caverly, S., Polese, M.L., and Yang, J. (2021). A What Works Clearinghouse Rapid Evidence Review of Distance Learning Programs (WWC 2021-005REV). Washington, DC: U.S. Department of Education, Institute of Education Sciences, National Center for Education Evaluation and Regional Assistance, What Works Clearinghouse. https://ies.ed.gov/ncee/wwc/Docs/ReferenceResources/Distance_Learning_RER_508c.pdf.

Scardamalia, M., and Bereiter, C. (2008). Pedagogical biases in educational technologies. *Educational Technology, 48*(3), 3–11. http://www.jstor.org/stable/44429572.

Schneider, M. (2021). A year for reflection and continued transformation. IES Director's Blog. https://ies.ed.gov/director/remarks/1-12-2021.asp.

Schwabish, J., and Feng, A. (2021). *Do No Harm Guide: Applying Equity Awareness in Data Visualization.* Washington DC: Urban Institute. http://hdl.handle.net/20.500.11941/3898.

Schwartz, H.L., Grant, D., Diliberti, M.K., Hunter, G.P., and Setodji, C.M. (2020). Remote Learning Is Here to Stay: Results from the First American School District Panel Survey. Research Report. RR-A956-1. RAND Corporation. https://www.rand.org/pubs/research_reports/RRA956-1.html.

Scott, J., Siegel-Hawley, G., DeBray, E., Frankenberg, E., and McDermott, K. (2020). An Agenda for Restoring Civil Rights in K–12 Federal Education Policy. Boulder, CO: National Education Policy Center. https://nepc.colorado.edu/publication/restoring-civil-rights.

Scott, J., Moses, M.S., Finnigan, K.S., Trujillo, T., and Jackson, D.D. (2017). Law and Order in School and Society: How Discipline and Policing Policies Harm Students of Color, and What We Can Do About It. Boulder, CO: National Education Policy Center. http://nepc.colorado.edu/publication/law-and-order.

Shedd, C. (2016). *Unequal City: Race Schools and Perceptions of Injustice.* New York: Russell Sage Foundation.

Sibbald, S.L., Singer, P.A., Upshur, R., and Martin, D.K. (2009). Priority setting: What constitutes success? A conceptual framework for successful priority setting. *BMC Health Services Research, 9*(1), 1–12.

Sindelar, P., Brownell, M.T., and Billingsley, B. (2010). Special education teacher education research: Current status and future directions. *Teacher Education and Special Education, 33*, 8–24.

Skiba, R.J., Horner, R.H., Chung, C.-G., Rausch, M.K., May, S.L., and Tobin, T. (2011). Race is not neutral: A national investigation of African American and Latino disproportionality in school discipline. *School Psychology Review, 40*(1), 85–107.

Solis, M., Vaughn, S., Swanson, E., and McCulley, L. (2012). Collaborative models of instruction: The empirical foundations of inclusion and co-teaching. *Psychology in the Schools, 49*(5), 498–510.

Technavio. (2021). Edtech Market by Sector and Geography—Forecast and Analysis 2021–2025. Technavio.com.

Theobald, R., Goldhaber, D., Holden, K., and Stein, M. (2021). Special Education Teacher Preparation, Literacy Instructional Alignment, and Reading Achievement for Students with High-Incidence Disabilities. CALDER Working Paper No. 253-0621.

Treglia, D., Cutuli, J.J., Arasteh, K., Bridgeland, J.M., Edson, G., Phillips, S., and Balakrishna, A. (2021). Hidden Pain: Children Who Lost a Parent or Caregiver to COVID-19 and What the Nation Can Do to Help Them. COVID Collaborative.

Van Dijk, J. (2020). *The Digital Divide.* Cambridge, UK: Polity Press.

Viergever, R.F., Olifson, S., Ghaffar, A., and Terry, R.F. (2010). A checklist for health research priority setting: Nine common themes of good practice. *Health Research Policy and Systems, 8*(1), 1–9.

Waitoller, F., and Artiles, A.J. (2013). A decade of professional development research for inclusive education: A literature review and notes for a sociocultural research program. *Review of Educational Research, 83*, 319–356.

Wilson, S.M., Floden, R.E., and Ferrini-Mundy, J. (2001). Teacher Preparation Research: Current Knowledge, Gaps, and Recommendations. Research report prepared for the U.S. Department of Education and the Office for Educational Research and Improvement, No. R-01-3. University of Washington Center for the Study of Teaching and Policy.

World Health Organization. (2020). *A Systematic Approach for Undertaking a Research Priority-Setting Exercise: Guidance for WHO Staff.* Geneva: Author. https://apps.who.int/iris/handle/10665/334408.

Yamaguchi, R., and Hall, A. (2017). A Compendium of Education Technology Research Funded by NCER and NCSER: 2002–2014. https://ies.ed.gov/ncer/pubs/20170001/.

Zheng, N.-N., Liu, Z.Y., Ren, P.J., Ma, Y.Q., Chen, S.T., Yu, S.Y., Xue, J.R., Chen, B.D., and Wang, F.Y. (2017). Hybrid-augmented intelligence: Collaboration and cognition. *Frontiers of Information Technology & Electronic Engineering, 18*(2), 153–179. https://doi.org/10.1631/FITEE.1700053.

6

Methods and Measures

In this chapter, the committee responds to the third element in our charge: to identify new methods or approaches for conducting research supported by the National Center for Education Research (NCER) and the National Center for Special Education Research (NCSER) of the Institute of Education Sciences (IES). We include both measures (a project type, or goal, in the IES matrix) and methods (a separate competition) because of the close links between the two. We placed this chapter here for the sake of narrative flow and will return to the second element in our charge—how best to organize NCER and NCSER's request for application (RFA) process—in Chapter 8.

One of IES's hallmarks since its inception has been its continuous investment in advancing education methods and measures. IES has adopted three primary strategies aimed at improving the quality of research methods in education: (1) funding basic research on methodological innovation and measurement, (2) prioritizing specific applied research methods in its RFAs, and (3) fostering a community of scholars with the necessary skills to make use of new and innovative methods and measures.

IES's investments in methodological innovation has produced a wealth of knowledge in this arena. This investment is both through field-generated research via grants from NCER and NCSER, and through IES-driven research focused on the What Works Clearinghouse (WWC) via contracts from the National Center for Education Evaluation and Regional Assistance. While the committee focused on the first of these types of research, given the statement of task, there are clearly connections between the two.

These investments have produced core knowledge around estimating average treatment effects—in both randomized controlled trials (RCTs) and quasi-experimental designs (QEDs)—as well as models and data useful for planning studies with adequate power for hypothesis tests. This funding has also advanced research methods specifically appropriate for research on students with disabilities, including advances in statistical approaches to estimating effects in single-case designs.

IES has also invested in development of measures, largely through field-generated research funded through NCER and NCSER. They include new approaches for measuring student academic and behavioral outcomes in the context of research, as well as the expansion of available assessments for use in practice, including a number of universal screening and progress monitoring tools. There have also been advancements in the technologies of student assessments, including the use of adaptive testing.

IES has also established high standards that have been widely adopted across the field for how causal research is conducted. Through its RFAs and guidance to proposal reviewers—and in alignment with recommendations for internal validity through the WWC—IES encourages submitted studies to meet high technical standards. Examples include the requirement that Efficacy and Replication studies be adequately powered, that studies prioritize research designs aligned with causal inferences (e.g., experimental designs, quasi-experimental designs, single subject designs), and more recently, that Efficacy and Replication studies provide information on their generalizability and on the cost effectiveness of the intervention being studied (IES, 2021).

In addition to these formal avenues for research on methods and measurement, NCER and NCSER have worked to establish a community of education research scholars focusing specifically on methodology. It has done so in large part through its investment in methodological training opportunities, described in Chapter 7 of this report. IES also invested in the initial development and growth of the Society for Research on Educational Effectiveness, a research organization focused on increasing the field's capacity to design and conduct causal investigations, which, in 2008, launched the *Journal of Research on Educational Effectiveness* committed to publishing causal studies in education. Without such an investment, it is hard to imagine that causal studies in education would be anywhere close to where they are today.

Collectively, these three strategies converge to provide a roadmap for how IES can support the development of tools to conduct high-quality scientific research in education. But, as outlined across this report, as the educational landscape shifts, so too must IES's investments in methods and measures research. A focus on treatment heterogeneity, implementation and adaptation, knowledge mobilization, and equity means that IES will need to re-orient its investment in methods and measures.

We begin with underlying principles to guide our recommendations:

- **IES's charge as written into the Education Sciences Reform Act (ESRA) requires that the institute maintain its focus on causal research.** IES is uniquely situated—among other federal agencies and private foundations—to develop and test interventions in education settings. This focus should certainly continue.
- **Since causal questions are inherently comparative, descriptive work is also needed to conceptualize and describe current practices and the context of schools and districts.** This means IES will need to invest in other approaches beyond causal designs (e.g., descriptive, qualitative, mixed methods).
- **Questions of what works and how it works need to be pursued in concert.** Only by pairing different methodologies can researchers answer not only what works for improving student outcomes, but also how to make something work, for whom, and under what conditions. The committee's view is that each of these questions needs answering and each is necessary to inform the others.
- **Theoretical frameworks play an essential role in connecting research questions across studies.** The connections across causal and descriptive studies are strengthened when researchers are clear about the theoretical framework they are developing and testing.

THE FUTURE OF METHODS RESEARCH

Summary of Methods Research to Date

NCER and NCSER have invested in methodological innovation from their beginnings. This investment was first via unsolicited grants and later through a separate grant program, Statistical and Research Methodology in Education, that funded research relevant to both centers. From its beginning in 2002 through 2020, NCER awarded 93 grants to support methodological innovation in the education sciences. In an analysis of abstracts from these studies, Klager and Tipton (2021) revealed that funded studies have been roughly evenly divided across four categories:

- Psychometrics ($n = 28$), including value-added models ($n = 8$).
- Statistical Models for Analysis ($n = 23$), including multilevel models and missing data ($n = 13$).

- Randomized Controlled Trial Designs ($n = 28$), including power analyses ($n = 7$), effect size computations and interpretations ($n = 5$), and single-case designs, $n = 6$.
- QED Designs ($n = 14$), including regression-discontinuity ($n = 6$) and comparative interrupted time series ($n = 5$).

Overall, these studies have addressed a variety of difficult problems that occur in applied research. Abstracts indicate that most of these studies ($n = 48$) mention the development and availability of free software tools for use by applied researchers, providing a mechanism to increase the likelihood that methodological innovations get taken up in future IES-funded work. Further seeding the potential for methodological uptake, many of the funded studies have resulted in methodological workshops delivered at national research conferences in education. The committee thinks that this approach used to generate knowledge and use of statistical methods has been one of NCER and NCSER's considerable strengths.

Methods Research Moving Forward

In this report, we have argued that education research needs to focus on five crosscutting themes: the *heterogeneity* of contexts, experiences, and treatment effects; the *adaptation* of programs and policies to local contexts, leading to different degrees and types of implementation; the need to better understand and test new ways to support the development of knowledge that is *useful* for decision making; the continued need to take advantage of *education technologies;* and the need to focus directly on the goal of improving *equity* in educational experiences.

In this section, based upon what has been previously studied and these themes and goals, we propose areas that need new methodological development. Overall, each of these areas begins from the question: What methods are required for researchers developing and testing interventions to provide decision makers with the information they need regarding interventions?

Methods for Understanding Treatment Effect Heterogeneity

Current literature makes clear that there is no single effect of an intervention, and instead that effects likely vary across structures, contexts, cultures, and conditions (Joyce & Cartwright, 2020). As such, education research stands to benefit from studies that improve the ability to understand how treatment effects vary. Meeting this goal requires both quantitative methods and qualitative methods, as both are essential for developing theory and understanding mechanism.

IES is already a leader in building quantitative approaches to heterogeneity. Over the past decade, an increasing number of methods grants have focused on questions of treatment effect heterogeneity, understanding moderators of effects, and external validity ($n = 14$). These studies have provided methods for estimating and testing hypotheses about the degree of heterogeneity, as well as methods for improving generalizations from samples in studies to populations in need of evidence. This generalization literature, for example, has shown that if treatment effects vary, the average treatment effect estimated from a randomized trial in a sample of convenience can be as different from the true population average treatment effect as one estimated using a nonexperimental design. That is, external and internal validity biases can be of the same magnitude.

To date, much of this research has focused on how to improve estimates of average treatment effects (what is called generalization). Repeatedly, however, decision makers call upon research to provide them not simply an estimate of the average treatment effect, but also a prediction regarding if the intervention will work in their school, district, or community. To date, only three of the methods grants have focused directly on the development and testing of methods for the prediction of local treatment effects. Predicting local effects with precision will require both new statistical methods for analysis, such as machine learning and Bayesian Additive Regression Trees, and more complex research designs, such as factorial, crossover (Bose & Dey, 2009), and stepped-wedge designs (Hussey & Hughes, 2007). As these methods are better understood, and fit to the realities of education contexts, they may provide important insights into how studies should be conducted in the field. For example, it is likely that studies focused on heterogeneity and prediction will require larger samples than are typical in studies of the average treatment effect. In order to know exactly how much larger and what other trade-offs might be included, however, methods for study design, including determining power and precision, will be needed.

Finally, not all of the methods required are quantitative. In order to understand treatment effect heterogeneity—essential for the prediction of local causal effects—data are not sufficient on their own. Instead, the development and refinement of theory will be essential. Theory can help, for example, guide researchers in determining *why* treatment effects might vary, under what conditions interventions might be most useful, and the mechanism through which an intervention works. It is here that qualitative and mixed methods research especially offers promise.

Methods for Understanding Implementation and Adaptation

Tied to the concept of heterogeneity is the need to understand the implementation and adaptation of interventions. Decision makers need to know what adaptations implementers make and why, which adaptations are productive and which adaptations go "too far," and what kinds of supports are required to implement well. IES has shown interest in and encouraged methods development related to implementation, fidelity, and mediation. To date, six Statistical Models and Research Methods grants have focused on these topics. However, more methods are needed to study implementation and adaptations made as programs move across places and people (reconceived in Chapter 4 as Development and Adaptation grants).

There are several exciting possibilities for continued methods development in this burgeoning field. Methods for evaluating implementation build on many familiar designs for studying efficacy and effectiveness, while also expanding beyond them through a variety of randomized and nonrandomized designs (Brown et al., 2017). They include, but are not limited to, hybrid effectiveness-implementation designs (Curran et al., 2012), multiphase optimization strategy implementation trials (e.g., Collins, Murphy, & Stretcher, 2007), helix counterbalanced designs (Sarkies et al., 2019), and stepped-wedge trials (Brown & Lilford, 2006). Additional methods include survival analysis to evaluate sustainability (e.g., Brookman-Frazee et al., 2018) as well as system dynamics, network analysis, and agent-based modeling to assess diffusion and spread (Northridge & Metcalf, 2016; Burke et al., 2015; Mabry et al., 2008). Closely related to implementation research, a family of improvement approaches with roots in statistics, industry, and health care have migrated to education (Cohen-Vogel et al., 2018). Described by some as representing a fourth wave of implementation science, the approaches involve iterative tests of change in an increasingly larger number of classrooms, grades, and schools (e.g., Bryk, 2020; Bryk et al., 2015; Lewis, 2015). The approaches, which include but are not limited to improvement science, design-based implementation research, and design experimentation, share an emphasis on learning from adaptations that occur as programs are tested in an ever-growing number of settings as well as authentic collaborations between researchers and practicing educators that span innovation design, prototype testing, and implementation (e.g., Cohen-Vogel et al., 2015; Cobb et al., 2013; Donovan, 2013; Means & Harris, 2013; Anderson & Shattuck, 2012; Bryk, Gomez, & Grunow, 2011; Design-Based Research Collective, 2003). Methods for evaluating improvement projects include variants of trial designs, quasi-experimental designs, qualitative field techniques, and systematic reviews, as well as program, process, and economic evaluations (Portela et al., 2015).

Of particular interest for their rigor and sensitivity in detecting variation in a system are statistical process control methods, which distinguish between common-cause variation and special-cause variation to determine when changes are significant and when a process is out of control (see Provost & Murray, 2011; Deming, 1982; Juran, 1951; Shewhart, 1931, and later in this chapter for a discussion of methods for learning from and about education technologies). Closely related to interrupted time series designs, statistical process control can detect variation across subgroups and sites, not just over time, and displays information more intuitively for real-time monitoring and decision making in practice (Fretheim & Tomic, 2015). These methods also are especially valuable for highlighting the distinction in framing between enumerative studies that describe the current state and analytical studies that make predictions about a future state (Provost, 2011).

Finally, questions related to implementation and adaption are fundamentally questions of process, an area where qualitative and mixed methods excel. The power behind mixed methods research lies in integrating data from multiple sources. Qualitative methods can inform the development or refinement of quantitative instruments, for example, and quantitative data can inform sampling procedures for naturalistic observations, interviews, or case study (e.g., O'Cathain, Murphy, & Nicholl, 2010). Consequently, the committee believes that standards for the conduct and reporting of data from qualitative and mixed methods could be helpful for a future IES. The further development, testing, and refinement of these methods will enhance the ability of researchers to study implementation of evidence-based practices in education.

Methods for Knowledge Mobilization

As the committee noted in Chapter 1 of this report, if the research that NCER and NCSER fund is not useful to or used by its intended audience, it is not meeting the charge mandated under ESRA to effect change in student outcomes. In Chapter 4, we proposed the creation of a new project type focused on Knowledge Mobilization. The purpose of this project type is to continue to develop a science of decision making in education, in order to understand current practice and to develop and test new strategies for mobilizing knowledge produced from research so that it may be used to support improved practice in schools.

Studying knowledge mobilization can be difficult because it is a subtle and complex process, one that does not always lend itself to the kind of randomized controlled design common with other interventions (e.g., researchers do not have two sets of research-practice partnerships to test out one form of knowledge utilization in one group and a different form or control message in another group). Thus, it is necessary to continue to develop innovative methods to help make these kinds of comparisons and study strategies to mobilize knowledge. There are several opportunities for the development of methods (for a broader overview, see Gitomer & Crouse, 2019).

By far, the most common method for studying knowledge mobilization in education to date is survey and interview methods (e.g., May et al., forthcoming; Penuel et al., 2017; Weiss & Bucuvalas, 1980). While these approaches have been useful for descriptive studies of research use in nationally representative samples of educators and education leaders, they fall prey to social desirability bias and retrospective smoothing. In response, there are new efforts aimed at studying decision making in real time using observational methods (e.g., Huguet et al., 2021). These methods are labor intensive and, to date, limited to small N descriptive studies. However, there is great potential for adapting such methods for use in experimental design of interventions to foster knowledge mobilization that include observation or, for example, video analyses of nationally representative samples of school board meetings (see Box 6-1 for an additional need in the knowledge mobilization space).

Another key development in research on knowledge mobilization has been the use of social network methods to map the relationships between producers and consumers of research and the intermediaries who knit them together (Frank et al., 2020; Gitomer & Crouse, 2019; Finnigan, Daly, & Che, 2013). This approach allows researchers to identify who the powerful

---

BOX 6-1
Knowledge Mobilization and Data Visualization

In the Knowledge Mobilization space, there is a need for studies of the best practices regarding communication around the use of new and improved statistical and research methods in practice. Questions include: Are workshops effective? Is a software package an effective approach, or is a webtool better? Is it better to convey findings using statistics or using data visualizations?

To these ends, there is a pressing need for studies regarding data visualization. As a result of almost two decades of funding and research, IES is now at a place in which there are many studies and interventions a decision maker might need to choose between when selecting an intervention. These findings are typically provided for decision makers using online dashboards (e.g., WWC), data visualizations, and webtools. The committee observes that often these tools are conceived of and developed by statistical research methodologists, who are experts in understanding and working with data and statistics. However, research on data visualization—found in journalism and cognitive psychology—shows that the best approaches for displaying findings for experts are often far from optimal for nonexperts (Eberhard, 2021; NRC, 2000). The existing literature highlights that appropriate visualizations and data exploration tools for one field are not necessarily appropriate for another (Li, 2020; Padilla et al., 2018). Altogether, this suggests that research comparing different types of visualizations, both static and dynamic, is itself worthy of scientific study.

actors are and how information flows across systems. Outside of education, there are researchers who have used natural language processing and other strategies to track the uptake of research studies or ideas in legislation or policies (Weber & Yanovitsky, 2021; Yanovitsky & Weber, 2020; Weber, 2018), an approach that could profitably be adapted for scholarly studies of knowledge mobilization in education. Network methods and natural language processing methodologies applied to knowledge mobilization face a number of challenges, some that are general to network methods, such as sampling concerns, and some that are distinctive to knowledge mobilization, such as adequately capturing information flows (Gitomer & Crouse, 2019). IES investments in network methods and natural language processing for knowledge mobilization studies could fuel important advances in this area.

Additionally, one of the arguments the committee makes in Chapter 4 of this report is that "connectors" between project types are needed to help surface promising findings and interventions. This suggests that one area of growth will be the need for methods for systematic review and meta-analytic studies. Given the scope of the WWC, it is perhaps surprising that outside of single-case designs, there has only been one *single* Statistical and Research Methods grant focused on the development of meta-analytic methods. Many possible types of syntheses—and thus methods—are necessary. Perhaps the most obvious is the need for methods for synthesizing findings from impact studies; this includes methods for very small meta-analyses (as found in the WWC) and for very large meta-analyses focused on understanding variation (including 50 or more studies). Given the growing trends toward open data and data science, integrated data analysis and other data harmonization methods (Kumar et al., 2021, 2020; Musci et al., 2020) may be particularly valuable for synthesizing findings across disparate studies. Less obvious, but equally important, is the need for methods for synthesizing descriptive studies (Discovery and Needs Assessment) and for surfacing promising interventions (Development and Adaptation).

Supporting all of these is the need for methods research that informs various aspects of the meta-analysis process, including, for example, methods for efficiently and systematically searching the literature (e.g., using machine learning algorithms), efficient and standardized coding and reporting, presenting and conveying the results to nonexperts, and measuring knowledge mobilization and research use. It is likely, for example, that the best syntheses do not focus solely on quantitative summaries of the field, but also provide rich examples and information on the intervention mechanisms and components—again, a combination of both quantitative and qualitative methods.

Finally, the importance of studying knowledge mobilization motivates strengthening participatory research methods, which highlight the value of including the voices, perspectives, and questions originating from those who are intended to benefit from the research. Examples include participatory design, action research, youth participatory action research, and community-based participatory research (Stringer & Aragón, 2020; Balazs & Morello-Frosch, 2013; Robertson & Simonsen, 2012; Cammarota & Fine, 2010; Shalowitz et al., 2009). How best to engage with the range of stakeholders when discovering, innovating, and adapting, or evaluating a new educational experience may vary by research goal, emphasizing the importance of considering these perspectives throughout the research, not merely at its "end." Yet such methods may carry significant time and resource costs, not just for researchers but also for practitioners and community members. Refining these methods allows elucidating when and how to engage in co-production in a manner that is not only beneficial, but ethical and equitable.

Methods for Learning from and about Education Technologies

Since the founding of IES, determining how, when, and under what conditions education technology can improve student outcomes has been at the fore. It is perhaps surprising, then, that to date *zero* IES methods grants have explicitly focused on methods for working with data from education technologies. This is not to say that IES has not invested here, however. For example, NCER recently awarded five grants under the Digital Learning Platforms to Enable Efficient Education Research Network that will redesign existing digital learning platforms to support research.

Education technology data differ from typical data in randomized trials in that they include a vast amount of process data. For example, in addition to a pre-test and a post-test, an education technology product may also collect "click" data regarding every single item, the pathway taken through the intervention, and even data on attention. These new data bring new opportunities for understanding student learning. The committee anticipates a continued need for learning analytic methods.

But education technology research is broader than simply studying how to use technology to deliver learning experiences to students. Here we also include the promise of new and emerging data sources, including big data. These sources include administrative data, as well as data scraped from the web and from learning platforms. They also include data not only about students, but also about teachers, schools, and communities. We anticipate that these data will become increasingly useful in all types of projects, from answering descriptive questions about how systems work (Discovery and Needs Assessment), to how students' progress and learn (Development and Adaptation), to how to understand treatment effect heterogeneity and predict local treatment effects (Impact and Heterogeneity Analyses), to the networks through which teachers and leaders interact and share knowledge

(Knowledge Mobilization). We anticipate an ongoing need for methods development in all of these areas.

Methods for Centering Equity in Research

Throughout this report we have argued that equity should be front and center as the primary goal for research funded by IES. To date, this has not been an explicit focus of methods development grants at IES (though certainly questions of equity have motivated the development of many methods). Below we provide examples of several possible areas for methods development to support this work.

Interventions focused on small subgroups or communities, such as students with low-incidence disabilities (e.g., traumatic brain injury), are often hampered by the fact that recruiting large samples is simply not feasible. In these cases, the resulting studies will need to be smaller than usual and may have additional considerations for recruitment. The development and testing of new research designs and statistical analysis methods for conducting *small* causal studies, both randomized and quasi-experimental, are needed.

In Chapters 4 and 5, we argued that focusing on interventions that can be studied by randomized trials severely limits the type of interventions that IES-funded studies can focus upon and learn about. Some of the largest effects on student outcomes may, in fact, arise from structural changes that are difficult to randomize. To date, IES has invested heavily in the development of quasi-experimental methods ($n = 20$ grants to date), but several important questions remain. For example, this work might address the conditions under which common quasi-experimental methods, such as difference-in-difference, instrumental variables, and synthetic control groups, perform well and where they do not. This might also include methods for not only conducting quasi-experimental studies on existing data, but also planning future quasi-experimental studies that involve collecting new data. Importantly, as with randomized trials, this next wave of methods development needs to focus both on estimating the average treatment effect using these designs and on methods for understanding heterogeneity and generalizability.

Generally, a methodological focus on equity can proceed in two ways: either via an examination of changes over time (or across treatment and control groups) in disparities between groups, such as the subgroups articulated in the No Child Left Behind Act and the Every Student Succeeds Act, or through a focus on creating conditions to enhance the performance of a traditionally underserved community, without explicitly measuring disparities but relying on the research literature to identify an underserved community, as expressed in President Biden's Executive Order on Advancing Racial Equity. For example, Atteberry, Bischoff, and Owens (2021) have developed statistical approaches for gauging progress toward racial and ethnic achievement equity in U.S. school districts, focusing both on performance relative to other groups within the same district and in comparison to statewide averages.

Finally, schools have increasingly begun to rely upon education technology products to diagnose, assess, and place students (at all age levels). Here there is the opportunity for algorithmic biases to enter the systems. This creates an increased need for the development of methods and approaches to study and improve these algorithms, including the data these systems are developed upon and how to ensure that methods that perform well in the sample in which they were developed also perform well and without bias in new samples that might be quite different.

THE FUTURE OF MEASUREMENT RESEARCH

Summary of Measurement Research to Date

Studies that develop, evaluate, and scale measures are currently funded at NCER and NCSER within each topic area. Through 2020, the centers have funded 176 measurement studies.[1] An analysis of the abstracts of these studies indicates that they can be categorized by their unit of analysis: students, teachers, or "other" (Table 6-1).[2]

Collectively, these studies have provided the field with a number of measures related to student outcomes and student characteristics. These measures have expanded the field's understanding of the ways interventions impact students. At the same time, there is a need for further research

TABLE 6-1 Proportion of Measurement Grants Funded by NCER and NCSER, by Target

Table 21. Proportion of Measurement grants by target - NCER and NCSER

	NCER	NCSER
Student	77%	95%
Teachers	18%	4%
Other	5%	2%
Total Grants	121	55

SOURCE: Klager & Tipton, 2021 [Commissioned Paper]. Data from https://ies.ed.gov/funding/grantsearch/.

[1] This analysis is based on studies with GoalType = Measurement. This excludes investments via center grants, networks, or studies with multiple goals.

[2] This sentence was modified after release of the report to IES to indicate that this tally of funded studies runs through 2020.

on measures related to education systems, education leaders, and teachers. Detailed information on students only limits understanding of the mechanisms by which interventions lead to changes in student outcomes, as well as whether specific school or teacher characteristics moderate the impact of interventions. As we lay out a measurement agenda moving forward, we give careful attention to measurement tools across the education system and identify where IES might want to consider additional work.

Methods and measures are closely linked. Often new methods require new measures, and sometimes new measures spur the creation of new methods or the improvement of existing methods. Therefore, many of the issues we point to throughout this report will also require the development of additional measures. While we do not offer specific recommendations on which measures to invest in, we acknowledge in Chapter 9 that IES will need to consider strategic investments in support of our other recommendations.

Emerging Needs in Measurement Research

As noted above, the committee sees a number of areas where the development of new measures would facilitate IES's work as it continues to grow. In this section, we identify a few areas where we believe investment from IES could support emerging fields.

Expanding the Range of Student Outcome Measures

When it comes to measuring "what works," IES has in the past 20 years emphasized a broad range of student outcomes beyond standardized test scores and grades alone. This is evidenced in the broad range of measurement studies focused on student outcomes. At the same time, IES-funded researchers still frequently use standardized test scores and grades as the primary outcomes of their studies. This focus is easy to understand as these metrics are regularly collected by education institutions and agencies, relatively easy to access by researchers, and currently prioritized as outcomes in some education policies. Indeed, even research focused on social-emotional learning (SEL) often includes test scores or grades as the ultimate result or outcome in models and research designs. However, an overreliance on these narrow measures of learning make it difficult to understand the mechanisms and processes by which interventions have impact. Moreover, grades and achievement are the tip of the iceberg when it comes to assessing student learning.

However, there is now a deep knowledge base about the links between "upstream" affective, psychological, and behavioral processes that play a role in the "downstream" distal achievement of students (NASEM, 2018).

Moreover, there are many more ways to measure learning, both inside and outside the classroom, than test scores and grades. SEL, motivation, and behavior (e.g., persistence, engagement, disciplinary behavior)—and the processes and moderators that shape these outcomes—are important to study in and of themselves.

Developing and Validating Measures beyond the Student Level

Measures of the structural and contextual factors that shape student outcomes. It is important to measure the opportunities that education systems provide and the context in which learning occurs, in addition to how students perform. Rather than narrowly focusing on direct-to-student interventions (that often locate the problem within students), studies of the learning environment, systems, and contexts can also be valuable. Examples of such foci include federal, state, district, school, and classroom policies and practices that influence effective teaching and learning; school leaders and the educational opportunities they foster; and how the instructional environment and interactions between students, teachers, administrators, and staff shape students' learning and experience.

Measures of the context in which children develop and in which students learn, from birth through college, would be valuable. Of the 176 grants awarded by IES over the last 20 years, only four grants (2%) have focused on measuring qualities of schools as the primary question of interest. Studies that develop and validate structural and contextual measures that assess how these factors influence students' SEL, engagement, motivation, behavior, and performance—and how these systemic and contextual factors may differentially impact students from structurally disadvantaged backgrounds—would be valuable.

Measures of teacher development, practice, and effectiveness. Research on the measurement and assessment of teacher development, teacher practice, and teacher effectiveness in creating more equitable learning environments where all students are valued, engaged, and perform to their potential—regardless of their background and social identities—is important. The classroom climates that teachers create can predict students' experiences and learning; moreover, teacher practice can be observed, measured, improved, and intervened upon in an interactive fashion over the course of terms and years.

Of the 176 measurement grants awarded by IES over the past 20 years, only 16 grants (9%) included measures of teachers or teacher practice. The vast majority of IES grants (89%) focus almost exclusively on measurement of students and student-level characteristics.

To understand how students learn and develop in the American education system, it is essential to understand what goes on with schools and teachers inside and outside the classroom. Research on how teachers create the learning environment of their classes has centered on three core aspects that many professional development efforts variously target: (1) *teachers' intentions* to enact changes to their practice; (2) *teachers' implementation* of those intended changes/practices in their classrooms; and (3) *students' perceptions and experiences* of those enacted practices (e.g., Murphy et al., 2021). Implementation measurement is labor intensive and more work is needed to build on recent IES-supported advances in automated measurement of instructional practice (e.g., Kelly et al., 2018).

Measurement research focused on teachers' practices is an important step in identifying which practices positively influence *students'* SEL, engagement, motivation, behavior, and performance. In addition, it will be helpful to develop measures of teacher professional development (PD) in order to identify what kinds of PD are effective in creating changes and improvements to teachers' intentions and implementation of policies, practices, interactions with students, interactions with parents, and other aspects that mitigate group-based experience and achievement gaps in their classrooms and support all students' learning and development.

Measures of knowledge mobilization. As discussed in Chapter 4, the committee identified knowledge mobilization as a project type. In the past, IES has funded efforts to measure knowledge use through the creation and support of two knowledge utilization centers. Work from these centers resulted in validated survey measures of instrumental, conceptual, and symbolic use (Penuel et al., 2016) and measures of depth of research use (May et al., forthcoming, 2021). The work also highlights the psychometric challenges of measuring practitioner knowledge of research quality (Hill & Briggs, 2020). These measures, developed for survey research, could be built upon and extended by developing measures that could be used in observational data (including longitudinal observational data, video data, and observation in the context of experiments) as well as tracing the impact of research in policy and practice (e.g., Farrell et al., 2018; Huguet et al., 2017). In order to advance this work, IES will need to consider how to leverage existing work and what kinds of additional measures to support new knowledge mobilization project time.

Developing and Validating Measures of Equity and Inequity

Given the urgency of improving educational equity, the field needs more informative measures of the range of inequities in inputs, processes, and outcomes to help monitor and spur progress across all of these areas. How can it be known when systems, learning environments, and opportunities inside and outside the classroom (e.g., curricula, textbooks, instructional practices, teacher-student interactions) are equitable or inequitable? While school systems are generally required to report student outcomes disaggregated by various demographic characteristics, measuring and comparing between-group gaps in experiences, achievement, and proficiency rates (and growth over time) face multiple challenges, due to small subgroup sizes, distortion in binary measures, lack of a clear criterion for comparison, and ambiguity in interpreting changes in absolute gaps (Ho, 2008). For example, structurally disadvantaged student populations often experience the classroom setting differently than their structurally advantaged peers; thus, should measures of equity in such student experiences always include an advantaged comparison group? Many quantitative critical race scholars argue that requiring White and other advantaged "quasi-control groups" or "comparison groups" is a racist practice that assumes that the experiences of advantaged groups serve as a normative standard by which to compare other groups (e.g., Flanagin et al., 2021; Sablan, 2018; Garcia et al., 2017). Other measures of gaps, disparate impact, and disproportionality exist (e.g., Reardon & Ho, 2014) but are not consistently used across the field, whether due to technical complexity or limitations in applicability. Developing clearer measures of differences would support more effective and transparent monitoring of equity in outcomes.

A growing body of frameworks and tools have emerged for measuring equity in education, highlighting a range of dimensions and indicators for school systems to monitor (e.g., Hyler et al., 2021; Alliance for Resource Equity, 2020; NASEM, 2019). These include student, teacher, and staff inputs; funding and infrastructure; curricula; school climate; leadership; and teaching practices. Measurement along any single dimension could constitute an accounting of strengths and needs, documenting evidence on a checklist, comparing group differences, or calculating more complex metrics. For example, student composition may be measured in terms of its diversity (e.g., Keylock, 2005), its similarity to the broader population (e.g., Reardon & Firebaugh, 2002; Atkinson, 1970), or each group's exposure to other groups (e.g., Massey & Denton, 1988). Examining the relationship between dimensions, such as between demographics and inputs, then allows for measuring the extent to which all groups have equal access to those resources and opportunities. This could be calculated as correlations or as probability distributions (e.g., Shannon, 1948). Assessing the distribution of individuals and resources across organizational structures, or the distribution of individuals' participation in and experience of various interactional processes, could serve as measures of inclusion. Other challenges emerge when measuring growth and gaps.

Building on these measures of diversity, equality, and inclusion to assess equity requires tracking change over time. A key conceptual distinction between equality and equity is that while equality focuses only on the present, equity recognizes the influence of past experiences. Although the above measurement approaches account for situational differences, they do not capture historical differences. Tracking past and future change is critical, both to account for compounding historical inequalities and to assess whether investments are successful in subsequently reducing gaps. Future projections are essential for anticipating what is needed to achieve more equitable outcomes. The field needs reliable and transparent measures of equity from birth to college, not only to make sense of the multiple dimensions and indicators that influence outcomes, but more importantly, to guide policy and practice in providing the resources, opportunities, and supports necessary for educational equity.

Using Technology to Develop New Approaches and Tools for Measurement

The field of education has largely benefited from new and emerging technology that allows researchers and practitioners to understand the mechanisms that improve students' learning and development. Education technology has the potential to be a powerful tool for measurement and assessment allowing new insights into learning and teaching. For instance, data can shed light on the learning process (e.g., observational data such as classroom audio or video recordings, learning management system behavior, analyses of electronic documents, etc.). Web-scraping tools, education data mining, and learning analytics and the data that result from these approaches also offer new opportunities for measurement research.

Developing Common Measures

A major problem that the field of education encounters is a plethora of measures created by education researchers and practitioners. Understanding and effecting system-wide implementation and improvement demands a coherent set of measures that link processes and outcomes across levels. For example, measures that are calibrated across tests to a single scale of measurement support the same inferences about student performance from one locality to another and from one year to the next (National Research Council, 1999). Collectively, such measures could facilitate moving beyond simplistic deficit frames that attribute gaps to students, by revealing the opportunity gaps in what education systems provide. Systems of measures further enable researchers and practitioners to examine the relationships between processes across levels (Bryk et al., 2015; Provost & Murray, 2011).

At the same time, an overemphasis on common measures may force researchers to use measures that are not well suited to the outcomes they focus on and may limit creativity and development of innovative measures. For this reason, the committee concluded that encouraging, but not requiring, common measures is ideal and allows investigators to pursue innovative measures as called for by theory and the needs of particular studies.

RECOMMENDATIONS

IES's investments over the past two decades have led to substantial methodological advancements in education research, particularly with respect to how to conduct randomized controlled trials. To continue to set the standard for research and respond to the current needs of education writ large, IES will need to expand the range of research on methods it funds. The committee recognizes that ESRA calls for IES to maintain a focus on causal research. At the same time, descriptive research is needed to be able to fully understand the context of interventions and the nuances of implementation. This means IES will need to invest in research on methods and approaches beyond causal designs that can help to answer questions about how and why interventions work or do not work across varying contexts (e.g., descriptive, qualitative, and mixed methods).

RECOMMENDATION 6.1:
IES should develop competitive priorities for research on methods and designs in the following areas:
- Small causal studies
- Understanding implementation and adaptation
- Understanding knowledge mobilization
- Predicting causal effects in local contexts
- Utilizing big data

RECOMMENDATION 6.2:
IES should convene a new competition and review panel for supporting qualitative and mixed-methods approaches to research design and methods.

In order to respond to the new study types and priority topics and to support the continued growth of methods, new measures and new approaches to measurement will be required. IES has funded numerous studies focused on development of measures, and these studies have provided the field with a number of measures related to student outcomes and student characteristics and have expanded the field's understanding of the ways interventions impact students' learning and achievement. At the same time, there is a need for research on measures of other student outcomes such as motivation, behavior and social-emotional development as well as measures related to educational systems, education leaders, and teachers. For this reason, we offer a recommendation for IES to consider related to measurement research that will support continued growth in other parts of NCER and NCSER's portfolio.

RECOMMENDATION 6.3:
IES should develop a competitive priority for the following areas of measurement research:
- Expanding the range of student outcome measures
- Developing and validating measures beyond the student level (e.g., structural and contextual factors that shape student outcomes; teacher outcomes; knowledge mobilization)
- Developing and validating measures related to educational equity
- Using technology to develop new approaches and tools for measurement

REFERENCES

Alliance for Resource Equity. (2020). Dimensions of Equity. https://www.educationresource-equity.org/dimensions.

Anderson, A., O'Rourke, E., Chin, M., Ponce, N., Bernheim, S., and Burstin, H. (2018). Promoting health equity and eliminating disparities through performance measurement and payment. *Health Affairs, 37*(3), 371–377. https://doi.org/ 10.1377/hlthaff.2017.1301.

Anderson, T., and Shattuck, J. (2012). Design-based research: A decade of progress in education research? *Educational Researcher, 41*(1), 16–25. https://doi.org/10.3102/0013189X11428813.

Atkinson, A.B. (1970). On the measurement of inequality. *Journal of Economic Theory, 2*(3), 244–263.

Atteberry, A., Bischoff, K., and Owens, A. (2021). Identifying progress toward ethnoracial achievement equity across U.S. school districts: A new approach. *Journal for Research on Educational Effectiveness, 14,* 410–441.

Balazs, C.L., and Morello-Frosch, R. (2013). The three R's: How community based participatory research strengthens the rigor, relevance and reach of science. *Environmental Justice (Print), 6*(1). https://doi.org/10.1089/env.2012.0017.

Bose, M., and Dey, A. (2009). *Optimal Crossover Designs.* Hackensack, NJ: World Scientific Publishing.

Brookman-Frazee, L., Zhan, C., Stadnick, N., Sommerfeld, D., Roesch, S., Aarons, G.A., Innes-Gomberg, D., Bando, L., and Lau, A.S. (2018). Using survival analysis to understand patterns of sustainment within a system-driven implementation of multiple evidence-based practices for children's mental health services. *Frontiers in Public Health, 6,* 54. https://doi.org/10.3389/fpubh.2018.00054.

Brown, C.A., and Lilford, R.J. (2006). The stepped wedge trial design: A systematic review. *BMC Medical Research Methodology, 6,* 54. https://doi.org/10.1186/1471-2288-6-54.

Brown, C.H., Curran, G., Palinkas, L.A., Aarons, G.A., Wells, K.B., Jones, L., Collins, L.M., Duan, N., Mittman, B.S., Wallace, A., Tabak, R.G., Ducharme, L., Chambers, D.A., Neta, G., Wiley, T., Landsverk, J., Cheung, K., and Cruden, G. (2017). An overview of research and evaluation designs for dissemination and implementation. *Annual Review of Public Health, 38,* 1–22. https://doi.org/10.1146/annurev-publhealth-031816-044215.

Bryk, A.S. (2020). *Improvement in Action: Advancing Quality in America's Schools.* Stanford, CA: Carnegie Foundation for the Advancement of Teaching.

Bryk, A.S., Gomez, L.M., Grunow, A., and LeMahieu, P.G. (2015). *Learning to Improve: How America's Schools Can Get Better at Getting Better.* Cambridge, MA: Harvard Education Press.

Bryk, A.S., Gomez, L., and Grunow, A. (2011). *Getting Ideas into Action: Building Networked Improvement Communities in Education.* Stanford, CA: Carnegie Foundation for the Advancement of Teaching.

Burke, J.G., Lich, K.H., Neal, J.W., Meissner, H.I., Yonas, M., and Mabry, P.L. (2015). Enhancing dissemination and implementation research using systems science methods. *International Journal of Behavioral Medicine, 22*(3), 283–291. https://doi.org/10.1007/s12529-014-9417-3.

Cammarota, J., and Fine, M. (2010). *Revolutionizing Education: Youth Participatory Action Research in Motion.* New York: Routledge.

Cobb, P., Jackson, K., Smith, T., Sorum, M., and Henrick, E. (2013). Design research with educational systems: Investigating and supporting improvements in the quality of mathematics teaching and learning at scale. *National Society for the Study of Education, 112*(2), 320–349.

Cohen-Vogel, L., Allen, D., Rutledge, S., Harrison, C., Cannata, M., and T. Smith. (2018). The dilemmas of research-practice partnerships: Implications for leading continuous improvement in education. *Journal of Research on Organization in Education, 2*(1).

Cohen-Vogel, L., Tichnor-Wagner, A., Allen, D., Harrison, C., Kainz, K., Socol, A.R., and Wang, Q. (2015). Implementing educational innovations at scale: Transforming Researchers into continuous improvement scientists. *Educational Policy, 29*(1), 257–277.

Collins, L.M., Murphy, S.A., and Strecher, V. (2007). The multiphase optimization strategy (MOST) and the sequential multiple assignment randomized trial (SMART): New methods for more potent eHealth interventions. *American Journal of Preventive Medicine, 32*(5 Suppl), S112–S118. https://doi.org/10.1016/j.amepre.2007.01.022.

Curran, G.M., Bauer, M., Mittman, B., Pyne, J.M., and Stetler, C. (2012). Effectiveness-implementation hybrid designs: Combining elements of clinical effectiveness and implementation research to enhance public health impact. *Medical Care, 50*(3), 217–226. https://doi.org/10.1097/MLR.0b013e3182408812.

Deming, W.E. (1982). *Quality, Productivity and Competitive Position.* Cambridge, MA: MIT Press.

Design-Based Research Collective. (2003). Design-based research: An emerging paradigm for educational inquiry. *Educational Research, 32*(1), 5–8.

Donovan, M.S. (2013). Generating improvement through research and development in education systems. *Science, 340*(6130), 317–319.

Eberhard, K. (2021). The effects of visualization on judgment and decision-making: a systematic literature review. *Management Review Quarterly.* https://doi.org/10.1007/s11301-021-00235-8.

Finnigan, K.S., Daly, A.J., and Che, J. (2013). Systemwide reform in districts under pressure: The role of social networks in defining, acquiring, and using research evidence. *Journal of Educational Administration, 51,* 476–497.

Flanagin, A., Frey, T., Christiansen, S.L., for the AMA Manual of Style Committee. (2021). Updated guidance on the reporting of race and ethnicity in medical and science journals. *JAMA, 326*(7), 621–627. https://doi.org/10.1001/jama.2021.13304.

Frank, K., Kim, J., Salloum, S., Bieda, K., and Youngs, P. (2020). From interpretation to instructional practice: A network study of early career teachers' sensemaking in the era of accountability pressures and Common Core State Standards. *American Educational Research Journal, 57,* 2293–2338.

Fretheim, A., and Tomic, O. (2015). Statistical process control and interrupted time series: A golden opportunity for impact evaluation in quality improvement. *BMJ Quality & Safety, 24,* 748–752.

Garcia, N.M., López, N., and Vélez, V.N. (2017). QuantCrit: Rectifying quantitative methods through critical race theory. *Race Ethnicity and Education, 21*(2), 149–157. https://doi.org/10.1080/13613324.2017.1377675.

Gitomer, D.H., and Crouse, K. (2019). *Studying the Use of Research Evidence: A Review of Methods.* New York: William T. Grant Foundation.

Hill, H.C., and Briggs, D.C. (2020). Education Leaders' Knowledge of Causal Research Design: A Measurement Challenge (EdWorkingPaper 20-298). Annenberg Institute at Brown University. https://doi.org/10.26300/vxt5-ws91.

Ho, A.D. (2008). The problem with "proficiency": Limitations of statistics and policy under No Child Left Behind. *Educational Researcher, 37*(6), 351–360.

Huguet, A., Coburn, C.E., Farrell, C.F., Kim, D.H., and Allen, A-R. (2021). Constraints, values, and information: How district leaders justify their positions during instructional deliberations. *American Educational Research Journal.* First published online February 20, 2021. https://doi.org/ https://doi/10.3102/0002831221993824.

Huguet, A., Allen, A-R., Coburn, C.E., Farrell, C.C., Kim, D.H., and Penuel, W.R. (2017). Locating data use in the microprocesses of district-level deliberations. *Nordic Journal of Studies in Education, 3*(1), 21–28.

Hussey, M.A., and Hughes, J.P. (2007). Design and analysis of stepped wedge cluster randomized trials. *Contemporary Clinical Trials, 28*(2), 182–191. https://doi.org/10.1016/j.cct.2006.05.007.

Hyler, M.E., Carver-Thomas, D., Wechsler, M., and Willis, L. (2021). *Districts Advancing Racial Equity (DARE) Tool.* Palo Alto, CA: Learning Policy Institute.

Institute of Education Sciences. (IES) (2021). About Standards for Excellence in Education Research. https://ies.ed.gov/seer/index.asp.

Joyce, K.E., and Cartwright, N. (2020). Bridging the gap between research and practice: Predicting what will work locally. *American Educational Research Journal, 57*, 1045–1082.

Juran, J.M. (1951). *Juran's Quality Control Handbook.* New York: McGraw-Hill.

Kelly, S., Olney, A.M., Donnelly, P., Nystrand, M., and D'Mello, S.K. (2018). Automatically measuring question authenticity in real-world classrooms. *Educational Researcher, 47*, 451–464.

Keylock, C.J. (2005). Simpson diversity and the Shannon–Wiener index as special cases of a generalized entropy. *Oikos, 109*, 203–207. https://doi.org/10.1111/j.0030-1299.2005.13735.x.

Klager, C.R., and Tipton, E.L. (2021). *Commissioned Paper on the Summary of IES Funded Topics.* Paper prepared for the National Academies of Sciences, Engineering, and Medicine, Committee on the Future of Education Research at the Institute of Education Sciences in the U.S. Department of Education. https://nap.nationalacademies.org/resource/26428/READY-KlagerTipton_IES_Topic_Analysis_Jan2022v4.pdf.

Kumar, G., Basri, S., Imam, A.A., Khowaja, S.A., Capretz, L.F., and Balogun, A.O. (2021). Data harmonization for heterogeneous datasets: A systematic literature review. *Applied Sciences, 11*, 8275. https://doi.org/10.3390/app11178275.

Kumar, G., Basri, S., Imam, A.A., and Balogun, A.O. (2020). Data harmonization for heterogeneous datasets in big data—a conceptual model. In R. Silhavy, P. Silhavy, and Z. Prokopova (Eds.), *Software Engineering Perspectives in Intelligent Systems. CoMeSySo 2020. Advances in Intelligent Systems and Computing* (Vol. 1294). Cham, Switzerland: Springer. https://doi.org/10.1007/978-3-030-63322-6_61.

Lewis, C. (2015). What is improvement science? Do we need it in education? *Educational Researcher, 44*(1), 54–61.

Li, Q. (2020). Overview of Data Visualization. *Embodying Data: Chinese Aesthetics, Interactive Visualization and Gaming Technologies*, 17–47. https://doi.org/10.1007/978-981-15-5069-0_2.

Mabry, P.L., Olster, D.H., Morgan, G.D., and Abrams, D.B. (2008). Interdisciplinarity and systems science to improve population health: A view from the NIH Office of Behavioral and Social Sciences Research. *American Journal of Preventive Medicine, 35*(2 Suppl.), S211–S224. (Erratum in: *American Journal of Preventive Medicine, 35,* 611).

Massey, D.S., and Denton, N.A. (1988). The dimensions of residential segregation. *Social Forces, 67*(2), 281–315. https://doi.org/10.2307/2579183.

May, H., Farley-Ripple, E.N., Blackman, H., Wang, R., Shewchuk, S., Tilley, K., and Van Horne, S. (forthcoming). Survey of Evidence in Education for Schools (SEE-S) Technical Report. Center for Research Use in Education, University of Delaware, Newark.

May, H., Blackman, H., Wang, R., Tilley, K., and Farley-Ripple, E.N. (2021). Characterizing Schools' Depth of Research Use. Paper presented at the Annual Meeting of the American Educational Research Association, April 2021.

Means, B., and Harris, C.J. (2013). Towards an evidence framework for design-based implementation research. In B.J. Fishman, W.R. Penuel, A.R. Allen, and B.H. Cheng (Eds.), *Design Based Implementation Research: Theories, Methods, and Exemplars. National Society for the Study of Education Yearbook* (Vol. 112, pp. 320–349). New York: Teachers College.

Murphy, M., Fryberg, S., Brady, L., Canning, E., and Hecht, C. (2021). Global Mindset Initiative Paper 1: Growth Mindset Cultures and Teacher Practices. https://ssrn.com/abstract=3911594 or http://dx.doi.org/10.2139/ssrn.3911594.

Musci, R.J. (2020). Integrated Data Analysis in Prevention Science. [PowerPoint Slides]. https://prevention.nih.gov/education-training/methods-mind-gap/integrated-data-analysis-prevention-science.

National Academies of Sciences, Engineering, and Medicine (NASEM). (2019). *Monitoring Educational Equity.* Washington, DC: The National Academies Press. https://doi.org/10.17226/25389.

———. (2018). *How People Learn II: Learners, Contexts, and Cultures.* Washington, DC: The National Academies Press. https://doi.org/10.17226/24783.

National Research Council (NRC). (2000). *How People Learn: Brain, Mind, Experience, and School: Expanded Edition.* Washington, DC: The National Academies Press. https://doi.org/10.17226/9853.

———. (1999). *Embedding Questions: The Pursuit of a Common Measure in Uncommon Tests.* Washington, DC: The National Academies Press. https://doi.org/10.17226/9683.

Northridge, M.E., and Metcalf, S.S. (2016). Enhancing implementation science by applying best principles of systems science. *Health Research Policy and Systems, 14,* 74. https://doi.org/10.1186/s12961-016-0146-8.

O'Cathain, A., Murphy, E., and Nicholl, J. (2010). Three techniques for integrating data in mixed methods studies. *British Medical Journal, 341,* c4587.

Padilla, L. M., Creem-Regehr, S. H., Hegarty, M., & Stefanucci, J. K. (2018). Decision making with visualizations: a cognitive framework across disciplines. *Cognitive research: principles and implications, 3,* 29. https://doi.org/10.1186/s41235-018-0120-9.

Penuel, W.R., Briggs, D.C., Davidson, K.L., Herlihy, C., Sherer, D., Hill, H.C., Farrell, C.C., and Allen, A.-R. (2017). How school and district leaders access, perceive, and use research. *AERA Open, 3*(2), 1–17. https://doi.org/ 10.1177/2332858417705370.

Penuel, W.R., Briggs, D.C., Davidson, K.L., Herlihy, C., Sherer, D., Hill, H.C., Farrell, C.C., and Allen, A.-R. (2016). Findings from a National Study of Research Use among school and district leaders. Technical report No. 1. Boulder, CO: National Center for Research in Policy and Practice.

Portela, M.C., Pronovost, P.J., Woodcock, T., Carter, P., and Dixon-Woods, M. (2015). How to study improvement interventions: A brief overview of possible study types. *BMJ Quality & Safety, 24*(5), 325–336. https://doi.org/10.1136/bmjqs-2014-003620.

Provost, L.P. (2011). Analytical studies: A framework for quality improvement design and analysis. *BMJ Quality & Safety, 20*(Suppl. 1), i92–i96.

Provost, L.P., and Murray, S. (2011). *The Health Care Data Guide: Learning from Data for Improvement.* San Francisco: John Wiley & Sons.

Reardon, S.F., and Firebaugh, G. (2002). Measures of multigroup segregation. *Sociological Methodology, 32,* 33–67. https://doi.org/10.1111/1467-9531.00110.

Reardon, S.F., and Ho, A.D. (2014). Practical issues in estimating achievement gaps from coarsened data. *Journal of Educational and Behavioral Statistics, 40*(2), 158–189.

Robertson, T., and Simonsen, J. (2012). Challenges and opportunities in contemporary participatory design. *Design Issues, 28.* https://doi.org/10.1162/DESI_a_00157.

Sablan, J.R. (2018). Can you really measure that? Combining critical race theory and quantitative methods. *American Educational Research Journal, 56*(1), 178–203. https://doi.org/10.3102/0002831218798325.

Sarkies, M.N., Skinner, E.H., Bowles, K.A., Morris, M.E., Williams, C., O'Brien, L., Bardoel, A., Martin, J., Holland, A.E., Carey, L., White, J., Haines, T.P. (2019). A novel counterbalanced implementation study design: Methodological description and application to implementation research. *Implementation Science, 14,* 45. https://doi.org/10.1186/s13012-019-0896-0.

Shalowitz, M.U., Isacco, A., Barquin, N., Clark-Kauffman, E., Delger, P., Nelson, D., Quinn, A., and Wagenaar, K.A. (2009). Community-based participatory research: A review of the literature with strategies for community engagement. *Journal of Developmental and Behavioral Pediatrics 30*(4), 350–361. https://doi.org/10.1097/DBP.0b013e3181b0ef14.

Shannon, C.E. (1948). A mathematical theory of communication. *Bell System Technical Journal, 27,* 379–423. https://doi.org/10.1002/j.1538-7305.1948.tb01338.x.

Shewhart, W.A. (1931). *Economic Control of Quality of Manufactured Products.* New York; London: Van Nostrand; MacMillan.

Stringer, E.T., and Aragón, A.O. (2020). *Action Research.* Thousand Oaks, CA: SAGE Publications.

Weber, M.S. (2018). Methods and approaches to using web archives in computational communication research. *Communication Methods and Measures, 12*(2–3), 200–215. https://doi.org/10.1080/19312458.2018.1447657.

Weber, M.S., and Yanovitzky, I. (Eds.). (2021). *Networks, Knowledge Brokers, and the Public Policymaking Process.* New York: Palgrave.

Weiss, C.H., and Bucuvalas, M.J. (1980). *Social Science Research and Decision Making.* New York, NY: Columbia University Press.

Yanovitzky, I., and Weber, M. (2020). Analyzing use of evidence in public policymaking processes: A theory-grounded content analysis methodology. *Evidence & Policy: A Journal of Research, Debate and Practice, 16*(1), 65–82.

7

Ensuring Broad and Equitable Participation in NCER and NCSER Research Training Programs

According to Section 112 of the Education Sciences Reform Act (ESRA), the Institute of Education Sciences (IES) is directed to "strengthen the national capacity to conduct, develop, and widely disseminate scientifically valid research in education." To fulfill this charge, over the past two decades, IES has funded programs that train researchers in the skills needed to carry out such research. Put another way, IES's training programs have "seeded" the field of education sciences with researchers who have the skills necessary to carry out its vision of scientific research. In the early 2000s, as a new agency encouraging the adoption of research methods not widely used in the field, IES decided it was crucial to invest in several types of highly competitive training programs, including those administered by the National Center for Education Research (NCER) and National Center for Special Education Research (NCSER). Although data on the outcomes of the NCER and NCSER training programs are not available, based on the high volume of participation, increases in the funding, and publication of research of the sort desired by IES, as well as the high quality of training experiences reported in testimony to the committee and witnessed by committee members themselves at first hand, these training programs seem to have paid off in advancing IES's goal to build a cadre of researchers capable of pursuing the sort of research it aimed to fund.

In this chapter, we re-examine the goals of NCER and NCSER's training programs, asking the question of what it would mean to "strengthen the national capacity" to carry out this report's vision of education research for the future. At minimum, the recommendations of this report are likely to require a broadening of the number and kinds of training opportunities made available to emerging researchers. We begin the chapter by examining the existing NCER and NCSER training programs at the undergraduate, predoctoral, postdoctoral, and early career levels, as well as the methods training program. This chapter also explores the impact of the research training programs and the continued need for these programs within the field. Finally, we discuss numerous ways NCER and NCSER can work to broaden participation in education research through these training programs.

DESCRIPTION OF EXISTING NCER AND
NCSER TRAINING PROGRAMS

A review of training program requests for applications (RFAs) over IES's 20-year history indicates that the NCER and NCSER research training portfolios have had three primary objectives: (1) to increase the number of scientists capable of conducting rigorous and relevant education research independently, (2) to increase the number of education researchers capable of conducting education research that can be funded by IES, and (3) to advance the field of education research statistically, methodologically, theoretically, and practically. Over the past 5–10 years, a fourth objective has emerged: to increase the diversity of researchers and institutions that participate in training opportunities provided by NCER and NCSER so as to increase the diversity of the education research workforce. To achieve these goals, NCER and NCSER offer several different types of training programs for education researchers at different points in their careers, including programs aimed at undergraduate students, predoctoral students, postdoctoral scholars, and early career faculty. There are also methods training programs that vary in their focus, providing opportunities for education researchers at any stage of their careers, including graduate students (NCER only), researchers and faculty at institutions of higher education, and researchers outside of institutions of higher education, like local education agencies (LEAs), state education agencies (SEAs), research institutes and centers, and other non-university entities. More recently, some training programs have been designed specifically to increase participation of individuals from groups who are traditionally underrepresented in education research, including faculty and undergraduate students at Minority-Serving Institutions (MSIs). Other training programs require fellows to work in or with SEAs and LEAs to gain practical experience. We summarize these programs in Table 7-1.

The training opportunities offered by NCER and NCSER are overlapping but distinct. For example, both centers provide training opportunities for postdoctoral researchers and specialized methods training. NCER and NCSER diverge in their offerings for junior scholars, with NCSER providing training programs for early career faculty and NCER providing training

TABLE 7-1 Research Training Programs at the Institute of Education Sciences, FY2002–Present

Program	Agency	Years	Goal	Program Reach
Pathways to the Education Sciences Research Training	NCER	2016–Present	To broaden participation of groups underrepresented in education research, focusing on undergraduate, master's, and postbaccalaureate students at MSIs.	12 grants at 7 institutions; $14.9 million
Predoctoral Interdisciplinary Research Training Programs in the Education Sciences	NCER	2004–Present	To increase the number of education researchers capable of producing research evidence that is both rigorous and relevant to the decisions that policy makers and practitioners make to support student learning and achievement in school.	47 grants at 21 institutions; $209 million
Postdoctoral Research Training Program	NCER NCSER	2005–Present (NCER) 2008–Present (NCSER)	To prepare doctoral graduates to conduct high-quality education, special education, and early intervention research independently and to be able to use and conduct research that is funded by IES.	NCER: 47 grants at 27 institutions; $30.3 million. NCSER: 20 grants at 13 institutions; $13.6 million
Early Career Development and Mentoring in Special Education	NCSER	2013–Present	To support early career early intervention and special education researchers capable of producing rigorous research relevant to the needs of infants, toddlers, children, and youth with or at risk for disabilities.	33 grants; $16.3 million

continued

TABLE 7-1 Continued

Program	Agency	Years	Goal	Program Reach
Training in Education Research Use and Practice	NCER	2014	To bring together policy makers, practitioners, and researchers around a specific issue in order to share the latest evidence on the issue with policy makers and practitioners and to provide policy makers and practitioners an opportunity to talk with researchers regarding their own informational needs.	1 grant; $1 million
Early Career Mentoring Program for Faculty at Minority-Serving Institutions	NCER	2021–Present[3]	To diversify the types of institutions that provide research training opportunities funded by IES and the faculty who are prepared to conduct high-quality education research independently and can conduct research that is funded by IES.	No awards announced to date
Methods Training for Educational Researchers	NCER NCSER	2002–Present[4]	To support current researchers in building and expanding their skills to design, analyze, and interpret rigorous education research.	NCER: 15 grants; $11.7 million[1] NCSER: 4 grants; $2.2 million[2]

SOURCE: Committee-generated based on data from IES.

NOTES:

[1] This includes five grants funded through the Unsolicited grant opportunity. Three of these were funded prior to the existence of the official Methods Training for Education Researchers topic area (R305U080001, R305U100001, R305U110001), and the other two include one grant to provide training for SEA and LEA research staff to conduct cost analysis (R305U180001) and one Methods training planning grant (R305U190001).

[2] This includes one grant funded through the Unsolicited grant opportunity (R324U140001), two grants funded under a competition called "Methods Training Using Single-Case Designs" (R324B160034 and R324B200022), as well as one grant funded under a competition called "Research Methods Training Using Sequential, Multiple Assignment, Randomized Trial (SMART) Designs" (R324B180003).

[3] The Early Career Mentoring Program for Faculty at Minority-Serving Institutions was announced, but no awards had been made in FY2021.

[4] Prior to establishing the Methods Training for Education Researchers program, NCER and NCSER supported methods training grants that were submitted under the unsolicited grants opportunity. We have included these grants in our total grants funded under this program, and therefore have noted the starting date for these grants as 2002.

programs for undergraduate, masters, and predoctoral students and, as of FY2022, for early career faculty as well. These differences are due, in part, to differences in the funding levels for both centers. With substantially less funding, NCSER directs its limited resources to the postdoctoral and early career levels.

UNDERSTANDING THE IMPACT OF
RESEARCH TRAINING PROGRAMS AT IES

IES has invested millions of dollars into its training programs to date. How impactful have these programs been? We know that hundreds of students, junior, early career, and senior scholars have participated in training programs, and many have carried these skills and competencies into education research careers (IES, 2021). Likewise, available data on the career-development aspects of the training programs suggest that the programs have brought scholars to education science who may not otherwise be in the field (IES, 2021).

Although some new information was provided in a recent report (IES, 2021), more data are needed for the committee and the field to fully understand who participates in these programs, how their participation has contributed to their success as education researchers, and how their participation has shaped the field. For example, it is not clear from the available data how many participants in the various training programs have matriculated through education research careers, how many have applied for and secured funding from NCER and NCSER, or how many have made use of the specific methodological and statistical techniques they were trained on in their research. Moreover, although recent RFAs specifically encourage training programs to recruit fellows from specific groups that are underrepresented in education research, information about the participation of individuals from these groups in the training programs is not available. It would be important to know if individuals from these groups are or are not applying for the NCER and NCSER programs, being accepted into the programs, or using their experiences in the programs to further their research careers (e.g., to secure IES funding as independent researchers). Data about each of these points are needed to better understand the success of the programs and to evaluate whether changes are needed.

Beyond the quantity of participants, data are also not readily available on different aspects of the training experiences provided by the programs. For example, all of the pre- and postdoctoral training programs are required to implement strategies to recruit and retain fellows from groups that are underrepresented in education research. In addition, many of the current IES training programs have an explicit interdisciplinary focus, including the predoctoral training programs. Further, over time, required activities for trainees have changed (such as the move toward apprentice-ships for predoctoral fellows). However, data on the success of these efforts are not readily available. We do not know which components of the training programs are most beneficial for trainees. We do not know the extent to which programs have succeeded at enrolling and retaining individuals from historically underrepresented groups. And, we do not have data to understand whether specific disciplines within the broad field of education are underrepresented in the training opportunities.

All in all, it seems likely that the training opportunities have led to many desired changes. However, in the absence of specific data related to each of the training programs' primary objectives, it is difficult to ascertain the impact of the training opportunities offered by NCER and NCSER on education research. It is worth noting that the training programs' reporting requirements imply that indicators of program success have been collected; however, the data are not publicly available currently and were not made available to the committee. These data represent a rich and robust resource that can be used to examine who is and who is not participating in education research training programs at different points in the pipeline; what practices are effective for recruiting and retaining scientists in successful education research careers; and what barriers and opportunities are important to consider in the development of a diverse cadre of interdisciplinary education researchers. These data need to be made available to realize this promise.

NEED FOR CONTINUED TRAINING
IN EDUCATION SCIENCES

The training portfolio that NCER and NCSER established to meet the charge issued within ESRA (Section 112) is impressive. Through these programs, IES has established a pipeline for developing education scientists, from undergraduate and graduate study and continuing throughout their research careers. It has also established a reputation for offering high-quality training opportunities that have advanced statistical and method-ological expertise in the broad interdisciplinary field of education research, equipping the field with the expertise, tools, and competencies required to produce rigorous research. The sheer volume of education researchers who have participated in these training programs would seem to indicate that IES has, indeed, strengthened the nation's capacity to develop, conduct, and disseminate scientifically valid education research widely. At historical moments such as the present one, strengths like the training programs can and should be leveraged to address both challenges and opportunities to improve student achievement and school success.

As noted in previous chapters, recent events associated with the global COVID-19 pandemic and civil rights violations have laid bare historical and structural inequities that are prevalent in many aspects of U.S. society. Emerging data make clear that education is no exception. Disparities in academic, behavioral, and social-emotional opportunities and outcomes are not new (Schneider, 2021) but have been exacerbated as student experiences in schools have continued to vary in unexpected, unpredictable, and unprecedented ways. These issues are complex, and evidence is only just now emerging on their impact on a variety of educational outcomes. When available, data indicate that, on average, students who were already more likely to experience poorer outcomes on most indicators of school achievement and success fared much worse, including students with disabilities, students growing up in poverty and low-income households, and students from minoritized groups.[1] If these trends hold, then the immediate and long-term impacts of this once-in-a-lifetime moment are likely to be felt for generations, making already stubborn disparities even more difficult to address.

Advances in education science are required to respond sufficiently to such complex challenges proactively and effectively. Now more than ever, the public demands that the field act quickly and strategically to produce research that is rigorous, relevant, and responsive to this moment. Doing so will require a balance of improvement and innovation—both hallmarks of training programs offered by NCER and NCSER.

Regarding improvement, NCER and NCSER's training programs were founded, in part, on the assumption that many education researchers did not have specific skills or competencies required to design, conduct, or disseminate causally informative research studies. As discussed in Chapter 2, although the field continues to debate what constitutes scientifically valid research, the number of IES-funded research studies that have employed experimental and quasi-experimental research designs has increased substantially over the past 20 years, allowing for an increasing number of effectiveness and efficacy studies, and allowing for meta-analyses and research syntheses on several interventions and instructional practices across elementary, secondary, and postsecondary education. It stands to reason that these advances were due, in part, to training opportunities provided by NCER and NCSER to develop and upskill scientists who could produce this research. IES has been successful in building the field's capacity for conducting education research, and this success should be celebrated and continued.

Relatedly, diversity has emerged as an important area of improvement for the training programs. In recent years, both NCER and NCSER have

---

[1]These summary statements about the effects of the COVID-19 pandemic on education rely on a background paper the committee commissioned from Hough et al. (2021).

made efforts to increase diversity in the field of education research by providing training opportunities for individuals and institutions historically underrepresented in education research. RFAs for all training programs now explicitly encourage providers to recruit participants from underrepresented groups, including individuals from racial and ethnic subgroups, individuals with disabilities, individuals working in smaller or less well-known institutions, individuals in MSIs, individuals who are first-generation college students, and individuals with nontraditional professional pathways into education research. Specific data on the characteristics of participants in the training programs have become available only recently and make clear that participation of individuals from underrepresented groups in the full array of NCER and NCSER training opportunities is limited (IES, 2021). Thus, intentional efforts to broaden participation are warranted and would constitute a substantive improvement for both centers.

Regarding innovation, a hallmark of NCER and NCSER's training programs is their capacity to evolve to respond to needs in education research and education practice. For example, although ESRA charges IES with disseminating scientifically valid research, growing evidence indicates that dissemination of research evidence does not always translate into the uptake and use of research evidence; practitioners and policy makers often require significant engagement with researchers, knowledge brokers, and other agents to use research in a manner that changes policy, practice, and student performance (e.g., Finnigan & Daly, 2014; Coburn, Honig, & Stein, 2009). Accordingly, the most recent training programs respond to this need to improve efforts to mobilize research evidence for policy and practice. The 2019 predoctoral training grants required trainees to apprentice with an education agency or organization (e.g., school district, nonprofit education organization, or postsecondary institution) for a minimum of 1 year. The postdoctoral training grants required mentors to develop trainees' ability to "communicate their research findings effectively to researchers, education policymakers, practitioners, and the public." In 2021, a Methods Training on implementation research was awarded to prepare researchers to gain skills for studying the use of research evidence by teachers, principals, and other school administrators, and a Methods Training on research to support program and policy decisions was awarded to prepare researchers in state and local education agencies. These training programs are intended to increase the likelihood that IES-trained researchers are prepared to work in collaboration with communities and schools in ways that lead to timely, relevant, and high-quality research. Future trainings could build on these recent advances by explicitly developing the knowledge and skills needed to, for example, understand practitioner or policy maker contexts, build trusting relationships with partners, clearly establish roles and responsibilities of researchers and collaborative stakeholders, and more broadly engage in rigorous research in partnership with schools and communities.

Relatedly, innovation will be required to develop training programs that will prepare researchers to grapple with the complex themes of equity, implementation, heterogeneity, usefulness, and technology that resonate throughout this report. Both NCER and NCSER have prioritized training that supports scholars to pursue lines of inquiry to develop generalizable knowledge about "what works." Yet, data on student achievement and school success before and during the global pandemic have made it increasingly clear that access to and availability of evidence-based programs and practices are not sufficient to support student achievement for all learners. There are many barriers as well as opportunities for advancing education science in a manner responsive to practitioners, policy makers, students, and families, including issues associated with heterogeneity of intervention effects, barriers and facilitators to implementation of evidence-based practices, measurement of inequitable outcomes, development of effective intensive interventions for students with disabilities, analysis and integration of "found" data, and production of products and tools that can be used at scale to support learning. In its definition of scientifically based research standards, ESRA, Section 102(18)(vii) charges IES with "using research designs and methods appropriate to the research question posed." Accordingly, both NCER and NCSER have begun to focus on training that supports scholars to develop scientific evidence about the processes and mechanisms that underlie not just "what works," but how it works, why it works, for whom it works, and under what conditions it works. For example, in 2020, a Methods Training on selecting, implementing, and evaluating evidence-based interventions was awarded to build the capacity of researchers working in or with high-need school districts to use evidence-based interventions effectively to improve student and school outcomes.

Such pursuits of improvement and innovation should continue in earnest, as the nation will continue to face many challenges to ensuring equitable educational outcomes for all learners. ESRA charges IES with applying science to improve education and to address achievement disparities among different populations of students in specific content areas (ESRA, 2002). Scientific investigations that inform these complex problems of policy and practice will require theoretical, statistical, and methodological approaches above and beyond those already in use. Training that employs innovative approaches to quantitative, qualitative, and mixed methodologies will be needed to advance the field. Therefore, NCER and NCSER's training programs should be prepared for continued improvement and innovation.

BROADENING PARTICIPATION IN EDUCATION RESEARCH THROUGH RESEARCH TRAINING PROGRAMS

With a mission of building the nation's capacity for designing, conducting, and disseminating scientifically valid education research, IES has always been responsible for broadening participation in the field. NCER and NCSER have been critical in the institute's strategic approach to taking on this challenge. It is reasonable to suggest that the training provided by NCER and NCSER has not only changed the way that basic and applied education research are conducted, but also has changed the way that scientists are trained in the broad and interdisciplinary field of education research. This reciprocal relationship is critical for the advancement of science and for the overall health and well-being of the field of education. In the following section, we discuss practices that can both demonstrate and expand NCER and NCSER's commitment to broadening participation in education research through training programs.

Transparency in Data

As noted earlier in the chapter, IES requires that training programs make targeted efforts to recruit participants from diverse backgrounds. For the most part, however, data about the backgrounds of applicants and participants in the training programs have not been made public. Very recently, information on participants in Pathways predoctoral and postdoctoral training programs was released in a Technical Working Group summary (dated December 2, 2020) that was linked on an IES blog post (IES, 2021). This summary report noted the limited racial and ethnic diversity among predoctoral and postdoctoral trainees (75% and 74% White, respectively). The report also noted that the predoctoral training programs are becoming more diverse over time (the percentage of predoctoral fellows who are African American increased from 4 percent in 2004–2009 to 12 percent in 2014–2020). In addition, IES has organized listening sessions since the report's release to better understand how it might enhance diversity, equity, inclusion, and accessibility. The report—and the actions that have followed—makes clear that IES is increasingly attending to the need to track its training practices and the participants in its training programs. We encourage IES to prioritize the routine collection and public reporting of these data.

To better understand how current practices affect recruitment, participation, and retention in the training programs and to develop appropriate solutions to broaden participation, more detailed data on the racial, ethnic, gender, disability status, disciplinary, and institutional backgrounds of applicants and participants in the training programs must be collected and published. At present, we cannot discern whether individuals from underrepresented groups are not applying for training programs, not being accepted into training programs, or not remaining in the field over career transition points (graduation, becoming faculty members or research scientists). To identify which issues are at hand will require appropriate data and data access.

In the future, it will be necessary to develop and publicly share the criteria used to evaluate the success of each training program, and to gather and share data on these measures. These actions are needed to inform continued development of training that responds to the needs of the field and of society.

Expanding Methods Training

Addressing inequities in education requires understanding not only what educational practices, intervention, and policies "work," but also how and why they work, for whom they work, and under what conditions. Given the importance of these questions, there is a clear need for training opportunities that focus on methods to address questions of how and why educational practices, interventions, and policies work. This will require training focusing on methodological approaches appropriate to these research questions, including qualitative methods, survey research, and mixed methods. To address these "how" and "why" questions with cutting-edge tools and approaches, researchers will also need training in methods for working with new data sources and "found data," including machine learning, predictive analytics, and natural language processing. In addition, researchers will need training in the implications of these new methods for equity concerns (e.g., issues of bias detection and correction). Finally, we emphasize the need for all methods training to address connections to theory, with consideration of how methodological choices and approaches relate to the theoretical conceptions of the constructs being studied.

These strands of methodological training are important both in dedicated methods training and as part of career development programs. Emerging scholars need to gain expertise in the new and advanced methodologies that they will encounter during and after graduate study. More advanced scholars may be better equipped to take on the risk of a "career change" and lead others in the field in new directions. Thus, training in these methodological approaches needs to be offered, both in methods training opportunities for early and mid-career scholars, and in undergraduate, predoctoral, postdoctoral, and career-development training programs.

Finally, the number of methods training opportunities needs to be increased. There is intense demand for such training opportunities, and the committee anticipates that demand will continue to grow. If demand for spaces in methods training workshops continues to outstrip supply, it is also important to consider how to allocate spaces to interested individuals, with attention to the implications of such decisions for equity concerns.

Additional Strategies for Broadening Participation

Some current training programs are effectively broadening participation, most notably the Pathways to Education Sciences programs and the Early Career Mentoring Program for Faculty at MSIs. These programs must be continued with increased funding. Building on these strengths, IES can implement additional strategies to further broaden participation in its training programs and in the field as a whole.

First, IES can develop new training mechanisms to provide opportunities for individuals who do not have access to training programs within the current structure. One such mechanism would be *supplements for existing research grants* that could create training opportunities for individuals at institutions that do not have organized training programs but that do have IES-funded principal investigators (PIs). For example, supplements could support undergraduates' participation in research grants (similar to the National Science Foundation Research Experience for Undergraduates supplement program) or could support graduate students' and postdocs' participation in research grants (similar to National Institutes of Health ([NIH] Minority Supplements). Another mechanism would be *short-term research opportunity programs for undergraduate students,* such as summer internships or formal training programs like the national McNair Scholars Program or the Big Ten's Summer Research Opportunities Programs. Such programs would provide career and talent/skill development opportunities to a different set of undergraduates than the current Pathways programs, which are longer term and more geographically limited. Summer internship programs frequently draw students from undergraduate institutions or regional universities that are not research intensive and that might not be able to support Pathways programs. Summer internship programs could also provide research opportunities for practicing teachers who wish to consider working in education research.

Several other changes can lead to shifts in who is served by existing career-development training programs. Toward this end, IES could consider implementing competitive priorities to incentivize broadened participation for existing training programs. IES could institute competitive priorities for institutions underrepresented within the training grant portfolio (e.g., MSIs, Hispanic-Serving Institutions, Historically Black Colleges and Universities [HBCUs]); for programs that graduate a high percentage of individuals from underrepresented groups; for predoctoral programs that recruit scholars from the IES Pathways Programs; or for programs that include doctoral training in understudied or priority areas of education research.

It is also important to set increased expectations for continued funding for training programs at institutions that have previously received training grants. Training grants serve to enhance infrastructure and improve capacity; therefore, institutions that have received funding multiple times should be in a better position to take on greater responsibility for broadening participation. IES could encourage this greater responsibility, for example, by requiring institutions to implement practices to yield a greater percentage of participants from underrepresented groups admitted, retained, and successfully launched in education research careers postgraduation. Institutions that hold training programs could also be required, in subsequent applications, to partner with MSIs and HBCUs, to include faculty at MSIs and HBCUs as co-PIs or multiple PIs, to offer training programs at both campuses, or to establish extended in-person and/or remote research apprenticeship opportunities in MSIs and HBCUs.

The committee also recommends supporting engagement and interaction of scholars across different career stages—in a sense, creating "intergenerational" learning ecologies in which scholars can work together to learn new skills and to build broader and deeper networks. IES currently encourages interactions between predoctoral training programs and Pathways undergraduate training programs, for example, by asking applicants for training sites to formally describe their plans for such interactions. This practice could be continued and expanded. More broadly, career-development training programs can build in opportunities for trainees to engage with scholars at different career stages, as these opportunities may open new possibilities for trainees to receive mentoring or to gain skills via research site visits, "shadowing" opportunities, or research apprenticeships. These strategies focus not only on getting people into the field, but also on retaining them as they transition from undergraduate and graduate study into research careers in academic and nonacademic organizations.[2] By leveraging their training programs for researchers at different career stages, NCER and NCSER would be well positioned to promote sustained career development and thereby support retention of education researchers (Byrd & Mason, 2021).

---

[2] Education faces a shortage of well-trained research-active doctoral graduates. Though education produces more doctorates than all other fields combined, less than 10 percent of education doctoral recipients pursue research careers (Hedges & Jones, 2012). This faculty shortage is especially pronounced in the field of special education (Smith & Montrosse, 2012; Smith et al., 2011), which experiences substantial yearly losses of faculty to retirement and especially high attrition from doctoral training programs (Robb, Moody, & Abdel-Ghany, 2012). The shortage of special education faculty has cascading effects on the persistent shortages of special education teachers (Smith et al., 2011).

IES might also consider other avenues to broaden access to its training programs, particularly its methods training for education researchers. The methods training programs have proven to be highly desirable (as evidenced by the large number of participants annually). IES could elect to provide online access to these training materials, or coaching and/or technical assistance could be delivered remotely. IES might also consider approaches that would give faculty guidance on how to better navigate the grant proposal process, particularly for early career scholars who may not have mentors who had previously submitted IES proposals. For example, potential grantees might be able to observe panel discussions to better understand how proposals are reviewed. Or, successful grant applications could be made available (after sufficient time has passed) to give potential grantees models from which to learn.

Finally, another critical means to broaden participation in education research is to provide targeted funding for topics that scholars from underrepresented groups are interested in addressing. Some recent research (e.g., Hoppe et al., 2019) focusing on research portfolios at NIH has suggested that some of the challenges NIH faces in creating a diverse pipeline of scholars is that the agency has not tended to prioritize issues or research topics that are of interest to diverse scholars or the populations they serve. The same may be true for IES, although evidence is not yet available to discern if there is a mismatch between education researchers and IES's funding priorities. Therefore, IES may consider broadening the focus of its research portfolio to prioritize such topics, including those topics highlighted in Chapter 5 of this report. This broadening of focus will also require diversifying the reviewer pool and training reviewers to evaluate proposals to study these priorities appropriately.

RECOMMENDATIONS

IES's training programs are a vital and important component of its efforts to strengthen the education research field, and it is imperative that these programs continue to be offered. Indeed, the committee heard overwhelming testimony regarding both the popularity and utility of the existing programming. The committee encourages IES to systematically document the success of these programs and to expand them.

RECOMMENDATION 7.1:
IES should develop indicators of success for training, collect them from programs, and then make the information publicly available. IES should report the data it already collects on the success of programs and the pathways of trainees post-training.

RECOMMENDATION 7.2:
IES should build on its current strengths in methods training and expand in the following areas:
- Methods to address questions of how and why policies and practices work
- Methods that use machine learning, predictive analytics, natural language processing, administrative data, and other like methods

To fully meet the needs of the field as outlined in ESRA, IES has a responsibility to ensure that its training programming is reaching populations of scholars and researchers who need it most. As the committee notes in this report, this is an important issue of equity in the education research community. In addition, there is tangible value in ensuring that the field of education research is diverse insofar as it improves the overall quality of eventual research, increases the likelihood that issues of equity will be taken up in research, and supports the ultimate identity building of future researchers.

RECOMMENDATION 7.3:
IES should collect and publish information on the racial, ethnic, gender, disability status, disciplinary, and institutional backgrounds (types of institutions including Historically Black Colleges and Universities and Minority-Serving Institutions) of applicants and participants in training at both the individual and institutional levels.

RECOMMENDATION 7.4:
IES should implement a range of strategies to broaden participation in its training programs to achieve greater diversity in the racial, ethnic, and institutional backgrounds of participants. These strategies could include
- Implementing targeted outreach to underrepresented institution types
- Supporting early career mentoring
- Requiring that training program applications clearly articulate a plan for inclusive programming and equitable participation
- Offering supplements to existing research grants to support participation of individuals from underrepresented groups
- Funding short-term research opportunities for undergraduate and graduate students

REFERENCES

Byrd, C., and Mason, R. (2021). *Academic Pipeline Programs: Diversifying Pathways from the Bachelor's to the Professoriate.* Amherst, MA: Lever Press. https://doi.org/10.3998/mpub.12216775.

Coburn, C.E., Honig, M.I., and Stein, M.K. (2009). What's the evidence on districts' use of evidence? In J.D. Bransford, D.J. Stipek, N.J. Vye, L.M. Gomez, and D. Lam (Eds.), *The Role of Research in Educational Improvement* (pp. 67–86). Cambridge, MA: Harvard Education Press.

Education Sciences Reform Act (ESRA). (2002). Title I of P.L. 107-279.

Finnigan, K.S., and Daly, A.J. (Eds.). (2014). *Using Research Evidence in Education: From the Schoolhouse Door to Capitol Hill.* Cham, Switzerland: Springer.

Hedges, L., and Jones, N. (2012). Research infrastructure for improving urban education. In W.F. Tate (Ed.), *Research on Schools, Neighborhoods, and Communities: Toward Civic Responsibility* (pp. 481–504). Lanham, MD: Rowan and Littlefield.

Hoppe, T., Litovitz, A., Willis, K.A., Meseroll, R.A., Perkins, M.J., Hutchins, B.I., Davis, A.F., Lauer, M.S., Valantine, H.A., Anderson, J.M., and Santangelo, G.M. (2019). Topic choice contributes to the lower rate of NIH awards to African-American/Black scientists. *Science Advances, 5.*

Hough, H.J., Myung, J., Domingue, B.W., Edley, C., Kurlaender, M., Marsh, J., and Rios-Aguilar, C. (2021). *The impact of the COVID-19 pandemic on students and educational systems, critical actions for recovery, and the role of research in the years ahead.* [Commissioned Paper].

Institute of Education Sciences (IES). (2021). Updates on Research Center Efforts to Increase Diversity, Equity, Inclusion, and Accessibility. IES Blog, September 16. https://ies.ed.gov/blogs/research/post/updates-on-research-center-efforts-to-increase-diversity-equity-inclusion-and-accessibility.

Robb, C.A., Moody, B., and Abdel-Ghany, M. (2012). College student persistence to degree: The burden of debt. *Journal of College Student Retention 13*(4), 431–456.

Schneider, M. (2021). If it wasn't for bad news, would there be any news at all? IES Blog, May 26. https://ies.ed.gov/director/remarks/5-26-2021.asp.

Smith, D.D., and Montrosse, B.E. (2012). Special education doctoral programs: A 10-year comparison of the suppliers of leadership personnel. *Teacher Education and Special Education, 35*(2), 101–113. https://doi.org/10.1177/0888406412444455.

Smith, D.D., Young, C., Montrosse, B., Tyler, N.C., and Robb, S.M. (2011, October). The Impending Shortage of Special Education Faculty: A Summary. Claremont, CA: Claremont Graduate University. www.cgu.edu/sefna.

8

Application and Review Process

While previous chapters focus on the content of grants funded by the National Center for Education Research (NCER) and the National Center for Special Education Research (NCSER), in this chapter we focus on the application and review process through which these grants are awarded. Understanding and making recommendations related to this process responds to the second element of the committee's charge.

OVERVIEW OF THE APPLICATION AND REVIEW PROCESS

Each year, NCER and NCSER oversee multiple grant competitions. In 2021, NCER and NCSER awarded more than 147 research grants to universities, research firms, developers, and other organizations. This total included grants focused on each of the five project types (Chapter 4) and a myriad of topics (Chapter 5), as well as those focused on research methodology (Chapter 6) and training (Chapter 7). The overall funding for FY2021 was roughly on par with that of 2020, although less than 2010. The total planned funding commitment for grants initially awarded in FY2021 was $226,469,425 in NCER and $79,314,071 in NCSER. Figure 8-1 indicates the total funding for NCER and NCSER for grants that were categorized as Exploration, Development & Innovation, Efficacy, Replication/Effectiveness, or Measurement from 2002 to 2020.

172

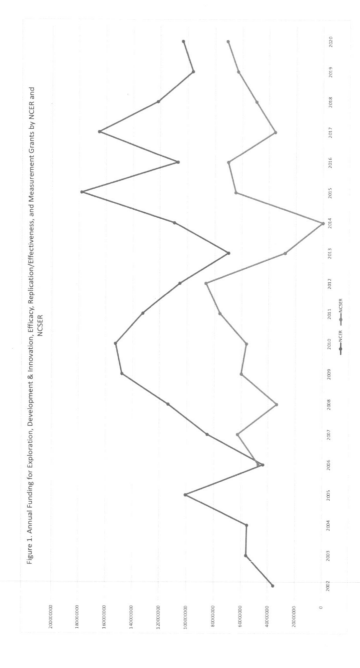

Figure 1. Annual Funding for Exploration, Development & Innovation, Efficacy, Replication/Effectiveness, and Measurement Grants by NCER and NCSER

FIGURE 8-1 Annual awards for NCER and NCSER, 2002–2020, for grants categorized as Exploration, Development & Innovation, Efficacy, Replication/Effectiveness, or Measurement.

SOURCE: Klager & Tipton, 2021 [Commissioned Paper]. Data from https://ies.ed.gov/funding/grantsearch/.

The annual grant process[1] for the main NCER and NCSER Education and Special Education Research competitions begins with a Notice Inviting Application (NIA) published each year in the Federal Register, along with an accompanying request for applications (RFA) published on the Institute of Education Sciences (IES) website. The NIAs and RFAs for many—but not all—of the research and research training competitions are typically released, advertised, and promoted in spring (~ April–June) of each year, leading to grant submissions in late summer/early fall (~ August–September). Additional reviewers for relevant panels are recruited beginning in the summer, applications are released to reviewers for initial conflict of interest identification in November, and applications are assigned to primary reviewers for initial reviews in December. IES maintains some standing review panels with some principal members who continue on each year. The Office of Science also recruits new principal and rotating members for those panels. The Office of Science also recruits reviewers for single-session panels that are newly constituted panels for one-off or irregularly run competitions.

Panels meet in mid-winter (~ February) and final decisions regarding funding are made in mid-spring of the following year (~ April–May). Applicants to the main competitions receive scores from the review panels about a week after the panel meetings end, and summary statements (narrative reviews and discussion summaries) about a month after the panel meetings. If selected for funding, a first disbursement usually occurs in late summer at the earliest, over a full year after the grant application was submitted. There are also smaller competitions that are run at different times and with different time frames that have much shorter turn-around times.

This research grant cycle thus includes three major activities for IES staff: the generation of the NIA and RFA (primarily the responsibility of NCER and NCSER, with input from the IES Director and the Office of Science); the application receipt, processing, and peer-review process (primarily the responsibility of the Office of Science with input from NCER and NCSER); and the funding decisions and obligation of new awards (primarily the responsibility of NCER and NCSER with IES Grants Administration staff).

In this chapter, we discuss the role and function of each purpose of the review process. We then turn to a discussion of three areas where the committee believes the current structure and organization of the review process

---

[1]The committee notes that this grant competition schedule represents a typical schedule for the main Education Research and Special Education Research grants. NCER and NCSER regularly run several other competitions that are competed on different time schedules. In FY2021, the Research Centers ran a total of eight grant competitions.

presents challenges to meeting NCER and NCSER's overarching goals, offering insight into how IES might consider each of these issues.

Elements and Functions of the Application and Review Process

The research community interprets IES's mission and values primarily through the application and review process. Indeed, the application and review process is the primary way that IES is able to convey its understanding of what research the field needs to improve outcomes for students and educators. By identifying a set of topic areas and requirements for what high-quality research looks like, the application and review process is a codex for a field looking to understand IES's priorities for research. Within those priorities, it is up to the applicants to determine the specific focus of their research. In this section, we discuss the purpose and functions of the three elements of the application and review process at IES: the request for applications (the RFA), panels and reviewers, and the review and scoring process.

RFAs

In FY2022, RFAs allowed grant proposals for NCER's Education Research Grants competition to include up to 22 pages of a narrative that included four required sections: Significance, Research Plan, Personnel, and Resources. The committee heard testimony that this length exceeds those allowed by other agencies, including the National Science Foundation (NSF) (maximum of 15 pages) and National Institutes of Health (NIH) (maximum of 12 pages). While some speakers urged the committee to recommend that IES adopt shorter proposal lengths, committee members were concerned that this might limit the level of detail in IES proposals that reviewers need to judge the proposals, especially in light of the committee's call for basing the significance of the research in the needs of the field as well as in disciplinary knowledge. In addition to this narrative, applications can include several required and/or optional appendixes on topics such as dissemination history (required), responses to reviewers (required for resubmissions), charts and figures, letters of agreement, and budget. In total, a grant proposal can thus include nearly 100 pages of material.

According to the committee's review, requirements found in the RFAs are more explicit than those provided by other funders, with clear directions for each section, as well as suggestions for the kinds of content that have been included in past successful applications. The committee carefully reviewed a range of RFAs from both NCER and NCSER over time: in addition to hearing testimony from IES staff and other speakers, the committee reviewed multiple iterations of the document itself, searching for places where the document was either unclear or redundant. Ultimately, the committee found that the explicit nature of the RFA's directions is one of the strengths of the IES grant review system, even if it precludes a shorter proposal. The requirements articulated throughout the document scaffold a complex process even for first-time applicants who might be working in institutions without strong, centralized support for grant submission. The committee was particularly impressed by the document's attention to detailed recommendations for strong proposals. For example, suggestions for Initial Efficacy studies include clear and explicit guidance regarding what should be reported regarding statistical power analyses (e.g., effect size selected).

Panels and Reviewers

Following the completion and submission of an application, each grant application that is responsive to and compliant with the requirements of the RFA to which the application was submitted is assigned to a specific review panel. The Standards and Review staff within the Office of Science at IES manages the entirety of the scientific peer-review process for NCER and NCSER's grant competitions. In order to ensure the integrity of the review process, and allow the program officers to provide intensive technical assistance to applicants, the Standards and Review team is completely independent from NCER and NCSER. A contractor provides support to IES and coordinates many aspects of the logistics of the review process, as well as maintains and enhances the online peer-review system. Standards and Review staff are responsible for all of the substantive activities related to peer review. Among other things, they "determine the number and type of review panels needed, select and recruit peer reviewers, assign grant applications to the appropriate review panels, [and] assign primary reviewers to each application" (IES, 2021a). Thus, at the same time that NCER and NCSER staff are working to develop RFAs, encourage applications, and provide technical assistance to applicants, the Standards and Review staff is working to complete recruitment of reviewers. The majority of these are standing panels that currently include a commitment of 5 years from the principal members of the panels (although the panels also include rotating members who serve for a particular session, and ad hoc reviewers who provide specialized expertise and review a small number of applications). Additional single-session panels also occur when necessary. Depending upon the number of applications received, each standing panel might need one or more sections, each with approximately 15 members, including both experts in the topic area(s) itself as well as experts in measurement and methods (research design, data analysis, cost analysis) in education research. For reviewers, this commitment includes serving as the primary reviewer on up to eight proposals, as well as reading and discussing *all* of the proposals that are forwarded after the triage process to the full panel for discussion and final scoring for the panel (between 10 and 20 typically).

Review Process and Scoring

The Office of Science oversees the review process. Prior to beginning the process, reviewers are provided with a variety of instructional materials to guide them through the premeeting, meeting, and postmeeting review process. Currently, the reviewer materials include an IES Guide for Grant Peer Review Panel Members, and a set of Review Notes with information specific to each panel or group of panels. In addition, the Office of Science now provides a set of three videos that explain what happens to an application after it is submitted, what the responsibilities are of an IES peer reviewer, and what panel meetings are like (including a mock panel meeting). Panel chairs are provided with the materials described above, as well as with a Panel Chair Supplement to the IES Guide for Grant Peer Review Panel Members. Before the panels meet, reviewers provide detailed feedback and scores (1–7, with 7 = Excellent) related to each of the review criteria specified in the relevant RFA, as well as an overall rating (1.0–5.0, with 1.0–1.5 = Outstanding). Based upon these initial primary reviews, the Standards and Review team "conduct[s] discrepancy analyses of initial rating scores, [and] conduct[s] the triage of applications to be considered by the full panel" (IES, 2021a). Applications above a given cut-score are then discussed by the full panel. For each application considered by the full panel, this includes a brief presentation by the primary reviewers (usually two to four reviewers per proposal), followed by a discussion by the full panel, panel discussion summary, reconsideration of initial scores by the primary reviewers, and final scoring by each panel member on both individual criterion (1–7, with 7 = Excellent) and overall (1.0–5.0, with 1.0–1.5 = Outstanding) scores. Importantly, each application is required to be reviewed on its own merits, relative to the expectations in the RFA, not in relation to other applications discussed. Given available funds, applications in the Outstanding and Excellent range, which generally corresponds to an average overall score of 2.0 or better, are considered for funding.

As noted above, this RFA and review process ensures that research funded through NCER and NCSER serves to advance the mission of promoting the development and evaluation of interventions to improve educational outcomes for students. Evidence of IES's success in using the RFA and review process toward these ends can be seen in a few ways. First, IES has iteratively improved the quality of causal studies funded by shifting its RFA requirements such that successful proposals reflect contemporary understandings around rigorous design. For example, requirements regarding assumptions and sensitivity testing for quasi-experiments, as well as sample size and statistical power requirements for randomized experiments, were not originally included in IES's first round of RFAs, but were added in later in order to incentivize higher-quality studies. Similarly, the requirements addressing concerns regarding the ultimate usefulness of research to practice were added over time, including requirements for addressing issues of generalizability and sample recruitment, data sharing, and most recently, inclusion of a dissemination plan. The committee thought that this use of the RFA for promoting best practices was a strength of NCER and NCSER.

Finally, throughout this process, IES has established procedures to ensure that the system is fair and objective. This can be seen in the explicit criteria in the RFAs, the separation of proposals and review by the SRO, the inclusion of a thorough conflict-of-interest process, and the focus on review conducted entirely by a panel of experts. Akin to NIH but unlike NSF, IES program officers have no role in the review process, other than to encourage applicants and provide guidance on the RFAs. Thus, the determination for funding arises only in relation to the final proposal score and the cut-score for that particular year. The committee found that these steps to ensure the independence of the enterprise are a considerable strength of the current system.

ISSUES WITH THE CURRENT
APPLICATION AND REVIEW PROCESS

As noted above, the annual process has served IES well in that it is predictable, investigators have ample information to write their proposals, and the procedures to score proposals and award funding provide all stakeholders with a common framework for assessing a study's potential for funding. Despite these strengths, the committee's assessment of the current application and review process revealed three issues that if addressed, may allow IES to build on its current strengths toward funding even stronger and more useful research: (1) IES does not consistently share demographic information on its applicants, reviewers, and grantees with the public, making it impossible to track whether the application and review process is resulting in an equitable distribution of awards and, if not, where in the process disparities are introduced; (2) the current procedures undermine IES's ability to be timely and responsive to the needs of the education research community; and (3) the current procedures do not allow for sufficient understanding of how well-proposed research addresses the needs of the field. We review these challenges in the section below, describing how current regulations or procedures may inadvertently create barriers to funding the best possible research proposals.

Data on Applicants, Reviewers, and Grantees

As with all aspects of its charge, the committee formulated its considerations around how well the current application and review process functions in the context of the crosscutting themes identified at the beginning of this report (see Chapter 1). In light of these themes, one of the first questions the committee asked was how equitable the review process is in terms of those who applied for and were ultimately funded. This issue is particularly important to the committee given President Biden's Executive Order, which asks agencies to assess "potential barriers that underserved communities and individuals may face to enrollment in and access to benefits and services in Federal programs" (Executive Order 13985, 2021). In order to better understand the implications of this order for funders, the committee heard testimony from IES staff, as well as from representatives from NSF and NIH.

The committee was surprised to find that in comparison to both NSF and NIH, IES reports very little data on equity. The most common source of data available is on *institutions* that receive IES grants. Tables 8-1 (NCER) and 8-2 (NCSER) provide overall funding (across years 2002–2020) by project type, and, within project type, by institution type.[2] These tables are inclusive of all NCER and NCSER grantmaking, including research centers, training, and research grants, but exclude funding for Small Business Innovation Research grants. These data indicate that overall, approximately 7 percent of NCER and 8 percent of NCSER grants have been held by Minority-Serving Institutions (MSIs); relative to other project types, MSIs were more likely to hold Exploration grants than any other type. By and large, most grants have been held by Carnegie-classified Research 1[3] universities (68% NCER, 72% NCSER).

IES collects and reports considerably less information on *applicants*. A recent IES blog post reported voluntarily submitted demographic information for the principal investigators (PIs) on applications submitted to the FY2021 competitions (IES, 2021b). Across NCER and NCSER, 59 percent of PIs who received funding were female (compared to 62% of applicants; 82% response rate). Only 13 percent of awardees were non-White or multi-racial (compared to 22% of applicants; response rate 75%). Similarly, 3 percent of awardees were Hispanic (compared to 5% of applicants;

---

[2] Although NCSER was not founded until 2006, Table 8-2 includes nine grants that were initially awarded at the Office of Special Education Programs but ultimately inherited by NCSER at its inception. The trends in these data do not qualitatively change when these nine grants are excluded from analyses. Given that NCSER includes these data in their list of funded research, the committee elects to include these grants as part of NCSER's portfolio.

[3] Research 1 universities may also be Minority-Serving Institutions, and so may be counted in both groups cited here.

response rate 72%). Finally, 4 percent of awardees identified as having a disability (compared to 3% of applicants; response rate 70%). As written in the blog post, "These data underscore the need for IES to continue to broaden and diversify the education research pipeline, including institutions and researchers, and better support the needs of underrepresented researchers in the education community" (IES, 2021b). Moreover, these data only represent a single year in the life of IES, leaving the committee unable to assess whether the state of information above is typical, or if the situation is improving or declining.

Finally it is important to highlight that while there are very limited data on applicants and awardees, to date there is *zero* publicly available information regarding the demographic background of members of review panels.

While there is very little information available regarding equity in the Application and Review process, the available data surface significant challenges. Clearly, both non-White and Hispanic researchers are less likely to submit applications (22% and 5%, respectively). Even when they do submit applications, they are less likely to receive funding (13% and 4%, respectively).

Review Panels

Available research suggests that that there are reasons to attend to the composition of review panels that extend above and beyond the rationales for attending to equity noted in the section above. There is much to learn about the role that multiple perspectives in the review process can play in supporting high-quality research, as the current literature on diversity in review panels[4] has come to suggest.[5] For example, Langfeldt and colleagues (2020) found that review panels with scholars from multiple disciplinary backgrounds and approaches more frequently supported diverse forms of research by extending definitions of quality beyond disciplinary norms. In contrast, Huutoniemi (2012) found that panels of researchers from similar backgrounds competed to establish their expertise and authority using narrow criteria to advance specific fields. Diverse groups, in terms of race, ethnicity, and research background, are less likely to fall prey to "groupthink," encouraging debate to counteract preformed preferences and biases (Esarey, 2017; Laudel, 2006; Antonio et al., 2004). Considering more diverse criteria of evaluation has been advocated to support innovative and risk-taking research (Azoulay and Li, 2020; Hofstra et al., 2020; Valantine

---

[4]This section draws on findings synthesized for the committee by Zilberstein (2021).

[5]The committee recognizes that attending to racial and disciplinary diversity in review panels in and of itself does not guarantee an equitable review process. Given the evidence about the importance of racial and disciplinary diversity in supporting high-quality research, we argue that this particular dimension of equity is of critical import.

TABLE 8-1 Average Proportion of NCER Funding by Project Type and Institution Type, 2002–2020[1]

Table 4. Proportion of funding by grant category and institution type - NCER

Grants	Exploration & Innovation	Development	Efficacy	Replication / Effectiveness	Measurement	Methods	RPP	Training	Other	All Grants
Grants	236	369	236	134	121	93	61	114	90	1454
Funding (Millions of $)	251.1	508.9	628.1	409.3	184.0	60.8	24.3	256.5	515.8	2838.9
University	86%	82%	66%	70%	84%	70%	69%	100%	74%	77%
MSI (vs Non-MSI)	13%	7%	3%	5%	9%	5%	2%	3%	11%	7%
R1 (vs Non-R1)	80%	68%	54%	60%	73%	59%	61%	97%	73%	68%
Private (vs Public)	24%	24%	23%	18%	19%	36%	20%	51%	25%	26%
Research Firm	12%	9%	26%	28%	13%	30%	21%	0%	21%	18%
Developer	1%	6%	5%	0%	3%	0%	3%	0%	4%	3%
Other	0%	3%	3%	2%	1%	0%	7%	0%	1%	2%

SOURCE: Klager & Tipton, 2021 [Commissioned Paper]. Data from https://ies.ed.gov/funding/grantsearch/.

[1] As discussed in Chapter 4 and in the Klager and Tipton (2021) paper, the categories identified here are delineated by project type and not grant-making program. For this reason, the RPP column only includes grants with the RPP project type specifically identified, and therefore does not include the entire suite of partnership investments.

TABLE 8-2 Average Proportion of NCSER Funding by Project Type and Institution, 2002–2020

Table 5. Proportion of funding by grant category and institution type - NCSER

Grants	Development			Replication /			Training	Other	All Grants
	Exploration & Innovation	Development	Efficacy	Effectiveness	Measurement				
Grants	54	191	70	56	55		48	33	507
Funding (Millions of $)	53.4	271.8	216.0	178.3	85.8		26.2	124.5	956.1
University	90%	94%	92%	80%	81%		100%	93%	90%
MSI (vs Non-MSI)	13%	12%	6%	3%	5%		13%	10%	8%
R1 (vs Non-R1)	76%	71%	76%	65%	65%		81%	76%	72%
Private (vs Public)	17%	12%	14%	20%	13%		12%	22%	16%
Research Firm	9%	2%	3%	19%	17%		0%	7%	8%
Developer	0%	3%	2%	0%	0%		0%	0%	1%
Other	1%	1%	3%	1%	1%		0%	0%	1%

SOURCE: Klager & Tipton, 2021 [Commissioned Paper]. Data from https://ies.ed.gov/funding/grantsearch/.

and Collins, 2015; Dezsö and Ross, 2012). Also notably, a lack of racially diverse reviewers perpetuates in-group bias and favoritism for the status quo, continually disadvantaging researchers from underrepresented groups whose research commonly lies outside of reviewers' areas of expertise (Hayden, 2015).

From their personal experiences, committee members noted IES review panels often include a range of disciplines, with panels typically including those in both the NCER and NCSER communities, researchers in multiple disciplines that pertain to the panel, and experts in methods and measurement. At the same time—in the committee members' experiences—most of the review panels were composed of researchers who had at some point been funded by IES. When considering this observation in concert with IES's reported data that the majority of awardees are White, it stands to reason that current review panels may not be able to access the benefits associated with racially diverse groups.

Given the role that both racial and disciplinary diversity on review panels can play in supporting high-quality research, the committee notes the importance of ensuring that review panels are, in fact, representative of multiple perspectives. In this case, a lack of consistently reported information has undermined the committee's ability to assess the degree to which IES has attended to these issues in its application and review process.

Timely and Responsive Application Cycles

The NCER and NCSER application and review processes takes, on average, 8–10 months from the time that a grant application is submitted until it is ultimately funded. Committee member experience (as reviewers and applicants) suggests that most grant proposals are not funded in their first submission but may take two or three submissions before ultimately being funded, resulting in a total process of as much as 3 years. While this timeline offers benefits in terms of both feasibility (for IES) and refinement of the proposal and research plan, it can impede the ability of researchers to be responsive to on-the-ground concerns of practitioners and decision makers in schools. Programs and interventions tend to move quickly within school districts, and it is likely that many programs that were ripe for research have been understudied due to the lack of federal funding at the crucial moment in time.

This timeline impacts proposals in that it makes it difficult to develop and maintain true partnerships with schools and districts. Currently, applications require letters of support from school district personnel indicating a commitment to take part in the study. However, school district superintendents and school leaders often move schools and school districts, as do teachers. From the researcher standpoint, the lengthy timeline means that the schools recruited for the first application may ultimately not be available for the second application, resulting in them investing less heavily in the partnership than they may otherwise. From the school district position, this means that most researchers who contact them are unlikely to lead to productive partnerships in a timeframe that matters to them or, even worse, valuable time invested into partnership building may be wasted. Finally, in the committee's experience, letters of support do not necessarily articulate a warrant for conducting research on a given topic in a given location, as support for conducting research is not always equivalent to identifying a rationale for why something is important. It is the committee's judgment that the current letters of support mechanism is not ideally suited toward guaranteeing participation or identifying the significance of proposed research.

Coherence with the Needs of the Field

The committee reviewed the current application and review process with an eye toward whether or not the process resulted in research that is ultimately useful to the field. In considering these questions, the committee noted a set of critical junctures wherein the current procedures do not allow for sufficient information to assess the significance of individual proposals and the extent to which proposals, if funded, are likely to serve the needs of the education community. In this section, we delineate several places in the application and review process where we see this problem emerge.

Reviewer Preparation and Scoring

Reviewers are encouraged to engage with a series of preparatory materials in advance of their review process. Reviewers are instructed to carefully read the RFA and evaluate applications based on the stipulations of the most current RFA text. Additional materials are provided to panel chairs who meet with the Office of Science prior to the panel meeting; however, it is the experience of members of this committee that chairs of review panels are left to their own discretion to lead and facilitate the conversation around individual applications. In addition, Office of Science staff attend and monitor the panel meetings to address questions or issues that arise, and to ensure that review criteria are appropriately applied. Reviewers are asked to draw upon their own expertise when evaluating how well applications respond to each aspect of the RFA.

Although the committee does not dispute the substantial expertise that each reviewer brings to the process, we note the absence of any kind of directive or orienting material that allows reviewers to gauge the significance of a proposal against expressed research priorities or notable needs in the field. Further, reviewers are also explicitly advised against attempting to build a complementary group of studies among those that they review and are asked instead to consider each study on its own individual merits. As a result, it is challenging for review panels to track whether a set of funded proposals coherently maps onto the needs of the field. This question, important as it is, is simply not structured into the review process.

Specific to scoring, the committee notes that after a proposal is discussed by the panel, the proposal's original reviewers are able to change their holistic scores for the proposal and then every panel member submits a score. As noted earlier in this chapter, these scores are between 1 and 7 to the tenth of a point. The committee notes that, in our experience, there is no real anchor for this scoring and that different reviewers may conceive of the meaning of scores differently; for example, the difference between a 1.9 and 2.1 is likely measurement error, not a precise difference. In the absence of clear and meaningful anchors for judgment, reviewers in different panels may be harsher or more lenient than others and, over the review panel meeting period, there may be drift in these scores.

Furthermore, the committee notes that while the scoring scale is continuous, it is understood by committee members who have participated in this process that a review score below 2.0 is typically considered "fundable" and a score above 2.0 is not, as noted earlier in this chapter. As a result, a repeated concern is that it is likely that reviewers are not simply providing a scale score of "merit" when providing an overall summary, but also a "vote" regarding whether they think the grant should be funded. It is thus possible to bias the merit review process by providing slightly lower scores (just below 2.0) for grants that reviewers prefer, or slightly higher scores (just above 2.0) for grants they do not, thus making it possible for reviewers to "game" the system in ways that may result in bias and inequities. The committee discussed these concerns at length, but observed that a comprehensive understanding of potential problems in this arena would require deeper analyses of data on applicants.

RFA: Significance

Applications submitted to NCER and NCSER typically include four parts: Significance, Research Plan, Personnel, and Resources. In the FY2022 Education Research Grants RFA (IES RFA, 2022), guidance for strong applications indicates that the Significance section should include a description of "how the factors you propose to study are under the control of education agencies" [Exploration], why the intervention would "be an improvement over what already exists" [Development], a description of the "population of learners and educators intended to benefit from this intervention" [Development], and "the learners who should benefit ... from this intervention" [Initial Efficacy]. The full RFA document contains additional relevant guidance intended to support strong applications.

While each of these suggestions encourages researchers to consider how their particular intervention or study might connect to improving practice, it does not ask them to provide rationale that the problem the intervention is attempting to address is one in need of additional research. That is, it is possible that there are problems and opportunities that education decision makers face that need research (that would clearly be "significant") and yet there are no studies conducted in this area (see Chapter 5 for our discussion about how current constraints impede the study of certain topics). At the same time, there may be many studies (each significant in a more narrow sense) on a single topic or intervention. Although the suggestions included in the RFA are intended to assist applicants in considering the current research landscape around a particular problem, they ultimately serve to direct applicants away from locating the value of their work inside the existing needs of educators and education stakeholders. Across many proposals and studies, the result of this framing is that it puts the interests of researchers above the needs of the field.

RFA: Dissemination

The Education Research Grant RFA includes a requirement that researchers identify a plan for how they will share the results of their study upon completion. The committee recognizes that this requirement represents an attempt to ensure that funded research ultimately makes its way into the hands of "end users." However, we have identified a set of ways in which the current dissemination requirement does not actually function to ensure that funded research will be useful to education stakeholders.

As with the Significance section described above, the RFAs include relatively open-ended instructions with minimal guidance for the required dissemination plan, and no clear direction for how reviewers should evaluate the dissemination requirement. In the absence of such guidance, research teams and review panels may be applying idiosyncratic judgments of the kind of dissemination that is appropriate and effective. Committee members note from their own experience on reviews that panels vary greatly in how they approach this portion of the application.

Additionally, the committee notes that current framing of the Dissemination section suggests a largely unidirectional kind of engagement around research results: that is, researchers tell stakeholders about their findings, and then stakeholders use those findings. However, as described in Chapter 4, contemporary scholarship around knowledge mobilization problematizes this unidirectional assumption. Stakeholders need to engage with the research at multiple stages of the process to interpret, adapt, and apply it in practice. Some projects with active partnerships may be well positioned for stakeholder engagement before, during, and after conducting the research. However, relying on a post-project dissemination plan alone may perpetuate inequities in access to relevant research. Further, the committee believes it is important to consider how dissemination and engagement extend beyond those who are immediately involved in the development and production of the research.

Role of Practitioners

Finally, the committee notes that the current application and review process does not have a consistent plan or procedure for engaging the education practice community. While some educators or policy makers may participate in the review process, the voices of practice stakeholders are not regularly integrated into review. Given the proximity of these professionals to the work of education, it is possible that the review process is missing a unique opportunity to ensure the application and review process yields useful research.

The issues highlighted above, taken together, point to a process wherein reviewers lack a clear north star by which to make calibrated judgments about what proposed research will be useful to stakeholders in the field, which can result in funded research that does not sufficiently meet the needs of education stakeholders and decision makers. We conclude this chapter with a set of recommendations for how IES might address this challenge.

RECOMMENDATIONS

In this chapter, we describe the elements and functions of each component of the application and review process. Given the role of the RFA as the primary mechanism through which NCER and NCSER signal their priorities to the field, the committee was particularly concerned with how to organize the review process. As noted in this chapter, the committee concluded that the RFA is well organized and purposeful, it is intentionally oriented toward providing applicants with an equitable experience, and its directions are clear and understandable.

Despite these successes, the committee did observe a few areas in which the current organization of the application and review process sets up a series of challenges: (1) IES does not publicly share information on its applicants, reviewers, and grantees, making it impossible to track whether the application and review process is resulting an equitable distribution of awards, and if not where in the process disparities are introduced; (2) the current procedures undermine IES's ability to be timely and responsive to the needs of the educational research community; and (3) the current procedures do not allow for sufficient understanding of how well-proposed research addresses the needs of the field. In this chapter, we described how these issues may inadvertently create barriers for NCER and NCSER in funding research that meets their stated goals. It is our sincere belief that with some modification to the process, IES will be even more successful in funding research that meets the needs of the field.

In regard to the first challenge noted above (i.e., lack of consistently reported data), the committee determined that given the centrality of equity issues to the mission and purpose of IES, it is critical that IES provide the field with transparent data on not only who is funded, but also who applies for funding and who is selected to review applications. Where this demographic data reveal inequitable inputs and outcomes into the review process, IES will want to craft immediate responses, but it is impossible to know what these problems are in the absence of a regular data report. For this reason, the committee recommends that IES takes immediate action related to the reporting of data.

RECOMMENDATION 8.1:
IES should regularly collect and publish information on the racial, ethnic, gender, disciplinary, and institutional backgrounds of applicants and funded principal investigators (PIs) and co-PIs, composition of review panels, and study samples.

Specific to the second issue noted in Chapter 8—timely and responsive application cycles—the committee found evidence that the current structure of a single annual review panel is not functional for the research community in education, and a September deadline for proposals is particularly problematic given the timing of the school year.

RECOMMENDATION 8.2:
IES should review and fund grants more quickly and re-introduce two application cycles per year.

The committee agrees that attending to the third challenge described in Chapter 8—ensuring that funded research is useful to the field—will require longer and more concerted effort. For a variety of reasons described in the chapter, reviewers in the current system do not have a way to calibrate their review of application materials toward any kind of shared understanding of what the field needs. It is therefore difficult to ensure that the work is relevant to policy and practice decision makers, which leads to funded research that meets the requirements of the RFA, but is not always aligned with the needs of education more broadly.

In general, the committee thinks that attending to the larger structural issues facing NCER and NCSER (see Recommendations 4.1 and 5.1–5.5) will serve to help ensure that funded research is ultimately positioned to be useful for the practitioners and policy makers. However, the effects of implementing these recommendations may take several years to emerge, and the committee notes that the field needs useful research as soon as possible. For this reason, we offer two recommendations that may help ameliorate some of the challenges related to usefulness that the committee laid out. First, in response to the current letter of support mechanism at work in the RFA, we considered how adjusting expectations around collaboration might better serve both researchers and involved communities. Below, we recommend an alternative approach to the letter of support that we believe will better map onto the current grantmaking timeframe, and also help better ensure that funded research is warranted in the community in which it is proposed.

RECOMMENDATION 8.3:
For proposals that include collaborating with local and state education agencies, the request for applications should require that applicants explain the rationale and preliminary plan for the collaboration in lieu of the current requirement for a letter of support. Upon notification of a successful award, grantees must then provide a comprehensive partnership engagement plan and letter(s) of support in order to receive funding.

The committee also noted the current lack of a consistent plan for engaging practitioner and policy-maker perspectives in the application and review process. The committee discussed multiple ways that IES might want to leverage these communities, ranging from consistent participation on panels to separate working groups, but notes that practitioner and policy-maker communities should be involved in determining the mechanism that works best for IES. Ultimately, the committee agreed that each approach has trade-offs to consider regarding the burden placed on policy makers and practitioners, as well as the logistics of working with school schedules. Importantly, the goal of this work is for IES to define a role for these communities that is both distinct and meaningful, such that these already burdened professionals can maximize their valuable time and effort.

RECOMMENDATION 8.4:
IES should engage a working group representing the practitioner and policy-maker communities along with members of the research community to develop realistic mechanisms for incorporating practitioner and policy-maker perspectives in the review process systematically across multiple panels.

The committee also discussed possible approaches to changing the review process to take on issues with rating described in this chapter. One idea was for IES to identify a person or entity to oversee and audit panel decision making. This person could, for example, review triaged proposals—ultimately pulling proposals out of triage when there appeared to be discrepancies or errors. They might also examine the final panel scores around the cut-point (2.0) and make substantive recommendations regarding priorities for funding. The committee, however, had difficulty determining who the right person for this position might be. Some thought that the program officer could take on this role; a problem, however, is that this changes the role of program officers, opening them up to have undue influence on funding decisions. Another idea was for the panel chair to take on this role; here the concern was that this would increase reviewer burden.

The committee also spoke about the problem of the cut-point at length. Some highlighted that another solution altogether was to shift from a known cut-point to a funding percentage instead, with such funding percentage cut-offs varying across panels. A benefit of this approach, some felt, was that it took into account differences in scoring across panels and did not allow for such clear gaming. Others worried, however, that there may be real differences across panels and that some panels may have stronger proposals than others, and that such a relative score would not be fair. Overall, while the committee declined to make a recommendation on the best approach to addressing these concerns, we agree that these problems require careful consideration in the future.

REFERENCES

Antonio, A.L., Chang, M.J., Hakuta, K., Kenny, D.A., Levin, S., and Milem, J.F. (2004). Effects of racial diversity on complex thinking in college students. *Psychological Science*, 15(8), 507–510.

Azoulay, P., and Li, D. (2020). Scientific Grant Funding. Working Paper 26889. National Bureau of Economic Research. http://doi.org/10.3386/w26889.

Dezsö, C.L., and Ross, D.G. (2012). Does female representation in top management improve firm performance? A panel data investigation. *Strategic Management Journal*, 33, 1072–1089. https://doi.org/10.1002/smj.1955.

Esarey, J. (2017). Does peer review identify the best papers? A simulation study of editors, reviewers, and the scientific publication process. *PS: Political Science & Politics*, 50(4), 963–969. doi:10.1017/S1049096517001081.

Executive Order 13985, 86 FR 7009 (January 25, 2021).

Hayden, E.C. (2015). Racial bias haunts NIH grants. *Nature*, 527(19), 286–287.

Hofstra, B., Kulkarni, V.V., Munoz-Najar Galvez, S., He, B., Jurafsky, D., and McFarland, D.A. (2020). The diversity-innovation paradox in science. *Proceedings of the National Academy of Sciences of the United States of America*, 117(17), 9284–9291. https://doi.org/10.1073/pnas.1915378117.

Huutoniemi, K. (2012). Communicating and compromising on disciplinary expertise in the peer review of research proposals. *Social Studies of Science, 42*(6), 897–921. https://doi. org/10.1177/0306312712458478.

Institute of Education Sciences. (IES) (2022). Education Research Grants Program Request for Applications.

—— (2021a). Peer Review of Grant Applications. https://ies.ed.gov/director/sro/peer_review/ application_review.asp.

—— (2021b). Updates on Research Center Efforts to Increase Diversity, Equity, Inclusion, and Accessibility. IES Blog, September 16. https://ies.ed.gov/blogs/research/post/ updates-on-research-center-efforts-to-increase-diversity-equity-inclusion-and-accessibility.

Langfeldt, L., Nedeva, M., Sörlin, S., and Thomas, D.A. (2020). Co-existing notions of research quality: A framework to study context-specific understandings of good research. *Minerva, 58,* 115–137. https://doi.org/10.1007/s11024-019-09385-2.

Laudel, G. (2006). Conclave in the Tower of Babel: How peers review interdisciplinary research proposals. *Research Evaluation* 15 (1), 57–68.

Valantine, H.A., and Collins, F.S. (2015). National Institutes of Health addresses the science of diversity. *Proceedings of the National Academy of Sciences of the United States of America, 112*(40), 12240–12242. https://doi.org/10.1073/pnas.1515612112.

Zilberstein, S. (2021). *National Academies of Science and Medicine: Diversity, equity, and inclusion in peer review.* [Commissioned Paper].

9

Concluding Observations

This committee was charged with providing guidance to the Institute of Education Sciences (IES) aimed at supporting the work of its National Center for Education Research (NCER) and National Center for Special Education Research (NCSER) in the years to come. The committee focused on four primary tasks outlined in its charge: (1) to identify critical problems or issues on which new research is needed; (2) to consider how best to organize the request for applications issued by the research centers to reflect those problems/issues; (3) to explain new methods or approaches for conducting research that should be encouraged and why; and (4) to identify new and different types of research training investments that would benefit IES. To carry out its charge, the committee gathered and reviewed evidence from multiple sources, including official documents from IES and federal legislation, testimony from IES leadership, perspectives of education stakeholders, and scholarly literature. Committee members also drew on their own expertise and their knowledge of and experience with NCER and NCSER in formulating the recommendations it offers throughout this report.

The reach and impact of NCER and NCSER over the past two decades is impressive. As of 2022, there is virtually no part of the education research enterprise in the United States that is not in some way influenced by IES-funded work. Moreover, the committee recognizes that it is due in large part to the efforts of IES that education research has achieved recognition as a robust science-based field. In formulating its recommendations, the committee kept these successes in mind while also working to identify areas where NCER and NCSER can improve their processes and be responsive to changes in the education landscape that have occurred over the past 20 years. In this chapter, we summarize several high-level observations about the landscape of education research in the United States, and point to two additional recommendations to support IES's ongoing work in building an education research enterprise equipped to serve the next generation of students.

TWENTY YEARS OF IES: A CHANGED LANDSCAPE

As the committee notes in the first several chapters of this report, the field of education research has changed substantially since the founding of IES. Any survey of education research over the past 20 years could point to a myriad of areas in which knowledge in education has grown, much of which is directly tied to IES-funded research. Beginning with the No Child Left Behind Act of 2001 and furthered by policies at all levels that require use of data in decision making, the field of education now has nearly two decades of data of all kinds. This abundance of data—on students, teachers, schools, and other education settings—has expanded the kinds of questions that education researchers can ask and answer.

As a result of two decades of research, the field now better understands the ways that students are nested within cultural contexts and the way those contexts matter for students' experiences. Similarly, the field is better positioned to understand the ways that nonacademic outcomes help support students' academic outcomes. Further, the field now has a more complete understanding of the way that education in the United States is a system, signifying that change needs to occur at multiple points in the system in order to bring about desired outcomes. Perhaps most importantly, the field now has decades of concrete evidence describing the undeniable role of structural inequality and systemic racism and discrimination in shaping educational experiences and outcomes of all kinds.

Of course, U.S. education and education research has seen tremendous upheaval in the past 2 years in particular. As the nation continues to reckon with the twin pandemics of COVID-19 and systemic racism, the committee encourages NCER and NCSER to shift to ensure that funded research is responsive to the challenges of the present moment. Recognizing that racial, ethnic, and economic inequality in education have always been present, and armed with new evidence that these divides have sharpened during the pandemic, it is more important than ever that IES prioritize research that advances equity. Likewise, we recognize the importance of addressing questions regarding access and inclusion of students with disabilities to ensure their meaningful academic progress and life chances.

In addition, knowledge of how research evidence is used in education settings has grown by leaps and bounds in the 20 years since the founding of IES. As discussed throughout this report, the field now recognizes that with rare exceptions, local decision makers do not tend to identify problems of practice and then turn to peer-reviewed research to find a "vetted" intervention to solve whatever the problem may be. In reality, mobilization of knowledge from research is a dynamic, multidirectional process that relies heavily on trusted relationships among researchers, practice partners, and individuals or organizations in knowledge broker roles.

As a result, the committee is concerned that the current reliance on a model for knowledge use that expects post-facto decision making by practitioners otherwise divorced from the production of knowledge simply does not map onto the realities of knowledge use in public education. This tension has the potential to substantially limit the ultimate utility of research funded by NCER and NCSER. In its recommendations, the committee offers insight into how IES might make changes to its current programming in order to better address the reality of how knowledge is and can be used in education. Throughout this report, the committee has identified recommendations that are intended to help IES continue to produce transformative education research and maintain its status as the premier funder of education research.

When the committee stepped back to look at NCER and NCSER's work within IES, it became clear that an organizational structure that once worked to build a national infrastructure of education research now constrains the issues and methods that are likely to be studied. Over time, NCER and NCSER have attempted to address these constraints as well as the shifting needs of the field by adding new and often unique or specific funding opportunities (such as Education Research grants in Special Topics) and altering institutional policies (Schneider, 2021). As the field continues to grow as a result of NCER and NCSER's investments, the ability to address ongoing challenges by adjusting the existing structure is unlikely to meet expanding needs. The recommendations identified by this committee are aimed at helping NCER and NCSER transform its infrastructure in a coherent and cohesive way to meet the present and future needs of this field.

IES has an obligation to adapt its work so that the centers' funded research continues to meet the objectives laid out in the Education Sciences Reform Act (ESRA) of 2002. In identifying these recommendations, we are describing a vision of NCER and NCSER that is distinctly appropriate for scientific research in education, based on two decades of cumulative knowledge building. If enacted in concert with one another, these recommendations will help IES continue to fulfill the obligations laid out in its founding legislation.

ENABLING RECOMMENDATIONS

The committee's recommendations are informed by our understanding of how the five crosscutting themes identified in Chapter 1 (equity in education, technology in education, usefulness in education research, attending to implementation in education research, and heterogeneity) bear on what IES needs to change or adapt in order to meet the current and future needs of education research. Some of our recommendations can be implemented rapidly, particularly those pertaining to topics, methods, and measures for future study, whereas other recommendations may require longer consideration by IES stakeholders.

By following our recommendations, IES will set a course for a productive and impactful body of education research in the future. To fully realize the vision, however, two additional conditions, if met, will enable IES to implement the recommendations we have offered. At face value, these additional recommendations may seem to go beyond our charge, but the committee determined that for IES to respond to the recommendations that respond directly to our charge, these additional recommendations are necessary. In that sense, these recommendations, too, fall within our charge. The first is directed to IES and the second is directed to the U.S. Congress.

First, as noted throughout this report, the committee has determined that given that ESRA clearly mandates that the work of NCER and NCSER attend to pernicious and stubborn gaps in achievement between groups of students, it is essential that the centers consider how to address equity issues in all aspects of their work. Such consideration would also be consistent with President Biden's Executive Order on Advancing Racial Equity. To build a diverse and inclusive field that is well positioned to meet the most difficult challenges facing education in the United States, IES should be continuously vigilant about how its activities relate to diversity, equity, and inclusion.

RECOMMENDATION 9.1:
In addition to implementing the recommendations highlighted above, NCER and NCSER should conduct a comprehensive investigation of the funding processes to identify possible inequities. This analysis should attend to all aspects of the funding process, including application, reviewing, scoring, and monitoring progress. The resulting report should provide insight into barriers to funding across demographic groups and across research types and topics, as well as a plan for ameliorating these inequities.

Second, the committee recognizes that meaningful and lasting change within an organization cannot occur without financial support. We are keenly aware of the realities of IES's budgetary constraints and have attempted to prioritize recommendations that would re-allocate existing resources, rather than require additional funding. That said, the committee knows that in order to achieve the overarching vision presented through these recommendations, IES will require additional investments. We were dismayed to learn about the modest size of IES's budget in comparison to the budgets of other like agencies throughout the federal government. The modest size seems particularly unwarranted in light of the high degree of success IES has demonstrated in pursuit of its mission, as outlined throughout this report. The committee's assessment was amplified in three of the six public comments received throughout the process of writing this report. These public comments, representing dozens of organizations, urged us to recommend higher funding levels for IES, particularly for special education research. In light of the committee's recommendations on project types, topics, methods, training, and the application process, the need for greater funding is even more acute. The committee recognizes that in the absence of additional funding, IES will need to make a series of challenging decisions related to how it will address the recommendations identified in this report. For this reason, the committee makes the following recommendation.

RECOMMENDATION 9.2:
Congress should re-examine the IES budget, which does not appear to be on par with other scientific funding agencies nor does it have the resources to fully implement this suite of recommendations.

The committee regards NCER and NCSER, under the auspices of IES, as well positioned to realize the vision laid out in ESRA: a federal agency squarely aimed at improving the experiences of students around the country. Building on the past accomplishments of IES, the committee offers this report as a series of recommendations to IES as a mechanism for continued improvement of its already good work.

REFERENCE

Schneider, M. (2021, January 21). A Year for Reflection and Continued Transformation. IES Director's Blog. https://ies.ed.gov/director/remarks/1-12-2021.asp.

Appendix A

Gathering and Assessing the Evidence

The committee drew on multiple sources of evidence in response to its charge. The Education Sciences Reform Act was a key reference, as was documentation of organizational structure and programming as provided by Institute of Education Sciences (IES) staff. The committee also held four public sessions with IES staff and experts from relevant areas of research. At the first session, on May 6, 2021, the committee heard testimony from Elizabeth Albro, commissioner of the National Center for Special Education Research [NCSER], and Joan McLaughlin, commissioner of NCSER, who provided an overview of the goals and organization of IES as well as insight into their goals for this study. At the second public session, on May 13, 2021, the committee heard from the director of IES, Mark Schneider, who shared his vision for this study and how he intends to use and engage with this report. The committee also heard from Anne Ricciuti, deputy director of science, who explained the review process for NCER and NCSER competitions, and NCER and NCSER program officers Katherine Taylor, Jacquelyn Buckley, Allen Ruby, Erin Higgins, and Emily Doolittle, who discussed their roles and responsibilities.

The third open session was comprised of a 2-day public meeting with multiple panels (June 29 and July 7, 2021). The first panel offered an opportunity for Elizabeth Albro, Joan McLaughlin, and Anne Ricciuti to update the committee and answer additional questions. The second panel provided the committee an opportunity to better understand where NCER and NCSER fit into the landscape of federal research agencies: the committee heard from James Griffin, chief of the Child Development and Behavior Branch at the National Institute of Child Health and Human Development;

Evan Heit, division director in the Division of Research on Learning at the National Science Foundation; and Gila Neta, program director for implementation science in the Division of Cancer Control and Population Sciences at the National Cancer Institute. Analogously, the committee heard from a series of private foundations that support education research in the third panel of the day, with speakers Bob Hughes, director of K–12 education at the Bill & Melinda Gates Foundation; Na'ilah Suad Nasir, president of the Spencer Foundation; and Jim Short, program director of leadership and teaching to advance learning at the Carnegie Corporation of New York.

The committee then turned to two panels focused on the education research needs of practitioners. In the first practitioner panel, the committee heard from "research brokers"—individuals whose job is to help "translate" researchers for practice communities. This panel included Carrie Conaway, senior lecturer at Harvard Graduate School of Education; Raymond Hart, director of research for the Council of Great City Schools; Emily House, executive director for the Tennessee Higher Education Commission; and Kylie Klein, director of research, accountability, and data in Evanston/ Skokie School District 65. The second practitioner panel focused on supporting beneficial research partnerships, and included Elaine Allensworth, Lewis-Sebring Director for the University of Chicago Consortium on School Research; Kingsley Botchway, chief of human resources and equity from the Waterloo Community School District; and Colin Chellman, university dean for institutional and policy research at the City University of New York.

The second day of the third meeting's public session focused on how and why education research is done. In the first panel, the committee heard about methods and measures in education research from Ryan Baker, associate professor at the University of Pennsylvania; David Francis, Hugh Roy and Lillie Cranz Cullen Distinguished University Chair at the University of Houston; Odis Johnson, Bloomberg Distinguished Professor at the Johns Hopkins University; and Elizabeth Stuart, associate dean for education and professor at the Johns Hopkins University. The next panel focused on assessing impact in education research, with panelists Ana Baumann, research assistant professor at Washington University in St. Louis; Becky Francis, chief executive officer of the Education Endowment Foundation; and Adam Gamoran, president of the William T. Grant Foundation and this committee's chair. Finally, the committee heard from a series of experts on research training in education: Curtis Byrd, special advisor to the provost at Georgia State University; Julie Posselt, associate professor at the University of Southern California; Sean Reardon, professor at Stanford University; and Katharine Strunk, professor and Erickson Distinguished Chair at Michigan State University.

Finally, the committee held a public session focused on topics in special education (August 10, 2021). As part of that panel, the committee heard from Beth Harry, professor emerita at the University of Miami; Karrie Shogren, professor and senior scientist at the University of Kansas; Patricia Snyder, distinguished professor at the University of Florida; and Vivian Wong, associate professor at the University of Virginia.

In addition to outside experts, the committee commissioned five short papers to help synthesize existing evidence in the field and frame our recommendations. First, we asked Heather Hough and colleagues at Policy Analysis for California Education to offer insight into the scope of loss, both personal and educational, facing the nation in the wake of the COVID-19 pandemic. Next, we asked Shirin Vossoughi, Megan Bang, and Ananda Marin to consider the ways that scholarly understandings of learning have evolved and grown since the founding of IES in 2001. Third, Kara Finnigan offered insight into what is known about how evidence is used in education policy and practice. Shira Zilberstein, under the supervision of Michelle Lamont, provided a paper on the impact of interventions aimed at supporting diversity, equity, and inclusion in academic peer-review processes. Finally, Christopher Klager, under the supervision of committee member Elizabeth Tipton, conducted an analysis of what research topics have been funded through NCER and NCSER since its founding in 2001. In addition to the full review provided by the committee for all five of these papers, the committee sent the Klager and Tipton paper to several external, independent coders under the supervision of committee member Nathan Jones. These external coders were asked to follow directions outlined in the Klager and Tipton paper to "spot check" 10 percent of the paper's original coding in order to ensure the coding process was both clear and accurate. This process resulted in 95 percent agreement between the original and external coders. For more information on how the Klager and Tipton paper is used in this report, as well as further details on coding processed, see Appendix D.

These papers and their findings have all been considered as scholarly input into the committee's work. As noted above, published, peer-reviewed literature remains the gold standard by which the committee made its judgments. The committee also received formal public comment from multiple scholarly organizations and individuals, including the deans of the schools of education associated with the LEARN Coalition, the American Educational Research Association, the National Center for Learning Disabilities, and dozens of others. Committee members have evaluated all documentation from IES as well as outside testimony through the lens of their scholarly expertise: these judgments ultimately form the basis of the committee's recommendations.

Following the completion of a draft report, the committee sent its work into the National Academies of Sciences, Engineering, and Medicine's review process. The report was reviewed by 15 independent reviewers, whose areas of expertise map onto and complement the study committee. The purpose of this independent review is to provide candid and critical comments that will assist the National Academies in making each published report as sound as possible and to ensure that it meets the institutional standards for quality, objectivity, evidence, and responsiveness to the study charge. The committee considered the full range of commentary from each reviewer, and made changes to the report draft in response to that commentary. The review of this report was overseen by Michael Feuer, George Washington University, and James House, University of Michigan. They were responsible for making certain that an independent examination of this report was carried out in accordance with the standards of the National Academies and that all review comments were carefully considered.

Concurrent to this review process, the committee shared a redacted version of the original draft with IES staff for fact-checking purposes. The redacted draft report contained the committee's understanding on matters of fact only: that is, IES staff were not privy to the committee's analytic work until after the report review process. Following a fact-checking process internal to IES, IES staff returned a set of comments and suggested edits. The committee considered those suggestions based on the following principles: (1) is the suggested edit an issue of fact or of characterization (facts were corrected as advised); (2) if the suggestion is a characterization, does it fit within the committee's shared understanding and judgment (suggestions for revised characterization that were aligned with the committee's judgment were adopted subject to the third principle); and (3) in either case, is the suggestion within the bounds of the committee's statement of task (if so and if the suggestion met either of the first two principles, the suggestion was adopted). Several committee members facilitated a first round of adjudications of these suggestions, and then each chapter was subjected to a second read for consideration by a different committee member. The entire report was then reviewed by the full committee, and submitted for final consideration to the National Academies' report review process.

Appendix B

Email Correspondence
Sent to the Committee

Due to the high interest in this consensus study, National Academies of Sciences, Engineering, and Medicine staff created a project email account to gather all public commentary. This account received a total of 20 email messages, most of which asked for information about how to attend planned open sessions. The following six messages contained substantive comments sent to the committee for consideration while answering its charge. They are reproduced below, in the order received.

- Kenji Hakuta, Stanford University (7/26/2021)
- Early career Special Education Researcher (8/6/2021)
- Soraya Zrikem, Learning and Education Academic Research Network (LEARN) Coalition (8/11/2021)
- Christy Talbot, American Educational Research Association (9/21/2021)
- Elizabeth Talbott, College of William and Mary (9/28/2021)
- Steve Pierson, American Statistical Association (10/5/2021)

From:	Kenji Hakuta
To:	IES Research Agenda
Cc:	Gordon, Edmund; Sonya Douglass Horsford; "Kent McGuire"; Na"ilah Suad Nasir
Subject:	Letter from Edmund W. Gordon re: IES ARP
Date:	Monday, July 26, 2021 11:55:19 AM
Attachments:	Letter to Director Schneider .pdf

Dear Colleagues:

We recently sent the attached letter to IES Director Mark Schneider, which speaks directly to the ARP funding, but more broadly makes a statement about educational research priorities and knowledge production capacity at HBCU's. Chair of the Committee Adam Gamoran suggested that we enter it into your public comment records.

Thank you.

Kenji

From: Kenji Hakuta <hakuta@stanford.edu>
Date: Monday, July 26, 2021 at 8:47 AM
To: Mark.Schneider@ed.gov <Mark.Schneider@ed.gov>
Cc: Gordon, Edmund <egordon@exchange.tc.columbia.edu>, Sonya Douglass Horsford <sdh2150@tc.columbia.edu>, 'Kent McGuire' <KMcGuire@hewlett.org>, Na'ilah Suad Nasir <nsnasir@spencer.org>
Subject: Letter from Edmund W. Gordon re: IES ARP

Dear Director Schneider:

Please find attached a letter from Prof. Gordon and his colleagues who are commemorating his centennial birthday, immediately regarding the ARP funds, and more broadly about priorities in education research. We would also like to request a follow-up meeting with you.

Thank you.

Edmund Gordon
Kenji Hakuta
Sonya Douglass Horsford
Kent McGuire
Na'ilah Suad Nasir

July 24, 2021

Director Mark Schneider
Office of the Director, IES
National Center for Education Statistics
Potomac Center Plaza
550 12th Street, SW
Room 4109
Washington, D.C. 20202

Dear Director Schneider:

We are writing as a collective of individual scholars, all concerned with equity and justice in the educational system that reflect the complex history of race and class in our nation. In addition to the historical moment captured in the recovery efforts from the magnification of these issues through the lens of COVID-19, we are also propelled by a celebratory note – the centennial birthday of one of the authors of this letter, Edmund Gordon – who has been addressing this issue for his entire career, recognized by scholars, practitioners, and policymakers.[1] His history of scholarship and advocacy on behalf of all disadvantaged students, particularly Black students, presents a vantage point from which to assess our current situation. As a celebration of Dr. Gordon's centennial, a large number of his students have been holding conferences and events over the course of the year. Research funders, notably the Spencer Foundation, the William T. Grant Foundation and the William and Flora Hewlett Foundation, have contributed to mark the moment as well.

As part of these events, we have been in conversations with the Congressional Black Caucus as well as staff from the House Education and Labor Committee, offering advice and seeking assistance with specific requests that promote our agenda. In our recent conversations with Congress in which we expressed our interests, they suggested that we contact you regarding ways of prioritizing the additional appropriations to IES that were made as part of the American Rescue Plan.

As might be expected from a long (and still continuing) career of a centenarian with a broad vision, a plethora of issues have been explored and advanced. But among them we would like to bring to your attention three simple priorities:

1. A synthesis of research that extend the report of the National Academies report _How People Learn II_ to specifically address implications of educational science to support the design of appropriate and sufficient pedagogical intervention. This would lead to a focus on educational opportunities that are equitable, and not just equal -- appropriate and sufficient to the needs and characteristics of the learning

525 W. 120TH STREET • BOX 67 • NEW YORK, NY 10027
HORSFORD@TC.COLUMBIA.EDU • (212) 678-3921
Prepublication Copy, Uncorrected Proofs

persons. The need to address this is particularly amplified by the evidence of COVID-19 gaps that are becoming increasingly apparent.[2]

2. An effort to expand the field of educational assessment to privilege the development of ability as much as it has promoted the measurement of ability. This has been a continuous theme of Dr. Gordon's life, ever since he began his career as a clinician conducting psychological testing of children in Brooklyn during the 1950's, extending into his leadership of The Gordon Commission on the Future of Assessment for Education (in contrast to "Assessment of Education."). This group advanced the notion that educational assessment can and should inform and improve learning and its teaching, as well as measure developed ability.

3. Developing a strong capacity in Historically Black Colleges and Universities (HBCU's) to engage in research and knowledge production in the education sciences (and the social sciences more generally) to enable strong alignment of the educational mission and purpose of these critical institutions with the K-12 needs of the Black community. Getting something akin to this in the social sciences was a long-term goal of one of Dr. Gordon's mentors, W.E.B. DuBois in the 1940's, and is something that could serve as an inspiration to this continuing need.[3]

We recognize your personal commitment as reflected in your memo of August, 2020, *Acting on Diversity*, highlighting ESRA legislation for "initiatives and programs to increase participation of researchers and institutions that have been historically underutilized in Federal education research activities of the Institute, including historically Black colleges or universities or other institutions of higher education with large numbers of minority students." We further applaud your emphasis on the Pathways program in working with minority-serving institutions, as well as comprehensively searching for opportunities across all of the IES programs. We truly applaud these actions, and encourage follow-through. As you do so, we hope that the three priorities indicated above help shape the ways in which the additional appropriations from the ARP are utilized.

We would like to request a meeting with you to further discuss our request, and to offer any assistance as appropriate. Thank you for your attention.

Sincerely,

Edmund W. Gordon
John M. Musser Professor of Psychology, Emeritus - Yale University
Richard March Hoe Professor of Psychology and Education, Emeritus - Teachers
College, Columbia University

Kenji Hakuta
Lee L. Jacks Professor of Education, Emeritus – Stanford University

Sonya Douglass Horsford
Associate Professor of Education Leadership
Teachers College, Columbia University

Kent McGuire
Program Director of Education
William and Flora Hewlett Foundation

[Electronic Signature TBA]

Na'ilah Suad Nasir
President, The Spencer Foundation

[1] Entered into the Congressional Record by Congressman Steven Horsford, Vice Chair of the Congressional Black Caucus: CELEBRATING PROFESSOR EDMUND W. GORDON'S 100TH BIRTHDAY

Mr. Speaker, I rise today to honor the life and legacy of Professor Edmund W. Gordon, an extraordinary professor of psychology whose career work has heavily influenced contemporary thinking in psychology, education, and social policy. Professor Gordon's research and initiatives have focused on the positive development of under-served children of color, including advancing the concept of the "achievement gap."

Professor Gordon grew up in a highly segregated area of North Carolina to parents who encouraged the importance of schooling. He received both his Bachelor's and Master's degrees from Howard University, and went on to pursue a PhD in psychology at the Teacher's College at Columbia University.

In 1956, after working with mentor and friend W.E.B. DuBois, Professor Gordon was commissioned by President Lyndon B. Johnson to help design the Head Start Program, aimed at providing early childhood education and family services to under-resourced families. After six months working on Head Start, Professor Gordon and his team had built a program to serve nearly half a million children. Professor Gordon also conducted research that would later be used to prove to the Supreme Court that school segregation had harmful effects on children. Professor Gordon strongly advocated the importance of understanding the learner's frame of reference in the development of education action plans.

Professor Gordon is the John M. Musser Professor of Psychology, Emeritus at Yale University, Richard March Hoe Professor, Emeritus of Psychology and Education and Founding Director of The Edmund W. Gordon Institute of Urban and Minority Education (IUME) at Teachers College, Columbia University.

From July 2000 until August 2001, Professor Gordon was Vice President of Academic Affairs and Interim Dean at Teachers College, Columbia University. Professor Gordon has held appointments at several of the nation's leading universities including Howard, Yeshiva, Columbia, City University of New York, Yale, and the Educational Testing Service. He has served as visiting professor at City College of New York and Harvard.

Currently, Professor Gordon is the Senior Scholar and Advisor to the President of the College Board where he developed and co-chaired the Taskforce on Minority High Achievement.

As a clinician and researcher, Professor Gordon explored divergent learning styles and advocated for supplemental education long before most scholars had recognized the existence and importance of those ideas. From 2011 to 2013, Professor Gordon organized and mentored the Gordon Commission, bringing together scholars to research and report on the Future of Assessment for Education.

Professor Gordon has authored 18 books and more than 200 articles on the achievement gap, affirmative development of academic ability, and supplementary education. He has been elected a Fellow of many prestigious organizations, including the American Academy of Arts & Science, and has been named one of America's most prolific and thoughtful scholars.

Approaching his centennial birthday, Professor Gordon still pays close attention to the state of education, and has stated that he would love to be able to change national education policy "to get a more equal focus on out-of-school and in-school learning."

On April 12, 2021, Professor Gordon was appointed as the first ever Honorary President of the American Educational Research Association.

I wish Professor Edmund W. Gordon the very best as he and his family celebrate his 100th birthday on June 13, 2021.

[2] See S. Douglass Horsford, L. Cabral, C. Touloukian, S. Parks, P. A. Smith, C. McGhee, F. Qadir, D. Lester & J. Jacobs (July 2021), Black Education in the Wake of COVID-19 & Systemic Racism: Toward a Theory of Change & Action. *Black Education Research Collective*, Teachers College Columbia University, July 2021. See also D. Bailey, G. J. Duncan, R. J. Murnane & N. A. Yeung (2021), Achievement Gaps in the Wake of COVID-19, *Educational Researcher, 50:* 266-275.

[3] David Levering Lewis (2019) in *W.E.B. Du Bois: A Biography 1868-1963* characterizes this push in 1943 as "a rebirth of the seminal Atlanta University Studies at the beginning of the century" (Du Bois was briefly at Atlanta then but the early studies he directed ran from 1896-1914 even as he was at NAACP). As Lewis wrote: "At the convention of the Presidents of the Negro Land Grant Colleges in Chicago that October [1943], Du Bois had rallied the association's seventeen presidents to formal endorsement and financial backing of an annual Atlanta University Conference. These were seventeen state-supported, racially restricted institutions founded as a result of the Morrill Act of 1862, to which the presidents of Hampton, Howard, and Tuskegee were affiliated." In his autobiography published posthumously in 1968 (*The Autobiography of W.E.B. Du Bois: A Soliloquy on Viewing My Life from the Last Decade of Its First Century*), Du Bois re-creates extensively his plan for knowledge generation and the capacity needed at HBCU's to do this work. What might have been had he successfully created the Black sociological empire focused on the problem of race is a matter of consideration, as it would have greatly affected where the state of educational research would be today.

From: ngb@ku.edu
To: Schweingruber, Heidi
Cc: Dibner, Kenne; Kelly, Margaret; Lammers, Matthew; Schweingruber, Heidi
Subject: IES Feedback [DBASSE-BOSE-20-07] - The Future of Education Research at the Institute of Education Sciences in the U.S. Department of Education
Date: Friday, August 6, 2021 3:14:28 PM

Thank you for taking the time to evaluate research activities and priorities for the future of IES. As an early career Special Education researcher, I believe these are two areas that deserve increased focus moving forward. Helping early career researchers become established in the field is critical for the future, and the current requirement that applicants in this award are within their first 3 years post-Ph.D. is extremely limiting given the competition is only held every 2 years. Additionally, Special Education research overall deserves increased support in the future. Effective instructional practices frequently used across this discipline (e.g., direct instruction) will become critical for all students as we work to decrease learning losses from the ongoing pandemic. I appreciate your consideration of these issues.

Open project information: DBASSE-BOSE-20-07

From:	Soraya Zrikem
To:	IES Research Agenda
Cc:	Alex Nock
Subject:	LEARN NAS Comments
Date:	Wednesday, August 11, 2021 12:43:59 PM
Attachments:	LEARN NAS Letter 8.11.21.pdf

Good Afternoon,

Attached please find the comments submitted by the Learning and Education Academic Research Network (LEARN) Coalition to the call for comment from the NAS panel on "The Future of Education Research at the Institute of Education Sciences in the U.S. Department of Education." Thank you for your consideration of LEARN's views.

Best,
Soraya Zrikem

--

Soraya Zrikem
Associate, Penn Hill Group
777 6th St NW, Suite 610 | Washington, DC 20001
szrikem@pennhillgroup.com
(734) 417-1796

LEARN™   Learning and Education Academic Research Network
Advancing the Sciences of Teaching and Learning

August 11, 2021

Adam Gamoran

Committee on The Future of Education Research at the Institute of Education Sciences
National Academy of Sciences, Engineering and Medicine
500 Fifth St., N.W.
Washington, D.C. 20001

Dear Dr.Gamoran:

     We are writing on behalf of the Learning and Education Academic Research Network (LEARN) Coalition to provide recommendations to the National Academies of Sciences, Engineering and Medicine (NAS) panel on "The Future of Education Research at the Institute of Education Sciences (IES)." LEARN, a coalition of 40 leading research colleges across the country, advocates for the importance of research on learning and development. As experts in the field, LEARN members provide evidence-based information to guide legislators and policy makers while advocating for an increased Federal investment in education research. With this letter, we hope to provide valuable insight on how this panel's recommendations should aim to improve IES and its critical work.

     As the education world works towards recovery from the COVID-19 pandemic, IES can play an important role in supporting education research on learning recovery. Consequently, the timing of this panel's recommendations should account for and address the challenges of the COVID-19 pandemic on the education world. While this response to the pandemic is critical, we also strongly urge the panel to consider a long term and broad view of its charge, so as not to lose momentum and focus on the many other domains of research that are so crucial for the nation's schools, students and communities. In short, IES's role in spurring high quality education research and discovery of knowledge across the full spectrum of education is more critical now than ever.

     After listening to both NAS public meetings, LEARN would like to respond to the four guiding questions asked in the afternoon of June 29 on "Knowledge Gaps in Education Research" and "Supporting Beneficial Research Partnerships." As Deans of Schools of Education from around the nation, LEARN provides a valuable perspective on the challenges and successes facing the education research world.

From your position in the field, what are the current knowledge gaps that could benefit from more robust research attention?
     While we know a great deal around certain areas of research (for example how children learn to read), other areas we have little to no knowledge. Additionally, as research is conducted, we are exposed to new factors that influence the education of children and adults, raising new areas in which we need to develop knowledge. Below are several areas we believe there are gaps in research that need additional attention.

     Overall, education research should investigate the student holistically; students need to learn about persistence, endurance and perseverance in addition to developing their content knowledge, cognitive skills, and problem-solving ability. This calls for a better understanding of effective interventions on student social and emotional learning (SEL), including school-based counseling interventions for significant mental health stressors. Schools need to develop confident and flexible learners and

 Learning and Education Academic Research Network
Advancing the Sciences of Teaching and Learning

problem-solvers, ones who can embrace ambiguity and nuance, who can move away from binary thinking and who can manage the complexity in challenging problems.

LEARN members also believe research is required on virtual learning at all ages. In addition to studying the effectiveness of current virtual programs, researchers should capitalize on the range of data and digital learning applications in their research and develop new ways for children to be learning with the use and assistance of technology. Virtual learning is still in its infancy. We must continue to tap into its potential to better help children learn. However, as we know, learning does not take place in isolation, and we note that it is also essential to conduct research that studies the systems of public education that support and/or inhibit improvement, and promising approaches and practices.

We need more research on successful interventions that can address the achievement gap. This is especially relevant after this past year when this gap grew and became much larger. How do we catch students up if they have fallen behind while still challenging students who are making good educational progress?

Lastly, we submit that there needs to be much more research around successful implementation and scale up of the contexts, structures, and approaches that support research take-up, including the conditions and types of research that are best aligned to research-practice partnerships.

Where are the human capital gaps that could benefit from better or more readily available training, and what kind of training is necessary?
LEARN believes it is critical to support the education research pipeline by training and providing grant opportunities to new researchers, including graduate students seeking to embark on a career in education research, as well as fellowships and training grants. The last two years have been highly detrimental to rising researchers, as projects and funding streams were paused in response to the COVID-19 pandemic. With the staggering learning loss being experienced by students due to the pandemic, it is important that IES provides researchers from a wide range of backgrounds with the grant opportunities to identify and develop innovative, evidence-backed and effective educational interventions. Using what we already know will only get us so far and not investing in our early career researchers will reduce our future potential at solving the problems facing education.

While a focus on research on the most effective interventions is important, we also need the nation's future generation of researchers to study educational systems, and policies that address complex educational challenges, including preparing teachers and leaders. Specifically, we note the need for more pre-doctoral training grants and a focus on mixed -methodologies as well as methodologies and approaches for research-practice partnerships, including improvement science. This strand of research can also include the development of researchers to focus on developing culturally relevant methodologies and approaches.

How does the field support and sustain mutually beneficial partnerships in education research?
The field, as well as IES as a federal grantmaking organization, must foster a greater number and more powerful set of partnerships. IES's research-practitioner partnerships are one example of IES seeking to foster partnerships in the education research space. However, the benefit of these partnerships is largely limited to only the organizations actively involved in the specific grant or research work envisioned by the partnership. To further drive the expansion of the partnership model, LEARN proposes that IES create a matching directory of locales, school districts, entities and organizations that are seeking research partnerships so that connections can be more efficiently and equitably made. This directory would not promise or require IES grant funding, but rather serve as a clearinghouse for those seeking to connect. Since the partnerships are reciprocal relationships, expanding access to this opportunity equally will benefit both the education and research field.

What are the conditions necessary for ongoing partnerships?
To identify the ingredients of a successful partnership, we need to identify the types of research that are best suited for partnerships. Additionally, there are multiple types and approaches to partnerships with

little research on the variation and the impacts. A broader research agenda into partnerships is warranted. Questions that must be asked as part of this agenda include:

- How can research funding balance response to local needs and priorities, and support research that is generalizable and builds a knowledge base all while providing clear standards of evidence and scientific merit?

- How is partnership and improvement science blended with, and used in concert with other types of research and knowledge funded by IES, rather than separate from research funded through other priorities?

Additional Comments on IES independence, RFP timing and IES Funding Levels
Outside of our immediate comments on the questions posed during the June 29th panel, we would also like to emphasize several other points. First, we view IES' independence from the U.S. Department of Education (ED) as critical as it allows for flexibility in quickly identifying and addressing research problems and issues. LEARN finds that this independent structure is most effective when IES is led by both a director and board. This structure is key to the integrity of IES and it is critical that IES populate the National Board for Education Sciences (NBES) which has been largely nonfunctional for the past several years due to few or no active members. We also want to emphasize the paramount importance of scientific merit and peer review in the funding process.

Second, we are concerned about the amount of time that IES generally permits between the release of a grant competition and the due date for proposals with respect to Request for Proposals (RFPs) that utilize partnerships. The time allotted generally does not sufficiently allow for developing the conditions for deep and ongoing partnerships. We recommend that IES consider establishing separate timeframes for issuance to proposal date when considering approaches for RFPs for new partnerships versus RFPs for established partnerships.

Finally, LEARN would be remiss to overlook the budget limitations IES currently faces. Conversations with IES staff have uncovered that they are working at capacity and straining to adequately operate competitions and identify priorities. As we have discussed above, there is a vast amount of research we need to conduct and knowledge we need to develop in order to address the education challenges of today's students. IES must be properly supported and staffed to allow for this work to occur intentionally and effectively.

This is especially critical in research on special education, which is presently spearheaded by IES's National Center for Special Education Research (NCSER). NCSER received over $71 million in FY 2010 but was misguidedly cut to less than $51 million in the subsequent fiscal year. NCSER's funding reached at high of $58.5 million in FY 2021, but that is $27.1 million short of the buying power of the FY 2010 NCSER funding level after factoring in inflation.

Likewise, Research, Development and Dissemination (R, D and D) funding, IES's largest research account, was $200.2 million in FY 2010. The FY 2021 R, D and D funding level is $195.9 million, which is $45 million short of what the FY 2010 amount would buy in today's dollars. Without an increase in funds for R, D and D and NCSER, IES will not be able to properly address this panel's recommendations nor drive the education research currently required. We hope the NAS panel will underscore the need for Congress to increase IES' funding in their recommendations.

Thank you for your commitment to sustaining and strengthening the nation's education research infrastructure. If you have questions, please do not hesitate to contact Alex Nock at 202 495-9497 or anock@pennhillgroup.com.

 Learning and Education Academic Research Network
Advancing the Sciences of Teaching and Learning

Respectfully Submitted,

Camilla P. Benbow, Ed.D.
Co-Chair, Learning and Education Academic Research Network (LEARN)
Patricia and Rodes Hart Dean of Education and Human Development of the Peabody College of
Education and Human Development, Vanderbilt University

Glenn E. Good, Ph.D.
Co-Chair, Learning and Education Academic Research Network (LEARN)
Dean of the College of Education, University of Florida

Rick Ginsberg, Ph.D.
Co-Chair, Learning and Education Academic Research Network (LEARN)
Dean of the School of Education, University of Kansas

From:	Christy Talbot
To:	IES Research Agenda
Cc:	Felice Levine
Subject:	Comments from Education Research Stakeholders - Future of Education Research at IES
Date:	Tuesday, September 21, 2021 1:08:25 PM
Attachments:	Comments from Education Research Stakeholders on the Future of Education Research at the Institute of Education Sciences (FINAL).pdf

Dear Dr. Gamoran and Committee Members,

Thank you for the opportunity to submit comments to inform the work of the National Academies of Science, Engineering, and Medicine Committee on the Future of Education Research at the Institute of Education Sciences (IES).

On behalf of 19 organizations with particular interest in IES research and training programs, please find attached comments that encourage the committee to address the underinvestment in IES over the past decade in its report and recommendations. Sufficient resources are critical for IES to meet both its mandated responsibilities and emerging priorities, including those discussed by this committee.

We specifically urge the committee to include two recommendations to Congress in its consensus report: (1) Advance strong, sustained funding levels for the Research, Development, and Dissemination (RD&D) and the Research in Special Education line items in appropriations legislation; (2) Include robust authorization levels for IES in a future reauthorization of the Education Sciences Reform Act.

Thank you for your consideration of these comments and recommendations. Please do not hesitate to contact Felice Levine (copied here) or me with any questions.

Warm regards,
-Christy

Christy Talbot
Senior Program Associate, Government Relations
American Educational Research Association
1430 K St. NW, Suite 1200
Washington, DC 20005
O: 202-238-3221 | M: 202-664-2737
ctalbot@aera.net

Comments from Education Research Stakeholders to the
National Academies of Science, Engineering, and Medicine
Committee on The Future of Education Research at the Institute of Education Sciences

September 21, 2021

On behalf of the 19 undersigned organizations, we appreciate the opportunity to provide comments on The Future of Education Research at the Institute of Education Sciences (IES) study by the National Academies of Science, Engineering, and Medicine. The organizations joining these comments represent scientific associations, K-12 and higher education organizations, universities, and organizations serving persons with disabilities.

We greatly appreciate the thoughtful work and deliberation that the committee has taken on over the past few months to examine the roles of the National Center for Education Research (NCER) and the National Center for Special Education Research (NCSER) in supporting rigorous and relevant education research. **As part of that effort, we encourage the committee to include recommendations that address the underinvestment in IES research and training programs over the past decade in its final consensus report.**

To enable NCER and NCSER to increase their respective capacities to support high-quality, innovative research and to build a diverse and inclusive education researcher workforce, we particularly encourage the committee to include two recommendations to Congress in its consensus report:

- Advance strong, sustained funding levels for the Research, Development, and Dissemination (RD&D) and the Research in Special Education line items in appropriations legislation.
- Include robust authorization levels for IES in a future reauthorization of the Education Sciences Reform Act (ESRA).

We are thankful for the $100 million provided through the American Rescue Plan to support education research and data collection as part of the response in education to the COVID-19 pandemic. We are also pleased to see strong proposals with significant and long-needed boosts for the investment in IES in President Biden's FY 2022 budget request and the House FY 2022 Labor, Health and Human Services, Education, and Related Agencies bill. These proposals show the commitment of the administration and Congress to the important role education research has in informing evidence-based policy and practice.

We urge you to address funding levels in your recommendations as sufficient resources are necessary for IES to meet its mandated responsibilities under ESRA and to support emerging priorities. The FY 2022 budget request and House bill serve as important steps to restore lost purchasing power that has constrained the ability of IES to award research grants and support training programs to advance essential knowledge on important educational issues and build the education research pipeline. Unfortunately, IES is still significantly behind the deep cuts borne by sequestration in FY 2011-2013, with the FY 2021 appropriation providing nearly $160 million less in purchasing power compared to the FY 2010 appropriation after adjusting for inflation.

The RD&D line item supports the research and training grants provided by NCER, yet funding for RD&D has remained relatively flat over the past five years. Funding in FY 2021 for RD&D was only $3 million above the FY 2016 level of $195 million. In that time, NCER launched new grant solicitations encouraging the use of innovative methods and open science best practices. As important as these programs are, appropriations levels have not kept up with the increased costs to incorporate the Standards for

Excellence in Education Research, resulting in larger, but fewer, grants for the field. NCER is also balancing awards for its core field-initiated education research grants with off-cycle competitions that promote replication of IES-funded research and use of state longitudinal data systems, among other programs. Postdoctoral and predoctoral training grants also provide professional development incorporating innovative methodological skills; additional funding could go toward increasing the reach of training programs to underrepresented institutions among IES grantees, including HBCUs, HSIs, and MSIs.

Funding has also remained relatively frozen for NCSER. The FY 2021 appropriated amount of $58.5 million is only $4.5 million above the FY 2014 funding level. Although NCSER will award research grants focused on accelerating learning recovery in special education with funding provided through the American Rescue Plan in FY 2022, it will not run its core special education research grant competition. This will be the second time since FY 2014 that NCSER has not been able to award new grants through its core research grant program due to limited funding.

Several of the organizations joining this statement will also be commenting separately on specific areas where there are gaps in research that could be supported by IES, new methods and approaches in education research, and new and different types of research and training. We have joined on these comments to collectively underscore that IES will require significant and sustained investment in order to meet those recognized needs. We thus urge the committee to include recommendations for Congress to increase appropriations and authorization levels to enable NCER and NCSER to support rigorous, timely, and innovative education research and training programs to develop a diverse education research workforce. In addition, we encourage the committee to provide language in the consensus report on the role of the executive branch to advance robust budget proposals for NCER and NCSER.

Thank you again for the opportunity to comment and for considering these recommendations. If committee members have any questions or need additional information, please contact Felice Levine (flevine@aera.net) or Christy Talbot (ctalbot@aera.net) at the American Educational Research Association.

Undersigned Organizations

Alliance for Learning Innovation (ALI)
American Educational Research Association
American Psychological Association
Association of Population Centers
Consortium of Social Science Associations
EDGE Consulting Partners
ETS
Institute for Educational Leadership
Institute for Higher Education Policy (IHEP)
Knowledge Alliance

LEARN Coalition
Lehigh University
National Center for Learning Disabilities
National Down Syndrome Society
National Education Association
Population Association of America
University of Florida
University of Washington College of Education
Vanderbilt University

From:	Talbott, Elizabeth
To:	IES Research Agenda
Subject:	Comments on the Future of IES-NCSER research
Date:	Tuesday, September 28, 2021 10:10:22 AM

To the National Academies Committee:

Thank you for providing a public recording of the panel presentation in August addressing future directions and priorities for IES-NCSER research. I watched the entire presentation and found it absolutely fascinating.

I know that 4 panelists commenting on needs for the field and future directions for IES-NCSER cannot possibly address all pressing issues. But the panelists did a terrific job of highlighting key ones, such as the need for systems change, funding for implementation science/team science and participatory research, and improving services provided to children and youth with disabilities from diverse backgrounds.

Yet I was struck by the fact that none of the panelists was an IES-funded expert in academic interventions, even as one of the most pressing and persistent needs for students with disabilities is the advancement of their academic skills leading to college and career readiness. OSEP has done a fantastic job of funding researcher and educator preparation in the area of intensive intervention, with the AIR providing technical assistance to leaders of school districts. However (and especially because of COVID), research addressing the academic and mental health needs of all students with disabilities becomes even more urgent, and we need IES NCSER to be a leader in funding intensive intervention research, in my opinion.

How do researchers and practitioners deliver intensive intervention in the context of instruction provided in inclusive settings? This question is absolutely critical for NCSER funding to address. Jade Wexler's IES-funded Project Cali provides direction to this end, with specific training for more effective co-teaching in literacy. Sharon Vaughn's work in individual and small group instruction with students who have LD also provides a helpful structure, as does Lynn and Doug Fuchs' work in peer tutoring. Special education researchers are well prepared to tackle this challenging question, as they are among the best in the nation. For example, both Chris Lemons, whose research focuses on intensive intervention in reading with students who have Down Syndrome and Sarah Powell, whose research addresses interventions for students with math disabilities, have received the Presidential Early Career Award for Scientists and Engineers.

These are a few examples of the significant accomplishments of researchers in our young field—yet the work clearly needs to accelerate and intensify and special education researchers, many of whom are funded by IES and OSEP, are well positioned to take on this challenge.

NCSER's struggle over the past decade has been its chronic under-funding by Congress. NCSER funding is 20% lower today than in 2010. Every few years or so (including 2021), NCSER has not been able to offer its regular competitions, creating lost momentum in critical areas such as career and technical education. There was no early career competition this year. I hope that the National Academy can reflect this urgent need for more funding in its report.

Thank you for providing this opportunity to comment. I wish the committee all the best in concluding its work.

Sincerely,
--
Elizabeth Talbott, PhD
Professor, Special Education
Associate Dean for Research & Faculty Development
School of Education
William & Mary

From: Pierson, Steve
To: IES Research Agenda
Subject: Comments from American Statistical Association
Date: Tuesday, October 5, 2021 12:08:49 PM
Attachments: NAS_IES_Research.pdf

Hello,

Please see the attached for your panel from the American Statistical Association.

Thank you,
Steve

Steve Pierson, Ph.D.
Director of Science Policy

American Statistical Association
Promoting the Practice and Profession of Statistics®
732 North Washington Street
Alexandria, VA 22314-1943
(703) 302-1841
www.amstat.org/policy
For ASA science policy updates, follow us on Twitter: @ASA_SciPol

AMERICAN STATISTICAL ASSOCIATION
Promoting the Practice and Profession of Statistics·

732 North Washington Street, Alexandria, VA 22314-1943
(703) 684-1221 ■ www.amstat.org ■ asainfo@amstat.org
f www.facebook.com/AmstatNews ◻ www.twitter.com/AmstatNews

October 5, 2021

Adam Gamoran
Chair, Committee on The Future of Education Research at the Institute of Education Sciences in
    the US Department of Education
National Academies of Sciences, Engineering, and Medicine
    [Transmitted electronically]

Dear Dr. Gamoran,

We are pleased to have the opportunity to provide input to your panel considering the future of
education research at the Institute of Education Sciences (IES) in the US Department of
Education. As the science of learning from data, statistics is fundamental to IES's mission to
"provide scientific evidence on which to ground education practice and policy." The role of
statistics in education research starts with framing the problem and designing the study and
continues through analyzing and interpreting the data and communicating the findings. We
believe emphatically that engagement of statisticians and the statistical perspective results in
better science.

The tremendous strides in education research over the past 25 years underscore the important
role of statistics both through the Statistical and Research Methodology in Education (SRME)
program and more broadly. One manifestation of this success is the What Works Clearinghouse
(WWC), which provides decision-makers with information about effective interventions in
reading, math, science, dropout prevention, and more. Many of these advances, and the
confidence in the studies reported in the WWC, would not be possible without strong statistical
methods underpinning the study designs and analyses and a solid research base for understanding
which designs and analyses yield accurate results.

Through the SRME program, we appreciate that IES has recognized—and indeed, fostered—the
importance of statistical methodology grounded in and disciplined by the context of education
research. Recognizing the need for statistical advances that respond to the specific challenges
faced by the field, SRMA-funded projects have ensured the following:

- Principled analyses of primary data collected in empirical studies
- More informative use of large-scale survey data routinely collected by IES
- Advances in methods for characterizing findings and synthesizing bodies of evidence
  from multiple studies

- Advanced power-analysis methodologies, with assumptions informed by empirical data, to ensure the money spent on research is put to good use
- Robust methods to determine what interventions work best for whom—again, a particularly important topic in times of limited resources

For IES to continue furthering education research, we recommend thoughtful implementation of the following statistical perspectives:

- More strategic use of existing administrative data, and new modalities for collecting and processing data, to provide practitioners and decision-makers with up-to-date information on student progress
- Study designs representing in more detail the heterogeneity of student and school characteristics to better inform local decisions
- Improved systems for archiving, accessing, and reanalyzing data collected from completed primary studies to better address emerging policy questions and improve the relevance of available evidence
- Continued development and improvement of methods for evaluating systemic and structural-level reforms that may not be easily randomized or evaluated using traditional quasi-experimental approaches currently examined by the WWC
- Further use of statistical methods and strategies for helping identify study design and analysis approaches most likely to yield accurate results, as has been done for the WWC to this point
- Development of methods that monitor or measure systems of discrimination
- Increased support of programs, workshops, and training initiatives in statistical and methodological research in education settings both generally and to increase the diversity of researchers engaged in statistical and methodological research in education settings

The following experts provided input and time to craft these recommendations: Vivian Wong, University of Virginia; Tracy Sweet, University of Maryland; Elizabeth Stuart, The Johns Hopkins University; James Pustejovsky, University of Wisconsin, Madison; and Luke Miratrix, Harvard University. My comments here echo the comments of some of those who presented to this committee over the summer.

Thank you for your consideration.

Sincerely,

Ron Wasserstein
Executive Director, American Statistical Association

Appendix C

Committee-Commissioned Papers

Finnigan, K.S. (2021). *The current knowledge base on the use of research evidence in education policy and practice: A synthesis and recommendations for future directions.*

This paper synthesizes what is known about use of research evidence (URE) in the United States educational system over the past decade as this knowledge base expanded and identified where gaps remain in the field's understanding of URE.

Hough, H.J., Myung, J., Domingue, B.W., Edley, C., Kurlaender, M., Marsh, J., and Rios-Aguilar, C. (2021). *The impact of the COVID-19 pandemic on students and educational systems, critical actions for recovery, and the role of research in the years ahead.*

This paper reported early findings on the impact of the pandemic and also offered an approach on how to potentially leverage research to address the differential impacts that were experienced during the pandemic.

Klager, C., and Tipton, E. (2021). *Summary of IES funded topics.*

This paper summarized the research studies funded by NCER and NCSER throughout the 20-year history of IES.

Vossoughi, S., Marin, A., and Bang, M. (2021). *Foundational developments in the science of human learning and their implications for educational research.*

This paper explored what was learned about human learning and development over the past 20 years from a sociocultural perspective, and what the implications of these new understandings mean for human communities.

Zilberstein, S. (2021). *National Academies of Science and Medicine: Diversity, equity, and inclusion in peer review.*

This paper addressed the state of knowledge about how diversity, equity, and inclusion are considered in the competing, reviewing and awarding of research grants, and how the review process influenced the outcomes of scholarly research.

Appendix D

Analysis of IES Funded Topics Commissioned Paper

As the committee began to discuss how to approach this consensus report, it identified the need for an analysis of Institute of Education Sciences (IES) past spending by topic area, with summary data on the topics studied by the National Center for Education Research (NCER) and National Center for Special Education Research (NCSER) grantees over the past 20 years. Chris Klager is a research associate at the Statistics for Evidence-Based Policy and Practice (STEPP) Center at Northwestern University. He was selected to write this paper because he researches the translation and communication of evidence about educational programs for policy makers and practitioners, and also has experience performing analyses related to projects funded by IES. This work was supervised in its entirety by committee member Elizabeth Tipton. This appendix details how the authors gathered the necessary data under six parameters to create summary tables that were utilized by the committee in the body of the report. A full copy of the final paper, which includes the Codebook that the authors created to develop the summary tables, is available at https://nap. nationalacademies.org/resource/26428/READY-KlagerTipton_IES_Topic_ Analysis_Jan2022v4.pdf.

The paper addressed a range of research questions listed below regarding the types of studies that have been funded across different time periods and categories:

- What *topics* have been studied in research funded by NCER and NCSER, and how has the distribution of funded topics shifted over time?
- How have studies of different *project types* funded by NCER and NCSER changed over time? How are studies connected to one another?
- What types of *interventions* are studied? Where are these interventions targeted?
- What is the relative *funding* distribution across topic areas, and what topic areas have received the highest levels of funding?
- What *institutions* receive grants from NCER and NCSER? How has this changed over time?
- What *Methods* and *Measurement* types have been studied under funded grants?

To answer these questions, Klager and Tipton reviewed publicly available data on IES-funded grants, which included information on each of these areas via the inclusion of study abstracts (IES, 2021). They also included data to classify institution types (R1, MSI, and Private) that came from the Carnegie Classification database which is based on information from the Indiana University Center for Postsecondary Research (n.d.).

The authors found that the complete dataset on the IES website has over 2,500 grants and contracts funded by NCER, NCSER, the National Center for Education Evaluation and Regional Assistance (NCEE), and the National Center for Education Statistics (NCES) from 2002 to 2021. The analysis completed was limited to grants funded by NCER and NCSER between 2002 and 2020. They noted that while 2021 awards were announced, it was unclear if all 2021 awards were present in the data that were downloaded at the time this paper was completed, so those awards were excluded. The analytic dataset also excluded awards funded by NCEE and NCES as this was not within the parameters that the committee was charged to examine in our statement of task. Contracts were also excluded, leaving only grants. All analyses in this paper exclude Small Business Innovation Research (SBIR) grants. Although NCER and NCSER issue SBIR awards, they differ from other awards in several ways. SBIR awards fall into either Phase I Development or Phase II Development. They are of a short duration and target small businesses with an emphasis on commercialization of the products that are developed. Many of them are also classified as contracts rather than grants. SBIR is a federal program that operates across federal agencies and is not unique to the Department of Education.

PROJECT TYPES

When trying to define project types, Klager and Tipton explained that over the past 20 years, NCER and NCSER have funded grants in a variety of categories based on two dimensions—the topic of the grant and project type. Over time, the project types have changed, and for much of the past 20 years, these were divided into numbered goals (1 through 5). More recently, this numbering was removed and some categories shifted. Because of these changes in the wording of the request for applications (RFA) and types of studies that fall under each project type, Klager and Tipton saw some simplification in terminology was required to communicate about each.

Historically, the core project structure included five goals:
- Goal 1 – Exploration
- Goal 2 – Development and Innovation
- Goal 3 – Efficacy
- Goal 4 – Effectiveness
- Goal 5 – Measurement

The categorizations that IES provides on its website include variations on these five goals. Additionally, IES funds grants in other programs such as researcher-practice partnerships (RPPs), Training, Methods, and various special programs including large "center" grants that engage in activities that cover multiple goals. The publicly available data on IES's website about funded grants includes a field called "GoalText," but not the actual Goal (i.e., 1, 2, 3, 4, 5, etc.) each grant was funded under. Instead, the GoalText field contains a description that characterizes the purpose of the grant. For the purposes of these analyses, Klager and Tipton categorized grants by their GoalText. This means that all grants that were marked by IES (in the GoalText) as Exploration were categorized as Exploration, regardless of the program the grant was funded under.

While Exploration and Development and Innovation projects have remained approximately the same over the history of IES, Efficacy and Effectiveness studies have changed over time. To explore trends over time, Klager and Tipton had to create new categories which involved combining categories in some cases. One important case is with regards to replication grants, which over time moved from Goal 3 to Goal 4 studies, and then to their own project type.

For purposes of comparison, the authors divided out "Initial Efficacy" studies into their own project type and then combined "Replication" and "Effectiveness" trials into a single category. This required them to determine which Efficacy studies were "initial" trials versus "replications." To do so, they turned to Chhin, Taylor, and Wei (2018), who categorized all Goal 3 and Goal 4 grants funded by NCER and NCSER between 2004 and 2016 as either a direct or conceptual replication, new evaluation, re-analysis, or longitudinal follow-up. They used the codes applied by Chhin and colleagues (2018) for the grants that they coded to identify replications.

All other grants with GoalText of Efficacy or Efficacy and Replication that were not coded by Chhin and colleagues were coded using the publicly available abstracts. Following the method described in Chhin et al. (2018), Klager and Tipton checked IES abstracts for evidence of the stated purpose of the evaluation and prior efficacy evaluations of the program. If a study cited pilot evaluations only, including previous Development and Innovation grants from IES, or provided no information about the purpose of the study regarding replication, it was coded as a non-replication and was classified as Efficacy for these analyses. If there was evidence of previous efficacy studies or if the stated goal of the grant was for replication, it was coded as a replication and classified as Replication/Effectiveness. The publicly available abstracts provide limited information about each grant. Chhin and colleagues had access to full grant proposals and were able to identify many replications (~50% of 307 grants). Using abstracts, Klager and Tipton identified 32 out of 189 (17%) additional grants that had Goal-Text indicating an efficacy trial. It is plausible that coding replications from abstracts undercounts the number of replications based on the disparity between Chhin and colleagues' rate and the rate Klager coded from abstracts. It is unclear, though, if the rate of replications is consistent across time and programs funded by IES.

Table D-1 shows how those GoalText descriptions were categorized for these analyses. Grants were categorized based on the GoalText rather than the programs under which grants were funded. For example, five grants funded as part of the Digital Learning Platforms to Enable Efficient Education Research Network program had GoalText of "Methodological Innovation" and were classified with other grants that also had the "Methodological Innovation" regardless of the programs they were funded under. The "Other" category includes special grant competitions, unsolicited grants, centers established for the study of particular topics, and other projects that cover multiple goals. All grants with GoalText that cover more than one goal (e.g., Efficacy and Development) were classified as meeting multiple goals and were categorized as Other.

TOPICS

Eight topics were formed using the program names that IES provides as the source of funding for each grant. (See Tables D-2 and D-3 for a list of program names where all grants were assigned to a particular topic and

TABLE D-1 Categorization of GoalText into Grant Categories

Table 1. Categorization of GoalText into grant categories	
Exploration	Exploration
Development & Innovation	Development and Innovation
Efficacy	Efficacy*
	Efficacy and Replication*
	Follow-Up
	Initial Efficacy
Replication/Effectiveness	Effectiveness
	Efficacy*
	Efficacy and Replication*
	Replication Effectiveness
	Replication Efficacy
	Scale-Up Evaluations
Measurement	Measurement
Methods	Methodological Innovation
RPP	Researcher-Practitioner Partnership
Training	Training
Other	Multiple Goals
	No Goal
	Other Goal
	Development and Evaluation
	Efficacy and Development
	Exploration and Efficacy
	Exploration and Measurement

a list of program names for which topics were coded by coders.) In some cases, the program names are descriptive and map well onto a topic, as is the case with the Science, Technology, Engineering, and Mathematics (STEM) program that maps onto the STEM topic used in this analysis. In other cases, the program name is not very descriptive, as in the case of Research Grants Focused on Systematic Replication. In the cases where the program name was not indicative of the type of intervention or idea being studied, the IES abstracts were coded to fit within the topic categories. Because the topics are not mutually exclusive (e.g., a STEM intervention that happens in an Early Childhood classroom could fall into both the STEM and Early Childhood categories), the authors gave preference to School Systems, Age (Early Childhood and Post-Secondary/Adult), then Cognition & Learning, Social & Behavioral, followed by content area (Reading, Writing, Language, Literacy, & ELL; STEM). School Systems was used for interventions that changed the structure of school operations, regardless of content area (e.g., State-wide remedial Algebra program). The Other category captures a small proportion of grants that do not fit well within the seven other topic categories.

TABLE D-2 Programs that Correspond to a Coded Topic

Topic	ProgramName
Early Childhood	• EARLY LEARNING PROGRAMS AND POLICIES • PRESCHOOL CURRICULUM EVALUATION RESEARCH • SUPPORTING EARLY LEARNING FROM PRESCHOOL THROUGH EARLY ELEMENTARY SCHOOL GRADES NETWORK • EARLY INTERVENTION AND EARLY LEARNING
Post-Secondary/Adult	• POSTSECONDARY AND ADULT EDUCATION • TRANSITION TO POSTSECONDARY EDUCATION, CAREER, AND/OR INDEPENDENT LIVING
Reading, Writing, Language, Literacy, & ELL	• ENGLISH LEARNERS • LITERACY • FOREIGN LANGUAGE EDUCATION • READING, WRITING, AND LANGUAGE
STEM	• SCIENCE, TECHNOLOGY, ENGINEERING, AND MATHEMATICS (STEM) EDUCATION • SCIENCE, TECHNOLOGY, ENGINEERING, AND MATHEMATICS
Cognition & Learning	• COGNITION AND STUDENT LEARNING • COGNITION AND STUDENT LEARNING IN SPECIAL EDUCATION
Social & Behavioral	• SOCIAL AND BEHAVIORAL CONTEXT FOR ACADEMIC LEARNING • SOCIAL AND CHARACTER DEVELOPMENT • SOCIAL, EMOTIONAL, AND BEHAVIORAL COMPETENCE
School Systems	• EDUCATION LEADERSHIP • EVALUATION OF STATE AND LOCAL EDUCATION PROGRAMS AND POLICIES • IMPROVING EDUCATION SYSTEMS • EDUCATORS AND SCHOOL-BASED SERVICE PROVIDERS • SYSTEMS, POLICY, AND FINANCE
Other	• ARTS IN EDUCATION • CAREER AND TECHNICAL EDUCATION • CIVICS EDUCATION AND SOCIAL STUDIES • SYSTEMIC APPROACHES TO EDUCATING HIGHLY MOBILE STUDENTS • UNSOLICITED AND OTHER AWARDS • AUTISM SPECTRUM DISORDERS • FAMILIES OF CHILDREN WITH DISABILITIES • SPECIAL TOPIC: CAREER AND TECHNICAL EDUCATION FOR STUDENTS WITH DISABILITIES

TABLE D-3 Programs for Which a Topic Was Coded

	ProgramName
Topic was coded	• EDUCATION TECHNOLOGY • EFFECTIVE INSTRUCTION • FIELD INITIATED EVALUATIONS OF EDUCATION INNOVATIONS • LOW-COST, SHORT-DURATION EVALUATION OF SPECIAL EDUCATION INTERVENTIONS • RESEARCH GRANTS FOCUSED ON SYSTEMATIC REPLICATION • RESEARCH GRANTS FOCUSED ON SYSTEMATIC REPLICATION IN SPECIAL EDUCATION • RESEARCH NETWORKS FOCUSED ON CRITICAL PROBLEMS OF POLICY AND PRACTICE IN SPECIAL EDUCATION: MULTI-TIERED SYSTEMS OF SUPPORT • SPECIAL TOPIC: SYSTEMS-INVOLVED STUDENTS WITH DISIBILITIES • TECHNOLOGY FOR SPECIAL EDUCATION

INSTITUTION TYPE

In categorizing institutions that have received IES funds (both NCER and NCSER), Klager and Tipton decided to have universities include hospitals and research centers that are affiliated with a university. Research firms were defined as nonuniversity institutions whose primary work is in the evaluation of products and programs that they did not develop themselves (i.e., external evaluations). This does not mean that they never engage in development of interventions, products, and techniques but that it is not their primary purpose. Developers, on the other hand, engage in basic research and evaluations, primarily on their own products and interventions. Within the Other category, there are several types of institutions although individually, they make up only a very small proportion of grants and funding awarded by IES. These types of institutions include education service providers, scientific organizations, state departments of education, and school districts. All institutions were coded into an institution type based on the description of the institution on its own website, if available, or other internet sources.

R1 classification was based on the classification given to the university at the time the grant was awarded. Classifications are recalculated every few years by the Indiana University Center for Postsecondary Research, with new releases in 2000, 2005, 2010, 2015, and 2018. Minority-Serving Institutions (MSIs) status is based on the 2018 data; thus, it does not reflect any changes in MSI status over time.

EXPLORATION CATEGORIES

Exploration studies include a range of possible study types. To learn more about these, Klager and Tipton divided these studies into different categories. First, they determined if the study involved collecting primary data or if it only included secondary data. If the former, the grant was classified as "primary," whereas grants that use only secondary data are classified as "secondary." Additionally, the authors divided the grants into categories based on study design. These designs were coded based upon information in the abstracts, resulting in the following categories: meta-analysis, correlational analyses, randomized experiments (including pilots), and quasi-experiments (causal questions). There were many Exploration grants that had multiple studies with varying analysis plans. In these cases, if there was any experimental study, the grant was classified as experimental. If there was any meta-analysis, the grant was classified as meta-analysis. If the grant did not use an experiment or conduct a meta-analysis, then if there was a quasi-experiment the grant was classified as such. All other grants were showing associations, correlations, or doing mediation analyses.

METHODS GRANTS

Publicly available IES abstracts for Methods grants were coded for type of statistical method employed/developed, products produced, and topic of study. Klager and Tipton classified studies as psychometric (28), statistical models for analysis (23), randomized control trial design (22), and quasi-experimental design (20). Within those classifications, the authors also noted some subclassifications that commonly were funded or which are of interest to the educational methods research community. Relevant subtypes that were coded include value-added models, multilevel models, missing data, power analysis, effect size computation/interpretation, regression discontinuity, interrupted time series, single-case design, heterogeneity, external validity, and local treatment effects. If the abstract indicated the grant dealt with any of the subtypes, the subtype code was applied. Klager and Tipton also coded if the grant mentioned development of software.

LEVEL OF INTERVENTION

Klager and Tipton also sought to understand the level at which an intervention was targeted. Coding the target of the grants from publicly available abstracts was difficult because ultimately, the authors acknowledge that virtually all IES grants seek to affect student outcomes. In many cases, even if the primary agent through which an intervention worked was someone other than the student, the outcome data used to measure impact was collected from students. Also, it is quite common for studies funded in these categories to have multiple components that target different people. For example, a common occurrence is to have teacher professional development that is accompanied by a curriculum intervention for students.

In cases where an intervention was clearly targeted only or primarily at students, the grant was coded as targeting students. If an intervention had components that affected someone other than students (e.g., professional development for teachers) but those actors were merely delivering an intervention (e.g., a math curriculum) to students, the grant was coded as students as the primary target.

Grants were coded as targeting teachers if they were meant to change teacher practice but did not otherwise affect students except through the changes seen in the teacher. These are primarily tools for teachers or professional development programs that are not intended to train teachers on the use or delivery of a product/intervention to students. The "other" category includes interventions focused on parents, administrator and principals, schools, and school systems. As with teachers, interventions were coded as other if they were designed to affect one of the aforementioned actors and did not otherwise affect students, except through the changes induced in the targeted individual or institution. Coding for parents and administrators as the primary target of the intervention worked in much the same way as teachers; the intervention needed to focus on changing beliefs, skills, or behavior or providing tools for the parents or administrators rather than simply having the parents or administrators deliver the intervention.

For schools and school systems, it is not enough for the program to be delivered to all students or staff in a school or for the unit of randomization to have been the school. Grants targeted at schools and school systems change the structure of schools (e.g., implementing a Montessori model) or are policies that affect schools (e.g., a new accountability system for schools in a state). Using this coding scheme results in most interventions funded by both NCER and NCSER across Development and Innovation, Efficacy, and Replication/Effectiveness targeting students.

This same coding scheme was also used to organize Measurement grants. Abstracts were coded for mentions of various actors for which the measures might be targeted. These include students, teachers, or other actors including schools or school systems.

LIMITATIONS

While Klager and Tipton were able to download the data that form the basis of the paper from the IES website, they noted that these data are limited in that there are categorizations and details about grants that may or may not be present in the public abstracts. The public abstracts tend to follow a format provided by IES, but it is still sometimes difficult to discern what a grant is about and what sorts of activities the researchers are engaged in. The fields that IES does provide are useful for categorizing by program, but there are many more fields that would clarify the types of grants IES has funded. More concrete categorizations would be useful instead of relying on principal investigators to include information in project abstracts.

REFERENCES

Chhin, C.S., Taylor, K.A., and Wei, W.S. (2018). Supporting a culture of replication: An examination of education and special education research grants funded by the Institute of Education Sciences. *Educational Researcher, 47*(9), 594–605.

Indiana University Center for Postsecondary Research. (n.d.). *The Carnegie Classification of Institutions of Higher Education*, 2018 edition. Bloomington, IN: Author.

Institute of Education Sciences (IES). (2021). Funded Grant Search. https://ies.ed.gov/funding/grantsearch/

Appendix E

Funding Information in NCER and NCSER Provided by the Institute of Education Sciences

Table 1 Number of Awards and Funding Investment by Grant Topic within Education Research Grants (84.305A)[1]

Topic within 305A	#Awards	$ Investment	Award Year	Notes
Career and Technical Education	11	$19,661,305	2017–present	Began as special topic, changed to "regular" topic in FY2019
Civics and Social Studies Education	6	$14,175,708	2019–present	Began as special topic, changed to "regular" topic in FY2021
Cognition and Student Learning	182	$258,797,210	2002–present	
Early Learning Programs and Policies	106	$211,946,505	2008–present	Data include 1 unsolicited award made in 2003; Before FY2011, topic was Early Childhood Programs and Policies.
Education Leadership	19	$36,002,238	2004–2012; 2015–2019	Applications related to education leadership can be submitted under other topics
Education Technology	48	$87,284,640	2008–2019	Applications focused on education technology prior to 2008 and after 2019 are accepted under other topics
Effective Instruction	107	$191,090,933	2003–present	Starting in FY2012, this topic incorporated Teacher Quality-Math/Science and Teacher-Quality-Read/Write
English Learners	49	$85,954,075	2010–present	Before FY2011, topic was English Language Learners
Improving Education Systems	83	$108,752,130	2004–present	In FY2006, FY2005 the topic was Education Finance, Leadership, & Management
Literacy	133	$241,226,872	2002–present	The name for this topic has changed over time from the Program of Research on Reading Comprehension to Reading and Writing to

				Literacy and includes a subset of projects funded under Adolescent and Adult Literacy. Projects specifically addressing Adult Literacy are now classified under the "Postsecondary and Adult Education" topic.
Postsecondary and Adult Education	88	$153,663,554	2007–present	This was originally two topic areas: Postsecondary education, which was first funded in FY2007, and Adult Education, which was first competed for FY2011 funding. The combined topic area was first funded in FY2012. Prior to their combination, Postsecondary did not allow for teaching/learning outcomes and Adult Education did not allow for policy/systems work.
Science, Technology, Engineering & Mathematics Education (STEM)	102	$201,908,928	2003–present	The name for this topic changed from Mathematics and Science Education to STEM in FY2018.
Social and Behavioral Context for Academic Learning	165	$338,205,052	2008–present	
Special Topics				

[1] Note that, prior to combining topics under a single request for applications (RFA) inviting applications in FY2007, many of these "topics" were competed as stand-alone competitions. An observant reader will also notice that many of these topics mirror the requirement for NCER to support research in 11 topic areas specified in Sec 133(c)(2). A full discussion of the decision and rationale to create a smaller number of RFAs with a larger number of topics is available in the FY2007 Education Research Grants RFA available here: https://www2.ed.gov/about/offices/list/ies/2007-305.pdf. Because of this, applications to the "A" competition were submitted under multiple RFAs between 2001 and 2005 for funding in FY2002–FY2006.

continued

Table 1 Continued

Topic within 305A	#Awards	$ Investment	Award Year	Notes
Arts in Education	2	$2,000,000	2017–2018	
Foreign Language Education	1	$1,400,000	2019	
Systematic Approaches to Educating Highly Mobile Youth	1	$1,399,914	2018	
TOTALs in 305A	1103	$1,953,469,063		

Note: In FY2016, NCER did not accept Development and Innovation (Goal 2) applications.

Table 2 Number of Awards and Funding Investment by Project Type within Education Research Grants (84.305A)[2]

Project Types within 305A	#Awards	% of total 305A awards	$ Investment	% of total 305A $ investment	Notes
Exploration	254	23%	$273,501,778	14%	
Development and Innovation[3]	390	35%	$549,553,768	28%	
Efficacy and Replication[4]	310	28%	$835,162,328	43%	Includes Efficacy, Initial Efficacy, Follow-up, and Efficacy and Replication. Beginning in FY2020, there was a separate competition (84.305R) for replication studies
Effectiveness/Scale-Up	19	2%	$94,371,925	5%	Includes "Replication Effectiveness"
Measurement	130	12%	$200,879,265	10%	
TOTALS	1103		$1,953,469,063		

Note: For each project type, we provide number of awards, percent of total awards, dollar investment, and percent of total dollar investment to illustrate the differing costs per project type. For example, NCER spends a greater proportion of the budget on Efficacy and Replication projects, even though we make fewer Efficacy and Replication awards than Development and Innovation projects. In addition, while the formal labeling of research project types did not occur until the FY2007 competition, IES reviewed the grant descriptions, identified the primary project type, and tagged them for type in the grant search engine.

[2] Prior to FY2007, "goals" were not specified in separate RFAs. However, NCER recoded projects on the public-facing abstracts for projects funded between 2002 and 2006 so as to (more clearly) identify the primary research questions of the project.

[3] In FY2016, NCER did not accept Development and Innovation (Goal 2) applications.

[4] For additional information see: Chhin, C.S., Taylor, K.A., & Wei, W.S. (2018). Supporting a culture of replication: An examination of education and special education research grants funded by the Institute of Education Sciences. *Educational Researcher, 47*(9), 594–605.

Table 3 Number of Awards and Funding Investment by Project Type within the Research Grants Focused on Systematic Replication (84.305R) Program

Research Grants Focused on Systematic Replication (305R)	#Awards	$ Investment	Award Years	Notes
Replication Efficacy	0		2020–present	This topic was competed, but no awards have yet been made.
Replication Effectiveness	2	$8,499,905	2020–present	
TOTAL	2	$8,499,905		

Table 4 Number of Awards and Funding Investment by NCER Grant Competitions

The table below shows the number of awards and amount of investment by funding cluster, corresponding to the clusters linked to on the NCER website (https://ies.ed.gov/ncer/research/). Beneath the clusters are individual competitions or funding opportunities for all but the Education Research Training cluster and the Education Research & Development Centers cluster, both of which have separate dedicated tables. The cluster-level name and details are in bold. The competition-level name and details are in italics. The competition RFA number (e.g., 305A, 305B) refers to the most recently used Assistance Listing Number (ALN) associated with the competition.

Competition Cluster and Program Name	#Awards	% of total awards	$ Investment	% of investment	Award Year	Notes
Education Research and Methods	1223	78%	$2,059,469	67%	2002–present	
Education Research Grants (305A)	1103	70%	$1,953,469,063	64%	2002–present	Includes programs initially competed separately for funding between FY2002 and FY2006 under multiple separate competitions that were combined into a single RFA for the FY2007 competition cycle. Includes all Project Types (see Table 1)
Statistical and Research Methodology (305D)	102	7%	$67,765,711	2%	2004–present	Note that between 2004-2008, research to support methodological innovation was funded via unsolicited grant opportunities. The stand-alone Stats and Methods competition was launched in FY 2009 and has been held annually except in FY2018.

continued

Table 4 Continued

Competition Cluster and Program Name	#Awards	% of total awards	$ Investment	% of investment	Award Year	Notes
Field Initiated Evaluations in Education (305F)	12	0.77%	$17,740,220	0.58%	2005	
Systematic Replication (305R)	2	0.13%	$8,499,905	0.28%	2020–present	
Transformative Research in Education (305T)	4	0.26%	$11,994,568	0.39%	2021	
Education Research Training Programs (305B)	122	8%	$266,882,547	9%	2004–present	Please see Table 7 (included in a separate file), which provides information about the NCER and NCSER investment in research training. This count includes some grants that were awarded under the Unsolicited Grant opportunity.
Education Research & Development Centers (305C)	**34**	**2%**	**$318,634,797**	**10%**	**2004–present**	As specified in ESRA, NCER is required to have 8 active R&D Centers in one of 11 pre-specified topic areas. Required by ESRA; includes topical foci. Note–the total also includes the Gifted Centers. Please see Table 5 for additional information.

Research Networks	49	3%	**$227,748,229.70**	7%		
Reading for Understanding Research Initiative (305F)	6	0.38%	$113,433,194	4%	2010	
Expanding the Evidence Base for Career and Technical Education	1	0.06%	$4,999,998	0.16%	2018	Network research team grantees were funded under "A" and are not counted here. This grant is for the network lead. The funds for this project came from the Office of Career, Technical, and Adult Education (OCATE) U.S. Department of Education.
Scalable Strategies to Support College Completion Network	4	0.26%	$13,915,461	0.46%	2016	
Supporting Early Learning From Preschool Through Early Elementary School Grades Network	7	0.45%	$26,491,692	0.87%	2016	
Building Adult Skills and Attainment Through Technology Research Network	6	0.38%	$20,700,363	0.68%	2021	Note: This network meets the requirement under ESRA for an R&D Center on Adult Literacy
Digital Learning Platforms to Enable Efficient Education Research Network	6	0.38%	$12,998,292	0.43%	2021	
Preschool Curriculum Evaluation Research (305J)	12	0.77%	$20,213,628	0.66%	2002–2003	This evaluation also included a contract for a multi-site coordinator, not included in this table or in the search tool.

continued

Table 4 Continued

Competition Cluster and Program Name	#Awards	% of total awards	$ Investment	% of investment	Award Year	Notes
Social and Character Development (305L)	7	0.46%	$13,595,688	0.44%	2004	*This evaluation also included a contract for a multi-site coordinator, not included in this table or in the search tool.*
Collaborations Between Researchers & Practitioners	111	7%	$158,810,754	5%		
Evaluation of State and Local Education Programs and Policies (305E/305H)	27	2%	$110,490,105	4%	2009–2015; 2017–2019	
Low-Cost, Short-Duration Evaluation of Education Interventions (305L)	9	0.58%	$2,207,185	0.07%	2016–2018	
Continuous Improvement (305H)	6	0.38%	$14,992,800	0.49%	2014–2015	
Using Longitudinal Data to Support State Education Policymaking (305S)	7	0.45%	$6,434,368	0.21%	2021–present	
Unsolicited (not included in other counts)	26	2%	$27,116,852	0.89%		
TOTAL NCER awards	1565		$3,057,262,733			

Table 5 Grants Awarded in Education Research & Development Centers (84.305C)[5]

Name of Center	Award FY	$ Investment	Project Type(s)[6]	ESRA Topic
Center for Data-Driven Reform in Education	2004	$9,997,674	Multiple Goals	Improving low-achieving schools
National Research and Development Center on School Choice	2004	$9,972,909	Multiple Goals: Exploration, Efficacy	Innovation in education reform
National Research Center on Rural Education Support	2004	$10,000,000	Multiple Goals: Exploration, Development, Efficacy	Rural education
Center for Research on Evaluation, Standards, and Student Testing (CRESST)	2005	$9,968,718	Multiple Goals: Measurement, Efficacy	Assessment, standards, and accountability research

[5] As specified in ESRA, Sec 133(c)(1)—In carrying out activities under subsection (a)(3), the Research Commissioner shall support not less than 8 national research and development centers. The Research Commissioner shall assign each of the 8 national research and development centers not less than 1 of the topics described in paragraph (2). In addition, the Research Commissioner may assign each of the 8 national research and development centers additional topics of research consistent with the mission and priorities of the Institute and the mission of the Research Center. (2) TOPICS OF RESEARCH.—The Research Commissioner shall support the following topics of research, through national research and development centers or through other means: (A) Adult literacy. (B) Assessment, standards, and accountability research. (C) Early childhood development and education. (D) English language learners research. (E) Improving low achieving schools. (F) Innovation in education reform. (G) State and local policy. (H) Postsecondary education and training. (I) Rural education. (J) Teacher quality. (K) Reading and literacy. (3) DUTIES OF CENTERS.—The national research and development centers shall address areas of national need, including in educational technology areas.

[6] Each R&D Center carries out multiple projects and has multiple goals including providing national leadership in their assigned topic area. Many, but not all, of the projects carried out by the R&D Centers align with the project types included in Table 3 and are listed here.

continued

Table 5 Continued

Name of Center	Award FY	$ Investment	Project Type(s)[6]	ESRA Topic
Center for Research on the Educational Achievement and Teaching of English Language Learners (CREATE)	2005	$9,897,290	Multiple Goals: Development, Efficacy	English language learners research
Center for Analysis of Longitudinal Data in Education Research (CALDER)	2006	$11,996,301	Multiple Goals: Exploration	State and local policy
National Center for Performance Incentives (Policy-NCPI)	2006	$10,835,509	Multiple Goals: Exploration, Efficacy	State and local policy; Teacher quality
National Center for Postsecondary Research	2006	$9,813,619	Multiple Goals: Exploration, Efficacy	Postsecondary education and training
National Center for Research on Early Childhood Education	2006	$11,016,009	Multiple Goals: Efficacy	Early childhood development and education
National Research Center on the Gifted and Talented[7]	2006	$8,706,200	Multiple Goals: Exploration, Measurement	
National Research & Development Center on Cognition and Science Instruction	2008	$9,995,038	Multiple Goals: Development, Efficacy	Innovation in education reform
National Research & Development Center on Instructional Technology: Center for Advanced Technology in Schools	2008	$9,833,451	Multiple Goals: Development, Efficacy	Innovation in education reform
National Research & Development Center on Instructional Technology: Possible Worlds	2008	$9,197,582	Multiple Goals: Development, Efficacy	Innovation in education reform

Center	Year	Amount	Goals	Topic
National Center for Teacher Effectiveness: Validating Measures of Effective Math Teaching	2009	$9,997,888	Multiple Goals: Measurement	Teacher quality
The National Center for Research on Rural Education	2009	$9,997,852	Multiple Goals: Exploration, Efficacy	Rural education
National Research & Development Center on Cognition and Mathematics Instruction	2010	$9,998,406	Multiple Goals: Development, Efficacy	Innovation in education reform
National Research and Development Center on Scaling Up Effective Schools	2010	$13,573,066	Multiple Goals: Exploration, Development	Improving low-achieving schools
The Center for Analysis of Postsecondary Education and Employment	2011	$9,951,362	Multiple Goals: Exploration, Efficacy	Postsecondary education and training
Center for the Study of Adult Literacy (CSAL): Developing Instructional Approaches Suited to the Cognitive and Motivational Needs for Struggling Adults	2012	$9,999,985	Multiple Goals: Exploration, Development	Adult literacy
National Center for Analysis of Longitudinal Data in Education Research (CALDER)	2012	$10,000,000	Multiple Goals: Exploration	State and local policy

[7]Note: IES has managed the Department's requirement to host a National Research Center for the Education of Gifted and Talented Children and Youth since 2006. As stated in the FY2020 Education Research and Development Center's RFA: "In fulfillment of the requirement in the "Jacob K. Javits Gifted and Talented Students Education Program" in the Every Student Succeeds Act (ESSA) (SEC. 4644. ø20 U.S.C. 7294 [d]) for a National Research Center for the Education of Gifted and Talented Children and Youth."

continued

Table 5 Continued

Name of Center	Award FY	$ Investment	Project Type(s)[6]	ESRA Topic
Center for the Analysis of Postsecondary Readiness	2014	$9,989,803	Multiple Goals: Exploration, Efficacy	Postsecondary education and training
National Center for Research in Policy and Practice	2014	$4,995,352	Multiple Goals: Measurement, Exploration	Innovation in education reform
National Center for Research on Gifted Education	2014	$5,000,000	Multiple Goals: Exploration, Efficacy	
Center on Standards, Alignment, Instruction and Learning (C-SAIL)	2015	$9,999,999	Multiple Goals: Exploration, Measurement, Efficacy	Assessment, standards, and accountability research
The Center for Research Use in Education (CRUE)	2015	$4,999,958	Multiple Goals: Measurement, Exploration	Innovation in education reform
Precision Education: The Virtual Learning Lab	2016	$8,908,288	Multiple Goals: Measurement, Efficacy	Innovation in education reform
The National Center for Research on Education Access and Choice	2018	$9,998,565	Multiple Goals: Exploration	Improving low achieving schools
The National Center for Rural Education Research Networks (NCRERN)	2019	$9,994,246	Multiple Goals: Exploration, Development, Efficacy	Rural education

	Year	Amount	Goals	Topic
The National Center for Rural School Mental Health (NCRSMH): Enhancing the Capacity of Rural Schools to Identify, Prevent, and Intervene in Youth Mental Health Concerns	2019	$9,999,729	Multiple Goals: Development, Efficacy	Rural education
WRITE Center for Secondary Students: Writing Research to Improve Teaching and Evaluation	2019	$5,000,000	Multiple Goals: Exploration, Development	Reading and literacy
National Center for Research on Gifted Education	2020	$5,000,000	Multiple Goals: Exploration, Efficacy	
National Research and Development Center to Improve Education for Secondary English Learners	2020	$10,000,000	Multiple Goals: Exploration, Development, Efficacy	English language learners research
Transdisciplinary Approaches to Improving Opportunities and Outcomes for English Learners: Using Engagement, Team-Based Learning, and Formative Assessment to Develop Content and Language Proficiency	2020	$9,999,999	Multiple Goals: Exploration, Development, Efficacy	English language learners research
Postsecondary Teaching with Technology Collaborative	2021	$9,999,999	Multiple Goals: Exploration, Development	Postsecondary education and training
TOTAL (R&D Centers)		$318,634,797		

Table 6 Number of Awards and Funding Investment by Grant Topic within Special Education Research Grants Program (84.324A)

Topic within 324A	#Awards	$ Investment	Years competed	Notes
Autism Spectrum Disorders	28	$55,460,024	FY2007–FY2013, FY2015–2020	In FY2021 ASD topic was removed from the RFA and applicants interested in research with children with ASD could apply to any topic area.
Cognition and Student Learning in Special Education	17	$29,062,362	FY2009–2013, FY2015–2021	
Early Intervention and Early Learning	106	$210,745,720	FY2006–2013, FY2015–2021	
Educators and School-Based Service Providers	37	$60,299,829	FY2006–2007, FY2009–2013, FY2015–2021	Before FY2011, topic was Teacher Quality. From FY2011–FY2020, topic became Professional Development for Teachers and Related Service Providers. In FY2021 this topic was changed to Educators and School-Based Service Providers.
Families of Children with Disabilities	2	$3,805,693	FY2012–2013, FY2015–2021	
Reading, Writing, and Language Development	59	$117,367,866	FY2006–2013, FY2015–2021	
Science, Technology, Engineering, and Math	31	$57,476,538	FY2006–2013, FY2015–2021	Before FY2019, topic was Math and Science.
Social, Emotional, and Behavioral Competence	80	$178,457,206	FY2009–2013, FY2015–2021	Before FY2021, topic was Social and Behavioral Outcomes to Support Learning.

Topic	Count	Amount	Fiscal Years	Notes
Systems, Policy, and Finance	28	$43,393,489	FY2009–2013, FY2015–2021	Before FY2011, topic was Systemic Interventions & Policies. From FY2011–FY2020, topic was Special Education Policy, Finance, and Systems.
Technology for Special Education	11	$16,356,486	FY2012–2013, FY2015–2021	In 2021 the Technology topic was removed from the RFA and applicants interested in technology research could apply to any topic area.
Transition to Postsecondary Education, Career, and/or Independent Living	38	$59,224,562	FY2006–2013, FY2015–2021	Before FY2011, topic was Secondary & Postsecondary Transitions. From FY2011–FY2021, topic was Transition Outcomes for Special Education Secondary Students. In FY2021, topic changed to Transition to Postsecondary Education, Career, and/or Independent Living.
Special Topics				
Career and Technical Education for SWD	3	$2,955,747	FY2019–FY2020	
Systems-Involved SWD	1	$3,299,326	FY2019–FY2020	
TOTALS	441	$837,904,848		

Note: SWD is Students with Disabilities. Due to funding constraints, there were no NCSER funding competitions in FY2014. In FY2017, again due to funding limitations, NCSER restricted the focus of the 324A RFA to research on teachers and other instructional personnel. In FY2019 and FY2020 there was a third Special Topic: English Learners with Disabilities that received applications, but none were rated highly enough in the peer review process to be considered for funding.

Table 7 Number of Awards and Funding Investment by Project Type within Special Education Research Grants (84.324A)

Project Types within 324A	#Awards	% of total 324A awards	$ Investment	% of total 324A $ investment	Notes
Exploration	58	13%	$58,725,260	7%	
Development and Innovation	198	45%	$285,688,284	34%	
Efficacy and Replication	125	28%	$389,257,633	46%	Beginning in FY2020, a separate competition (84.324R) was held for replication studies
Effectiveness/Scale-Up	3	1%	$16,399,131	2%	Beginning in FY2020, Effectiveness Replications were included in the Systematic Replication RFA (84.324R)
Measurement	57	13%	$87,834,540	11%	
TOTALS	441		837,904,848		

Note: For each project type we provide number of awards, percent of total awards, dollar investment, and percent of total dollar investment to illustrate the differing costs per project type. For example, NCSER spends a greater proportion of the budget on Efficacy and Replication projects, even though we award fewer Efficacy awards than Development and Innovation projects.

Table 8 Number of Awards and Funding Investment by Project Type within the Research Grants Focused on Systematic Replication in Special Education (84.324R) Program

Project Types within Systematic Replication 324R	#Awards	% of total 324R awards	$ Investment	% of 324R $ investment	Notes
Replication Effectiveness	4	50%	$16,992,435	54%	FY2020–present
Replication Efficacy	4	50%	$14,755,488	46%	FY2020–present
TOTALS	8		$31,747,923		

Table 9 Number of Awards and Funding Investment by NCSER Grant Competitions

NCSER Research Grant Competitions	#Awards	% of total awards	$ Investment	% of total $ investment	Notes
Special Education Research Grants (324A)	441	83%	$837,904,848	84%	All Project Types (See Table 1)
Research Training Programs in Special Education (324B)	56	10%	$31,790,528	3%	Training (Early Career, Postdoctoral, and Methods Training for Special Education Research)
Special Education Research & Development Centers (324C)	6	1%	$62,015,787	6%	Multiple project types within and across R&D Centers, including efficacy as well as development and/or exploration and/or measurement
Accelerating the Academic Achievement of Students with Learning Disabilities Research Initiative (324D)	1	<1%	$10,000,000	1%	Development and Efficacy
Low-Cost, Short Duration Evaluations (324L)	6	1%	$1,452,956	<1%	Efficacy Studies in partnership with state and local education agencies
MTSS Research Networks (324N)	5	1%	$17,496,507	2%	1 Development and Evaluation, 1 Efficacy, 1 Efficacy and Development, 1 Measurement, 1 Network Lead
NAEP Process Data (324P)	2	<1%	$ 1,399,340	<1%	Exploration
Systematic Replication in Special Education (324R)	8	2%	$31,747,923	3%	Replication Effectiveness, Replication Efficacy (See prior table)

255

Pandemic Recovery (324X)	—	—		—		As of January 2022, two awards have been made in the first round (324X-1); peer review of applications for the second round of (324X-2) is currently under way.
Unsolicited (324U)	—	9	2%	$3,857,426	<1%	
TOTALS		534		$997,665,315		

Note: Early Career grants within the Special Education Training Program (84.324B) include research projects with varying project types.

Table 10 Grants Awarded in Special Education Research & Development
Centers (84.324C)

Name of Center	Fiscal Year of Award	$ Investment	Project Type(s)
Center for Response to Intervention in Early Childhood	2008	$10,000,000.00	Multiple
National Research and Development Center on Serious Behavior Disorders at the Secondary Level	2008	$10,447,669.00	Multiple
National Research and Development Center on Improving Mathematics Instruction for Students with Mathematics Difficulties	2010	$ 9,896,532.00	Multiple
National Research and Development Center on Assessment and Accountability for Special Education	2011	$11,677,134.00	Multiple
Center on Secondary Education for Students with Autism Spectrum Disorders	2012	$ 9,994,452.00	Multiple
Special Education Research and Development Center on Reading Instruction for Deaf and Hard of Hearing Students	2012	$10,000,000.00	Multiple
TOTALS	6	**$62,015,787.00**	

Appendix F

Committee and Staff Biographies

COMMITTEE

ADAM GAMORAN (*Chair*) is president of the William T. Grant Foundation. Previously, he held the John D. MacArthur Chair in Sociology and Educational Policy Studies at the University of Wisconsin–Madison where, among other roles, he chaired the department of sociology, directed the Wisconsin Center for Education Research, and spent three decades engaged in research on educational inequality and school reform. He is a past grantee of the Institute of Education Sciences, the National Science Foundation, the National Institute of Child Health and Human Development, and several private funders. His research contributions have been honored by the Association for Public Policy Analysis and Management, the American Educational Research Association (AERA), and the Sociology of Education Section of the American Sociological Association. He is an elected member of the American Academy of Arts and Sciences and the National Academy of Education, which he currently serves as vice president. He was also twice appointed by President Barack Obama to the National Board for Education Sciences and is past chair of the Independent Advisory Panel of the National Assessment of Career and Technical Education. Gamoran received his Ph.D. in education from the University of Chicago.

MARTHA W. ALIBALI is a Vilas Distinguished Achievement Professor of Psychology and Educational Psychology at the University of Wisconsin-Madison, and she is a principal investigator (PI) at the Wisconsin Center for Education Research. Her research is situated at the interface of developmental psychology, cognitive psychology, and mathematics education. Her primary line of work investigates mathematical learning and development, with a special focus on the roles of gesture and action in mathematical cognition, learning, and instruction. She has published more than 130 journal articles and book chapters, co-edited two books, and co-authored a textbook on cognitive development. Her research has been funded by the Institute of Education Sciences, the National Science Foundation, and the National Institutes of Health. She is a fellow of the Cognitive Science Society and a past recipient of the Friedrich Wilhelm Bessel Research Prize from the Alexander von Humboldt Foundation. Alibali received her Ph.D. in developmental psychology from the University of Chicago.

ALFREDO J. ARTILES is Lee L. Jacks Professor of Education at Stanford University. He is the director of the Stanford Center for Opportunity Policy in Education and the director of research at the Center for Comparative Studies in Race & Ethnicity. His scholarship has been supported by many federal and philanthropic organizations to examine cultural-historical dimensions of disability and inclusive education and their implications for policy and practice. Artiles is the editor of the book series *Disability, Culture, & Equity*, and an elected member of the National Academy of Education, AERA fellow, previous resident fellow of the Center for Advanced Study in the Behavioral Sciences, and previous member of the White House Commission on Educational Excellence for Hispanics. He has received numerous honors for his scholarly work and mentoring activities including being named an honorary professor at the University of Birmingham (United Kingdom) and receiving an honorary doctorate from the University of Göteborgs (Sweden). He holds a Ph.D. in special education from the University of Virginia.

CYNTHIA E. COBURN is a professor in the School of Education and Social Policy at Northwestern University. She studies the relationship between instructional policy and teachers' classroom practices in urban schools, the dynamics of school district policy making, and the relationship between research and practice for school improvement. She is a fellow of AERA and received an honorary doctorate (Doctor Honoris Causa) from CU Louvain in Belgium. She is also a member of the National Academy of Education, among other recognition for her scholarship. Coburn holds a B.A. in philosophy from Oberlin College, and an M.A. in sociology and Ph.D. in education from Stanford University.

LORA A. COHEN-VOGEL is the Frank A. Daniels Distinguished Professor in the School of Education at the University of North Carolina at Chapel Hill, where she is also director of interprofessional education. Her teaching and research focus on education policy and politics, teacher quality, continuous improvement research, and bringing to scale programs and processes for system-level improvement and equity. As associate director of the National Center for Research and Development on Scaling Up Effective Schools, Cohen-Vogel helped lead research-practice partnerships that used the science of improvement to raise schooling outcomes for traditionally underserved students in two of the nation's largest school districts. She is currently co-PI of a project looking to extend the early learning gains of students in the rural South as part of the Early Learning Network. Cohen-Vogel is immediate past vice president of the AERA and former president of the Politics of Education Association. Cohen-Vogel began her career in education as the executive director of a grassroots community organization dedicated to advancing music education in California schools. She has a Ph.D. in education from Vanderbilt University.

NATHAN D. JONES is an associate professor of special education and education policy in the Wheelock College of Education & Human Development at Boston University. His research focuses on teacher quality, teacher development, and school improvement, with a specific emphasis on conceptualizing and measuring teaching effectiveness in preservice and inservice contexts. Recent work is on special education teacher evaluation; the measurement of teachers' time use and affect; the impact of special education policies and programs on student outcomes; and the development of curricular materials to support preservice general education teachers in teaching students with disabilities. In 2018, he served as co-chair of the Institute of Education Sciences (IES) Principal Investigators Meeting. Jones is associate editor of the *Journal of Teacher Education* and co-editor of *The Elementary School Journal*. Prior to pursuing his doctoral training, Jones taught for three years as a middle school special education teacher in the Mississippi Delta. He received his Ph.D. in special education and education policy from Michigan State University.

BRIDGET T. LONG is dean and Saris Professor of Education and Economics at the Harvard Graduate School of Education. Long is an economist who studies educational opportunity with a focus on college access and success, including the role of affordability, academic preparation, and information. She is a research associate of the National Bureau of Economic Research, a member of the National Academy of Education, and an affiliate of the Abdul Latif Jameel Poverty Action Lab. Long has served as chair of National Board for Education Sciences, the advisory panel of the Institute of Education Sciences at the U.S. Department of Education, and testified multiple times before federal congressional committees and state government bodies. She earned her A.B. from Princeton University in economics with a certificate in Afro-American studies and M.A. and Ph.D. from the Harvard University Department of Economics.

NORMA C. MING is the supervisor of research and evaluation in the San Francisco Unified School District's Research, Planning, and Assessment Division, where she manages the research portfolio and leads internal evaluations. Her work focuses on establishing and studying the conditions and supports that enable integrating research and practice for continuous improvement in education. This includes developing learning agendas, drawing from existing evidence syntheses, coordinating research partnerships to generate relevant evidence, supporting improvement teams to innovate and iterate through disciplined inquiry, and facilitating the implementation of evidence-based policy and practice. Her current research addresses inequities in school attendance and engagement through youth-led inquiry, and her publications apply text mining to disciplinary records and online discussion forums, use statistical process control to visualize trends and outliers in educational data, and propose a framework for assessing research for educational policy making and practice. She is a former K–12 and university educator and researcher. Ming holds a B.A. in chemistry from Harvard and Ph.D. in cognitive psychology from Carnegie Mellon University.

MARY C. MURPHY is the Herman B. Wells Professor of Psychological and Brain Sciences at Indiana University. Her education research illuminates the situational cues that influence students' academic motivation and achievement with an emphasis on understanding when those processes are similar and different for structurally advantaged and disadvantaged students. She develops, implements, and evaluates social psychological interventions that reduce identity threat and spur students' motivation, persistence, and performance. Murphy also co-founded the College Transition Collaborative, a research-practice partnership housed at Stanford University. In the realm of organizations and technology, her research examines barriers and solutions for increasing gender and racial diversity in STEM fields, in particular the role of organizational mindset in companies' organizational culture, employee engagement and performance, and diversity, equity, and inclusion. In 2019, she was awarded the Presidential Early Career Award for Scientists and Engineers (PECASE). She earned a Ph.D. from Stanford University and completed a National Science Foundation postdoctoral fellowship at Northwestern University.

NICOLE S. PATTON-TERRY is the Olive & Manuel Bordas Professor of Education in the School of Teacher Education, director of the Florida Center for Reading Research, and deputy director of the Regional Education Lab—Southeast at Florida State University (FSU). Prior to joining

FSU, she was an associate professor of special education and the founding director of the Urban Child Study Center at Georgia State University. Her research, innovation, and engagement activities concern young learners who are vulnerable to experiencing poor language and literacy achievement in school, in particular African American children, children growing up in poverty, and children with disabilities. Patton-Terry currently serves as an associate editor for the *Journal of Learning Disabilities*, board member for the Society for the Scientific Study of Reading, and fellow of the American Speech-Language-Hearing Association. She was a special education teacher in the Evanston (Illinois) Public Schools. She earned a Ph.D. from Northwestern University's School of Communication Sciences and Disorders, with a specialization in learning disabilities.

JAN L. PLASS is a professor in the Steinhardt School of Culture, Education, and Human Development at New York University (NYU). He is the founding director of the Consortium for Research and Evaluation of Advanced Technology in Education and co-directs the Games for Learning Institute. He was also the inaugural holder of the Paulette Goddard Chair in Digital Media and Learning Sciences at NYU. Plass' work envisions, designs, and studies the future of learning with digital technologies, most recently involving simulations and games for desktops, mobile, and AR/VR/MR. He is the author of more than 120 journal articles, chapters, and conference proceedings, and has given more than 200 presentations at academic conferences. He has served as lead editor for several publications, as PI or co-PI on numerous projects, and editorial review member on a number of journal boards. He has been a reviewer for funding agencies around the world and chairs the IES panels on basic processes and math and science learning. Plass received his M.A. in mathematics and physics education and Ph.D. in educational technologies from Erfurt University (Germany).

NATHANIEL SCHWARTZ is a professor of practice at Brown University's Annenberg Institute for School Reform, where he leads a set of research partnerships focused on improving educator pipelines and student well-being in Rhode Island. He also co-founded the EdResearch for Recovery project, which collects requests for pandemic-related research guidance from education leaders and identifies teams of researchers across the country to build out quick-response evidence synthesis. Schwartz previously served as the chief research and strategy officer for the Tennessee Department of Education. In that position, he led the department's research and strategic planning teams, contributing to the launch of Tennessee Succeeds, a strategic plan and vision aimed at increasing postsecondary and career readiness, and to the creation of the Tennessee Education Research Alliance, a state-level research partnership with Vanderbilt University. Prior to his graduate education, Schwartz was a high school science teacher in Arkansas and Illinois. He received his Ph.D. in educational studies from the University of Michigan.

JANELLE SCOTT is a professor and the Robert C. and Mary Catherine Birgeneau Distinguished Chair in Educational Disparities at the University of California at Berkeley in the Graduate School of Education, African American Studies Department, and Goldman School of Public Policy. Her research investigates how market-based educational reforms affect demo-cratic accountability and equity in public education across several policy strands: (1) the racial politics of public education; (2) the politics of school choice, marketization, and privatization: (3) the politics of research evidence on market-oriented reforms; and (4) the role of elite and community-based advocacy in shaping public education and research evidence utilization. Her work has appeared in many edited books and journals, and she is the editor or author of numerous other publications. Scott is an AERA fellow and member of the National Academy of Education. Before earning her doctorate, she was a teacher in Oakland, California. She earned a B.A. in political science from the University of California at Berkeley and Ph.D. in education policy from the University of California at Los Angeles.

L. ELIZABETH TIPTON is an associate professor of statistics, co-director of the Statistics for Evidence-Based Policy and Practice Center, and fac-ulty fellow in the Institute for Policy Research at Northwestern Univer-sity. Her research focuses on the design and analysis of field experiments, with a particular focus on issues of external validity and generalizabil-ity in experiments; meta-analysis, particularly of dependent effect sizes; and the use of (cluster) robust variance estimation. She was previously a member of the faculty at Teachers College, Columbia University, for 7 years. Tipton is a board member of the Society for Research on Edu-cational Effectiveness and serves as an associate editor of the *Journal of Educational and Behavioral Statistics*. She earned a B.A. in mathe-matics from Transylvania University, M.A. in sociology from the Uni-versity of Chicago, and Ph.D. in statistics from Northwestern University.

SHARON VAUGHN is the Manuel J. Justiz Endowed Chair in Education and the executive director of The Meadows Center for Preventing Edu-cational Risk, a research unit that she founded with a "make a wish" gift from the Meadows Foundation. She is the recipient of numerous awards, including the first woman in the history of The University of Texas to re-ceive the Distinguished Faculty and Research Award. She is the author of more than 40 books and 350 research articles. She is currently PI on several Institute of Education Sciences, National Institute for Child Health and

Human Development, and U.S. Department of Education research grants. She works as a senior adviser to the National Center on Intensive Interventions and has more than six articles that have met the criteria of the What Works Clearinghouse. Vaughn was a classroom teacher for five years, and has worked with state departments of education across the United States including Florida, Texas, Colorado, and New York as well as more than 30 school districts to develop, identify, and implement research-based practices and policies. She earned a B.S. in education from the University of Missouri, and master's and Ph.D. in education and child development from the University of Arizona.

STAFF

KENNE A. DIBNER (*Study Director*) is a senior program officer with the Board on Science Education at the National Academies of Science, Engineering, and Medicine (the National Academies). She has served as study director for *Reopening K–12 Schools During the COVID-19 Pandemic: Prioritizing Health, Equity, and Communities* and *Science Literacy: Concepts, Contexts, and Consequences,* as well as a recently completed assessment of the NASA Science Mission Directorate's education portfolio. Prior to this position, she worked as a research associate at Policy Studies Associates, Inc., where she conducted evaluations of education policies and programs for government agencies, foundations, and school districts, and as a research consultant with the Center on Education Policy. She has a B.A. in English literature from Skidmore College and a Ph.D. in education policy from Michigan State University.

LETICIA GARCILAZO GREEN is a research associate for the National Academies Board on Science Education. As a member of the board staff, she has supported studies focusing on criminal justice, science education, science communication, and climate change. She has a B.S. in psychology and a B.A. in sociology with a concentration in criminology from Louisiana State University and an M.A. in forensic psychology from The George Washington University.

MARGARET KELLY is a program coordinator for the National Academies Board on Science Education. She has more than 20 years of experience working in the administrative field for the private sector, federal government, and nonprofit organizations, including American University, Catholic University, the Census Bureau, International Franchise Association, the Department of Defense, and the University of the District of Columbia. She has received numerous professional honors and awards throughout her career, including the 2020 DBASSE staff award for Citizenship/Spirit, a

Superior Performance of Customer Service Award, Sustained Superior Performance Cash Awards, and Air Force Organizational Excellence Awards and Certificates of Appreciations.

HEIDI SCHWEINGRUBER is the director of the National Academies Board on Science Education. She has served as study director or co-study director for a wide range of studies, including those on revising national standards for K–12 science education, learning and teaching science in grades K–8, and mathematics learning in early childhood. She also co-authored two award-winning books for practitioners that translate findings of Academies' reports for a broader audience, on using research in K–8 science classrooms and on information science education. Prior to joining the Academies, she worked as a senior research associate at the Institute of Education Sciences. She also previously served on the faculty of Rice University and as the director of research for the Rice University School Mathematics Project, an outreach program in K–12 mathematics education. She has a Ph.D. in psychology (developmental) and anthropology and a certificate in culture and cognition, both from the University of Michigan.